# AIR BAN
# RADIO HAND

G000154835

As part of our ongoing market research, we are always pleased to receive comments about our books, suggestions for new titles, or requests for catalogues. Please write to: The Editorial Director, Patrick Stephens Limited, Sparkford, Nr Yeovil, Somerset BA22 7JJ.

# AIR BAND RADIO HANDBOOK
## 6th edition

David J. Smith

Patrick Stephens Limited

First published in 1986
Second edition 1987
Reprinted (with revisions) July 1988
Third edition February 1990
Reprinted (with revisions) July 1990
Reprinted August 1991
Fourth edition October 1992
Reprinted (with revisions) August 1993
Fifth edition November 1994
Sixth edition February 1997

A Catalogue record for this book is available from the British Library

ISBN 1 85260 581 2

Library of Congress catalog card no 96-79741

Patrick Stephens Limited is an imprint of Haynes Publishing, Sparkford, Nr Yeovil, Somerset, BA22 7JJ.

Designed & typeset by
G&M, Raunds, Northamptonshire
Printed and bound in Great Britain by
Butler & Tanner Ltd, London and Frome

# Contents

# Introduction

Interest in air band listening has increased steadily since this book was first published in 1986, and is reflected in its continuing success. In addition, late in 1995 a companion volume, *International Air Band Radio Handbook*, was published. Its scope is worldwide, but there is much to interest the UK reader in the coverage of topics for which there is insufficient space in the current volume.

Prior to 1963 enthusiasts had to rely on their own eyesight, aided by binoculars or telescopes, to identify aircraft. A minor revolution occurred in that year when the first radios covering the VHF air band (then 108–136MHz) were put on the market. The messages between pilots and ground controllers could now be overheard by anyone who cared to buy one. More important, the majority of aircraft flying over could be identified by their registration or serial number.

Modern technology has improved those early sets beyond recognition. Current receivers, better known as scanners, are able to search the whole band automatically, or can be pre-programmed to scan any desired sequence of frequencies.

A great many people have bought air band radios, however, and found the jargon they hear almost incomprehensible. It is easy to pick out call-signs, but most VHF listeners to whom I have talked would like to build up a better picture of what is going on, and to unravel the 'mysteries' of Air Traffic Control. This book aims to do just that.

Similarly, people embarking upon a course of flying lessons for a Private Pilot's Licence would find it useful to acquire an air band radio and listen to how the professionals do their R/T. My experience shows that to the majority of trainee pilots learning how to use the radio is almost as big a hurdle as mastering their aircraft. The terse messages, so confusing at first hearing, follow a definite pattern known as 'standard phraseology'. This verbal shorthand is designed to impart the maximum amount of unambiguous information in the shortest possible time. Since English is the international language of Air Traffic Control, it must be understood easily by those with a different native tongue. With careful listening, and the aid of the examples in this book, the R/T exchanges on the air band will soon become both logical and familiar.

It must be emphasised that in the extremely complex world of Air Traffic Control, procedures are changing all the time; new air lanes may be brought into use, others replaced or re-routed. Similarly, new beacons and reporting points are always being introduced. Frequencies tend to stay the same for many years, although with the recent introduction of closer spacing between them there may be some upheavals in the future. The fact that radio navigation charts are updated every month or so shows just how frequently changes are liable to occur.

Since the 5th edition of the handbook appeared in 1994 there have been many developments in Air Traffic Control and air navigation. EATCHIP, the European ATC Harmonisation and Integration Programme, is now well under way and excessive delays are a thing of the past. The responsibility for flow control now rests with the Central Flow Management Unit in Brussels, which has replaced the previous fragmented system. The next phase of EATCHIP is the European Air Traffic Management System, which will use precision area navigation equipment in aircraft based on satellite navigation, inertial navigation and Mode S air/ground datalink. The ultimate aim is to provide aircraft with conflict-free paths between departure and destination. Much of the technology already exists and is on trial in various parts of the world, including over the North Atlantic.

The Central Control Function (CCF), the 'tunnels in the sky' concept designed to smooth and integrate the flows of traffic into and out of London's airports, continues on schedule. The approach radar functions of Heathrow and Gatwick have moved to the London Area and Terminal Control Centre. Construction of LATCC's replacement, the New En Route Centre (NERC) near Fareham in Hampshire, is now complete, but because of computer software problems it will not become operational until at least December 1997. In an effort to accommodate ever-increasing

traffic in LATCC's busiest sector, Daventry, two new sectors – Cowly and Welin – were introduced in February 1996 to replace the lower levels of the southern part of the Daventry Sector. This effectively extends terminal control to just south of Birmingham.

Since the last edition of this book, there have been many changes in the London Control sector frequencies, as well as fresh allocations for new sectors. Problems with interference have caused some frequencies to be abandoned soon after becoming operational, and in one or two cases the replacements have also been dropped. The situation seems to have stabilised, but there could be many more changes in the pipeline!

### Author's note

The reader is reminded that air band listening by unauthorised persons in the UK is technically illegal but there is evidence to suggest that officialdom regards it as an essentially harmless activity. The enthusiast is thus strongly advised not to use an air band receiver in public places other than airport viewing areas and at air shows.

# Acknowledgements

For their help in the preparation of this book I would like to thank the Civil Aviation Authority, British Airways Aerad, Siemens Plessey Systems, Lowe Electronics at Matlock, Transair (UK) Ltd at Fairoaks Airport, The Airband Shop at Heald Green near Manchester Airport, Raycom Communications, Waters and Stanton Electronics, and Nevada Communications. Also Ken Cothliff and Andy Rackham of Air Supply, near Leeds & Bradford Airport and Bob Sidwick of R. C. Simulations at Bristol Airport. I am particularly grateful to Ron Bishop of the Ulster Aviation Society for supplying much helpful advice and allowing me to draw freely on the material he has written about air band listening for the Society's magazine *Ulster Air Mail*. Other friends who have helped include Keith Crowden, Graham Innes, John Locker, Gary Nuttall, Steve Parsons, Margaret and Adrian Thompson, and Ken Rodgers. The magazine of the Merseyside Branch of Air-Britain, *North West Air News*, as always proved an invaluable source of information, particularly its 'Comscan' column and 'Airline News'. Finally, not forgetting Patrick Stephens who first suggested this book back in 1984 and whose input has been most useful ever since.

# Abbreviations and Q-Codes

* Abbreviations marked with an asterisk are normally spoken as a complete word.

| | |
|---|---|
| AAC | Air Arrivals Control |
| ACARS* | Aircraft Communications Addressing and Reporting System |
| ACAS* | Airborne Collision Avoidance System |
| ACC | Area Control Centre |
| ACMI* | Air Combat Manoeuvring Instrumentation |
| ADD | Allowable Deferred Defect |
| ADF | Automatic Direction Finder |
| ADR | Advisory Route |
| ADT | Approved Departure Time |
| AEF | Air Experience Flight |
| AFA | Air-to-Air Fuelling Area |
| AFIS* | Aerodrome Flight Information Service |
| AGL | Above Ground Level |
| AIS | Aeronautical Information Service |
| AM | Audio Modulation |
| AMSL | Above Mean Sea Level |
| APU | Auxiliary Power Unit |
| ARINC* | Aeronautical Radio Inc |
| ATA | Aerial Tactics Area |
| ATC | Air Traffic Control |
| ATD | Actual Time of Departure |
| ATIS* | Automatic Terminal Information Service |
| ATM | Air Traffic Monitor |
| ATU | Aerial Tuning Unit |
| ATZ | Aerodrome Traffic Zone |
| BAA | British Airports Authority |
| BFO | Beat Frequency Oscillator |

| | |
|---|---|
| CAA | Civil Aviation Authority |
| CAAFU* | Civil Aviation Authority Flying Unit |
| CAVOK* | (pronounced 'Cav okay') Ceiling and Visibility OK |
| CCF | Central Control Function |
| CDA | Continuous Descent Approaches |
| CHAPI* | Compact Helicopter Approach Path Indicator |
| CVR | Cockpit Voice Recorder |
| D/F | Direction Finding |
| DFR | Departure Flow Regulation |
| DGPS | Differential Global Positioning System |
| DME | Distance Measuring Equipment |
| DVP | Digital Voice Protection |
| EAT | Expected Approach Time |
| EATCHIP* | European Air Traffic Control Harmonisation Programme |
| EEPROM | Electronically Erasable Programmable Read-Only Memory |
| ETA | Estimated Time of Arrival |
| ETD | Estimated Time of Departure |
| FDPS | Flight Data Processing System |
| FDR | Flight Data Recorder |
| FIR | Flight Information Region |
| FISO | Flight Information Service Officers |
| FL | Flight Level |
| FM | Frequency Modulation |
| FMS | Flight Management System |

| | | | |
|---|---|---|---|
| FMU | Flow Management Unit | MDH | Minimum Descent Height |
| FTR | Fighter | MEDA | Military Emergency Diversion Aerodrome |
| FTU | Flying Training Unit | METRO* | US Military Met Office |
| GAT | General Air Traffic | MHz | Megahertz |
| GHFS | Global High Frequency System | MLS | Microwave Landing System |
| GLONASS* | Global Orbiting Navigation Satellite System | MNPS | Minimum Navigation Performance Specification |
| GMC | Ground Movement Control | MOR | Mandatory Occurrence Report |
| GMP | Ground Movement Planning | MRA | Military Reserved Airspace |
| GPS | Global Positioning System | MRSA | Mandatory Radar Service Area |
| GPU | Ground Power Unit | | |
| GPWS | Ground Proximity Warning System | MTA | Military Training Area |
| | | NDB | Non-Directional Beacon |
| HF | High Frequency | NERC* | New En Route Centre |
| HMR | Helicopter Main Route | NFM | Narrow (band) Frequency Modulation |
| HPZ | Helicopter Protected Zone | NM | Nautical Miles |
| IAS | Indicated Air Speed | NOTAM | Notice to Airmen |
| ICAO | International Civil Aviation Organisation | NPR | Noise-Preferential Routes |
| | | NRASA | Northern Radar Advisory Service |
| ICF | Initial Contact Frequency | | |
| IFR | Instrument Flight Rules | | |
| ILS | Instrument Landing System | OACC | Oceanic Area Control Centre |
| IMC | Instrument Meteorological Conditions | OAT | Operational Air Traffic or Outside Air Temperature |
| INS | Inertial Navigation System | OCA | Oceanic Control Area |
| IRVR | Instrumented Runway Visual Range | OCH | Obstacle Clearance Height |
| | | ORCAM* | Originating Region Code Assignment Method |
| kHz | Kilohertz | OTS | Organised Track System |
| LARS* | Lower Airspace Radar Advisory Service | PAPI* | Precision Approach Path Indicator |
| LATCC* | London Area and Terminal Control Centre | PAR | Precision Approach Radar |
| | | PIREP* | Pilot Report of weather conditions encountered en route |
| LDOCF | Long Distance Operational Control Facilities | | |
| LITAS | Low Intensity Two-Colour Approach Slope Indicator | PPR | Prior Permission Required |
| LJAO | London Joint Area Organisation | QAR | Quick Access Recorder |
| | | QDM | Magnetic track to the airfield with nil wind |
| LSB | Lower Side Band | | |
| MACS | Military Aeronautical Communication System | QFE | Barometric pressure at aerodrome level |
| MATO | Military Air Traffic Operations | QGH | Controlled descent through cloud |
| MATZ* | Military Aerodrome Traffic Zone | QNH | Barometric pressure at sea level |

| | | | |
|---|---|---|---|
| QSY | Change frequency to . . . | TA | Traffic Advisory |
| QTE | True bearing from the | TACAN* | Tactical Air Navigation |
| | aerodrome | TAD* | Tactical Air Designator |
| | | TAF* | Terminal Aerodrome Forecast |
| RA | Resolution Advisory | TAS | True Air Speed |
| RAS | Radar Advisory Service | TCA | See TMA |
| RCC | Rescue Co-ordination Centre | TCAS* | Traffic Alert and Collision |
| RIS | Radar Information Service | | Avoidance System |
| RIV | Rapid Intervention Vehicle | TMA | Terminal Control Area |
| RP | Reporting Point | | (formerly Terminal |
| R/T | Radio telephony | | Manoeuvring Area) |
| RTOW | Regulated Take-Off Weight | TOS | Traffic Orientation Scheme |
| RTTY* | (pronounced 'Ritty') Radio | TRACON* | Terminal Radar Control |
| | Teletype | | |
| RVR | Runway Visual Range | UAR | Upper Air Route |
| | | UAS | University Air Squadron |
| SAR | Search And Rescue | UHF | Ultra High Frequency |
| SID* | Standard Instrument | UIR | Upper (Flight) Information |
| | Departure | | Region |
| SLP | Speed Limit Point | USAF | United States Air Force |
| SMR | Surface Movement Radar | USB | Upper Side Band |
| SOTA* | Shannon Oceanic Transition | UTC | Universal Time Constant |
| | Area | | |
| SPECI | Special Observation | VASI* | Visual Approach Slope |
| | Approach | | Indicator |
| SRA | Surveillance Radar | VCR | Visual Control Room |
| SSB | Single Side Band | VDF | VHF Direction Finder |
| SSR | Secondary Surveillance | VFR | Visual Flight Rules |
| | Radar | VHF | Very High Frequency |
| STAR* | Standard (Instrument) | VMC | Visual Meteorological |
| | Arrival Route | | Conditions |
| STCICS | Strike Command Integrated | VOR | VHF Omni-directional Range |
| | Communications System | VRP | Visual Reference Point |
| STOL* | Short Take-Off and Landing | | |
| | | WFM | Wide Frequency Modulation |

# Chapter 1

# Listening

What you can hear, and in turn relate to aircraft you see flying overhead, obviously depends on the position of your location relative to airports and air lanes. Since VHF radio waves follow approximate lines of sight, the higher the aircraft, the further away you can hear messages from it. Transmitter power is also a factor, but, generally speaking, high-flying aircraft can be received up to 200 miles away. As a rule of thumb, frequencies below 123MHz are allocated to Tower and Approach units and those above 123MHz to Area Control Centres (ACCs), although there are exceptions to this.

Ground stations may be screened by hills, buildings and other obstructions, so you may not be able to pick up the replies from the tower or approach if you live more than 10 miles away from the airport. The coverage for the ACCs at London, Manchester and Prestwick is very much better, however, there being few places in the flatter parts of the British Isles out of range of one or more of the powerful transmitters. This is because they are sited at some distance from their associated ground stations, usually on high ground. There may, however, be some 'blind spots' in reception for no apparent reason.

The first thing to do is to establish which ground stations are within range and which can help you to identify aircraft flying in your local area. If you are fortunate enough to own a scanning receiver you can set up the appropriate frequencies and monitor them when required. With experience you will soon know which station an aircraft is likely to be 'working', its height being a

good clue as to whether it is talking to the local airfield, ACC, radar unit, etc.

Unfortunately in parts of Britain there are so many ATC units capable of giving a radar service that it may be difficult to discover to which a transit aircraft is talking. A flight below airways in the North Midlands, for example, might be in contact with Birmingham, East Midlands or Shawbury Radar, or simply the London Flight Information frequency. Of course, the pilot might not be talking to anyone, nor does he need to if he keeps clear of aerodrome traffic zones and other restricted airspace.

If you have the good fortune to live beneath an airway and, even better, close to one of its reporting points, the relevant airways frequency can be selected and you can sit back and wait for something interesting to appear. Alas, rare aircraft seem to have a tendency to fly over when there is a solid cloud layer and only a tantalising drone or rumble can be heard! Unfortunately, it is not just a simple case of listening in, running outside at the right moment and rapidly filling up one's notebooks. Aircraft do not always use their registrations or serial numbers as call-signs, and most commercial flights use a call-sign totally unrelated to what is painted on the aircraft.

The answers to many of the questions that may arise from this procedure are to be found in the network of enthusiasts' magazines, which keep most airfields under surveillance and publish detailed lists of visitors, usually tabulated by call-sign as well as registration letters. The information

**Left** *View from the Air Traffic Control Tower at Southampton Eastleigh Airport* (Airports UK).

is normally acquired by courtesy of the airport management or ATC, the ranks of which are riddled with enthusiast 'moles'. Some private airfields, such as those run by British Aerospace that operate military aircraft, are understandably less co-operative, but there is often a local spotter who makes notes and passes them on! Since most transatlantic flights from North West Europe have to cross Britain at some point, even those anonymous airliners on contrails can be identified as there are several publications available that match the call-sign and registration of most of them.

Identifying military aircraft is very difficult as few use the actual serial number, USAF transports being one of the few exceptions. Military airfields generally use UHF frequencies to communicate with their own aircraft, but many scanners are able to receive UHF signals. Unfortunately, the call-signs of first-line aircraft are changed frequently for security reasons.

Bearing in mind that air traffic has its rush hours too, certain times of the day can be particularly rewarding for air band listeners. For example, the Heathrow peak period for arriving traffic is mid-morning, reflected in the increased landing fees at this time. Late afternoon, especially on Fridays, sees an even larger volume of traffic in the congested United Kingdom airways system, as the entire British executive fleet seems intent upon making for home!

For insomniacs there is plenty going on even in the smallest hours of the night, as aircraft flying the mail wend their way in and out of Liverpool, Coventry and East Midlands five nights a week to and from all points of the compass. Heathrow has a virtual ban on traffic after midnight because of noise restrictions, but Manchester, Luton, Glasgow and others send load after load of holidaymakers to the Mediterranean and further afield. Mixed in are the newspaper and general

cargo aircraft, most of them scheduled, but occasionally including special charters rushing some urgently needed parts for the motor industry.

Finally, a note about the law relating to air band listening. In a word, it is illegal for the unlicensed! It is also a myth that listening is permitted if one does not impart the information to another person. Judging by the number of radios one hears blasting out across public viewing areas at airports, it would appear that officialdom turns a blind eye to what is essentially a harmless activity. The law may be changed one day, but in the meantime do not telephone the newspapers if you overhear a hijack or some other emergency in progress. This sort of thing could end the authorities' tacit acceptance of air band listening. Be discreet!

In 1965 there was some trouble caused by cheap super-regenerative receivers that actually re-transmitted the received signal. The resulting carrier wave interfered with air-to-ground communications and air band radios were banned on Manchester Airport's public viewing galleries, unless the owner had a dispensation from the telecommunications section, which offered a free testing service. This appears to have been the only time when air band radios have ever been controlled in this country, and there is no evidence that it was done at any other British airport.

However, since modern air band receivers are totally passive, there is no chance of spurious transmissions jamming the air waves. Trouble may loom in another area because many scanners are able to monitor cellular telephone conversations. British Telecom and its competitors have complained about this to the Department of Trade & Industry, but no action has so far been taken to control the sale of scanning receivers. Listening to police messages is another illegal activity, and there have been a number of recent cases involving heavy fines and confiscated scanners. Merely having these frequencies in the receiver's memory is considered proof of guilt. You have been warned!

# Chapter 2

# *ATC terminology*

The majority of air band listeners use their radios as a means of logging aircraft registrations, but there are others for whom this is of no more than academic interest. Their listening pleasure is derived from learning how aircraft are controlled and the way the ATC system operates. Those in the second category will soon begin to grasp the principles, and will want to find out more, while those in the first will recognise that a basic knowledge of them will assist in tracking the aircraft in which they are interested.

Before I embark upon a more detailed description of ATC I should like first to cast some light on the jargon words that seem to puzzle the new air band listener. The most obvious are the terms QNH, QFE and Flight Level. The first two are codes rather than abbreviations and refer to the current atmospheric pressure at sea level and aerodrome level respectively. When the value in millibars is set on the aircraft's altimeter, the instrument will indicate the distance above the appropriate datum. The term QFE Threshold refers, by the way, to the barometric pressure converted to that at the end of the runway.

Above a point known as the transition altitude, normally between 3,000ft and 6,000ft in the United Kingdom, a standard setting of 1013.2 millibars is used, producing what is termed a Flight Level (abbreviated to FL). This ensures that all aircraft, particularly within controlled airspace, are flying on the same altimeter setting and can thus easily be separated vertically by the required amount. This obviates the necessity of continually adjusting the altimeter to allow for local pressure variations over the route, any error being common to all aircraft in the system. FL70 is roughly equivalent to 7,000ft, FL230 to 23,000ft and so on.

Times are given in the form of two figures: for example 14, pronounced one-four, indicates 14 minutes past the hour, four-two 42 minutes past the hour, and so on. The standard ATC time in the United Kingdom, and indeed in the entire aviation world, is Universal Time Constant (UTC). In the winter it is the same as local or 'Alpha' time in the United Kingdom, but British Summer Time is one hour ahead of it. This use of UTC ensures that there is no confusion with Flight Plans on aircraft flying through time zones.

The word 'squawk' is often heard, particularly in route clearances, along with a four-figure code. This is set on the aircraft's transponder, a device that responds to automatic interrogations from a ground station by sending a return signal in coded form. The information appears on the radar screen as a label giving call-sign, height and destination, adjacent to the appropriate aircraft position symbol. The word 'blip' is obsolete, the image on the display (screen is obsolete too!) on modern radars being produced electronically via a computer. The centre sweep familiar in films is now rarely seen, as even relatively old radar equipment can be processed to produce an excellent picture.

The term 'clearance' or 'cleared' is a legal one meaning that the aircraft may proceed under certain explicit conditions and that it will not be impeded by other traffic. It has,

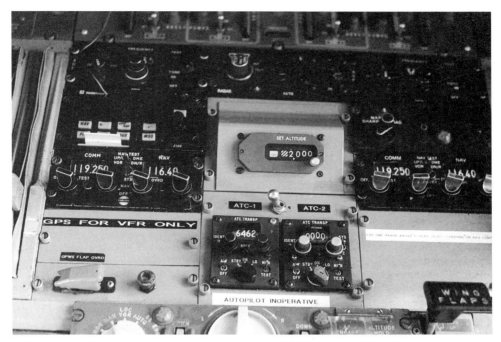

*An Air Atlantic DC-6 coms panel with the Coventry Tower frequency and Honiley VOR selected. The transponder in the foreground is showing a UK domestic squawk code* (Steve Parsons).

in the past, been rather over-used by controllers in circumstances where its use was unnecessary, so the authorities have narrowed it down considerably. It is now confined mainly to route clearances and runway occupancy for take-off and landing, thus avoiding any possible confusion with the meaning.

Directions are given in degrees magnetic, so that if an aircraft is heading 360° it is flying due north, 090° due east, and so on. Note the difference between 'heading' and actual path over the ground ('track'). If there is a strong cross-wind an aircraft may be pointing ('heading') in a particular direction but travelling over the ground in a considerably different direction. There is an analogy here with rowing a small boat across a fast-flowing river; although you may be aiming for a point on the opposite bank, the current will also be deflecting you sideways. Simple 'right' and 'left' are used

for direction changes, as in the instruction 'Turn right heading 340°; 'port' and 'starboard' are long outmoded in aviation.

Speed is expressed in knots, 1 knot being equal to 1 nautical mile per hour. The exception to this is on transatlantic and similar long-haul flights where a Mach number is employed, speed being expressed as a ratio of the speed of sound. Above 25,000ft, this overcomes considerable airspeed indicator errors caused by low air density and varying temperatures. Jet transports cruise at around Mach 0.8 and Concorde at Mach 2, twice the speed of sound.

Distances are measured in nautical miles (approximately 2,025yd). References to DME, as in 'Report 8 DME Wallasey', relate to the Distance Measuring Equipment carried aboard aircraft. This receives radio transmissions from ground beacons and enables the distance to or from the particular position to be presented automatically to the pilot as a continuous read-out in miles and tenths of a mile. In some systems, the 'time to go' to the beacon can also be displayed to the pilot.

Runways are designated by two numbers derived from the heading in degrees magnetic. The runway at Manchester, for example, is '06/24', which is rounded up from the actual direction of 057/237° magnetic, and the end zero omitted. Similarly a heading of 054/234 would be presented as 05/23. Other familiar examples are 09 Right/27 Left and 09 Left/27 Right at Heathrow, and 08 Right/26 Left at Gatwick. Note that small annual changes in the bearing of the Magnetic Pole can affect the designation of runways. For example, Heathrow's directions were 10/28 until 1987, when the exact alignment became nearer to 090/270° than 100/280° magnetic.

Somewhat confusing to the layman are the terms VFR, IFR, VMC and IMC; these are of paramount importance in ATC, so I shall explain them at some length. Flight conditions are divided thus:

a   Visual Flight Rules (VFR), which apply under Visual Meteorological Conditions (VMC), and
b   Instrument Flight Rules (IFR), which apply under Instrument Meteorological Conditions (IMC).

The minima for VFR flight are quite complicated, but can be summarised as follows. At or below 3,000ft AMSL at an indicated air speed (IAS) of 140 knots or less, an aircraft must remain in sight of ground or water and clear of cloud in a flight visibility of at least 1,500 metres. If the IAS is more than 140kt up to a limit of 250kt, the flight visibility must be at least 6km. Above 3,000ft up to FL100 the minima are 5km visibility and at least 1,500 metres horizontally, or 1,000ft vertically clear of cloud. At FL100 and above, the speed limit no longer applies and the visibility minimum is increased to 8km.

Since it is his or her responsibility to keep clear of other traffic, the pilot must maintain a good look-out. Furthermore, so as to expedite traffic, under certain conditions climbs or descents maintaining VMC may be authorised for aircraft flying under IFR; it is then the pilot's responsibility to avoid other traffic. In R/T transmissions the terms VFR, or 'Victor Fox', are used freely. In the same way, VMC may be referred to as 'Victor Mike'. The phrase 'VMC on top' means that the aircraft is flying in VMC conditions above a cloud layer.

IFR comes into force when the visibility requirements described above cannot be met, and at all times during the hours of darkness. It is then mandatory for an aircraft to be flown on instruments by a suitably qualified pilot. It must also carry a minimum scale of navigational and other equipment. Within controlled airspace, responsibility for separation from other aircraft is in the hands of the ground controllers.

Outside controlled airspace, pilots flying above the transition altitude of 3,000ft must reset their altimeters to the standard setting of 1,013 millibars and fly in accordance with what is known as the quadrantal rule. This is intended to ensure that aircraft on converging headings at levels below 24,500ft remain clear of each other by at least 500ft, as the following table explains:

| *Magnetic track* | *Cruising level* |
| --- | --- |
| Less than 90° | Odd thousands of feet |
| 90° but less than 180° | Odd thousands of feet plus 500ft |
| 180° but less than 270° | Even thousands of feet |
| 270° but less than 360° | Even thousands of feet plus 500ft |

*Above 24,500ft the semi-circular rule applies:*

| *Magnetic track* | *Cruising level* |
| --- | --- |
| Less than 180° | 25,000ft<br>27,000ft<br>29,000ft or higher levels at intervals of 4,000ft |

180° but less than 360°   26,000ft
28,000ft
31,000ft or higher
levels at intervals of
4,000ft

A further variation on the IFR/VFR theme is Special VFR, an authorisation by ATC for a pilot to fly within a control zone, even though he is unable to comply with IFR, and in certain airspace where provision is made for such flights. Depending on the visibility, amount of cloud and its height, and the limitations of the pilot's licence, a Special VFR clearance may be requested and issued.

Standard separation is provided between all Special VFR flights, and between such flights and other aircraft operating IFR. In practice much use is made of geographical features to keep Special VFR traffic apart, for instance by routeing along opposite banks of an estuary. When flying on this type of clearance a pilot must comply with ATC instructions and remain at all times in flight conditions that enable him to determine his flight path and to keep clear of obstructions. It is implicit in all Special VFR clearances that the aircraft stays clear of cloud and in sight of the surface. ATC almost always imposes a height limitation that will require the pilot to fly either at or below a specific level. A typical clearance at Liverpool, for example, is 'GYE is cleared to the zone boundary via Chester, Special VFR not above altitude 1,500ft Liverpool QNH 1002'.

## The phonetic alphabet

The use of phonetics on radio to overcome the problems of confusion between similar-sounding letters like 'B' and 'P', or 'M' and 'N', dates back to the First World War, when it was essential that such information as map references were passed accurately by aircraft spotting for the artillery. The phonetic alphabet of the time began 'A-Ack, B-Beer . . .' and has left us with such familiar phrases as 'Ack-Ack' for Anti-Aircraft fire. By the Second World War it had been replaced by an alphabet beginning 'A-Able, B-Baker, C-Charlie. . .' In the 1950s, by international agreement, the British wartime code was superseded by a new alphabet designed to be more easily pronounced by aircrew whose native language was other than English. Some of the original phonetics were retained but a number of words known throughout the world were now employed. The resulting alphabet was almost identical to that in use today, the exceptions being M-Metro, N-Nectar and X-Extra. The new offering sparked off some ribald comment that its originators seemed to have spent a lot of time hanging around in bars and dance-halls, such was the emphasis on these admirable pursuits! The alphabet was overhauled once more in 1956 and remains in use to this day.

My only subjective criticism is that 'Juliet' and 'Zulu' can be confused, admittedly not very often, when used by certain foreign nationals against a background of engine noise. 'Papa' is another weak point; correctly it should be pronounced 'Pah-*Pah*', but this is more difficult to say and most pilots and controllers pronounce it with equal emphasis on the two syllables.

Certain universally accepted codes and abbreviations, such as QNH, QFE, ILS, SRA, QDM are not put into phonetics but said as written. There is also a standard way of pronouncing numbers, and the word 'decimal', as used in radio frequencies, is supposed to be pronounced 'dayseemal', although this rarely happens in practice.

*Current phonetic alphabet*

| | | |
|---|---|---|
| A – Alpha | J – Juliet | S – Sierra |
| B – Bravo | K – Kilo | T – Tango |
| C – Charlie | L – Lima | U -Uniform |
| D – Delta | M – Mike | V – Victor |
| E – Echo | N – November | W -Whiskey |
| F – Foxtrot | O – Oscar | X – X-Ray |
| G – Golf | P – Papa | Y – Yankee |
| H – Hotel | Q – Quebec | Z – Zulu |
| I – India | R – Romeo | |

### Transmission of numbers

| | | |
|---|---|---|
| 0 – Zero | 4 – Fower | 8 – Ait |
| 1 – Wun | 5 – Fife | 9 – Niner |
| 2 – Too | 6 – Six | Thousand – |
| 3 – Tree | 7 – Seven | Tousand |

Examples of number transmissions include: 10 – Wun Zero; 583 – Fife Ait Tree; 2,500 – Too Tousand Fife Hundred; 3,000 – Tree Tousand. (I once heard an Irish pilot who, after the controller used the word 'tree', accused him of 'takin' da mickey'!)

An exception is Flight Level One Hundred, said in this way to avoid the confusion that has sometimes taken place in the past. Frequencies are passed in the form: 118.1 – Wun Wun Ait Dayseemal Wun; 120.375 – Wun Too Zero Dayseemal Tree Seven (the final digit being omitted).

## The Q-Code

A further note concerns the Q-Code, long obsolete in aviation apart from certain enduring terms like QGH, QNH and QFE. This was an expansion of the Q-Code already in use by the merchant marine, and it became possible to exchange information on practically all subjects that might be needed in aviation communications. These three-letter groups could be sent by wireless telegraphy (W/T) in morse with great speed, and overcame any inherent language difficulties. For example, an operator would send the code 'QDM' to a ground station, which meant 'What is my magnetic course to steer with zero wind to reach you?' The ground operator would transmit 'QDM' and the appropriate figure.

## Standard words and phrases used in R/T communications

| Word/Phrase | Meaning |
|---|---|
| Acknowledge | Let me know that you have received and understood this message |
| Affirm | Yes |
| Approved | Permission for proposed action granted |
| Break | Indicates the separation between messages |
| Cancel | Annul the previously transmitted clearance |
| Check | Examine a system or procedure (no answer is normally expected) |
| Cleared | Authorised to proceed under the conditions specified |
| Confirm | Have I correctly received the following? or Did you correctly receive this message? |
| Contact | Establish radio contact with . . . (the obsolete code 'QSY', which meant the same thing, is often still used by pilots) |
| Correct | That is correct |
| Correction | An error has been made in this transmission (or message indicated). The correct version is . . . |
| Disregard | Consider that transmission as not sent |
| How do you read? | What is the readability of my transmission? |
| I say again | I repeat for clarity or emphasis |
| Monitor | Listen out on (frequency) |
| Negative | No, or permission not granted, or that is not correct |
| Over | My transmission is ended and I expect a response from you |
| Out | My transmission is ended and no response is expected |
| Pass your message | Proceed with your message |
| Read back | Repeat all, or the specified part, of this message back to me exactly as received |
| Report | Pass required information |
| Request | I should like to know, or I wish to obtain |
| Roger | I have received all your last transmission (under no circumstances should this |

be used in reply to a question requiring a direct answer in the affirmative (Affirm) or negative (Negative)

*Say again* — Repeat all, or the following part of, your last transmission

*Stand by* — Wait and I will call you (no onward clearance should be assumed)

*Verify* — Check and confirm

*Wilco* — I understand your message and will comply with it (abbreviation for 'will comply')

In practice the words 'Over' and 'Out' are now rarely used. Also note that controllers who are recently ex-military sometimes use standard RAF phrases such as 'Wait' (for Stand by) and 'Wrong' (for 'Correction').

The clarity of radio transmissions is expressed by the following scale:

Readability 1 – unreadable
Readability 2 – readable now and then
Readability 3 – readable but with difficulty
Readability 4 – readable
Readability 5 – perfectly readable

Note that controllers in exasperation sometimes use non-standard phrases like 'Strength a half' for really awful radios! Another phrase in common usage is 'Carrier wave only', indicating that an unmodulated transmission is being received by the ground station, ie it is just noise without the accompanying speech.

## Communications

Aeronautical ground stations are identified by the name of the location, followed by a suffix that indicates the type of service being given.

| Suffix | Service |
|---|---|
| Control | Area Control Service |
| Radar | Radar (in general) |
| Director | Approach Radar Controller dealing only with arriving traffic |
| Arrivals | As Director but currently only used at Manchester |
| Approach | Approach Control |
| Tower | Aerodrome Control |
| Ground | Ground Movement Control |
| Delivery | Ground Movement Planning (Clearance Delivery) |
| Talkdown | Precision Approach Radar (Military) |
| Information | Flight Information Service |
| Radio | Aerodrome Air/Ground Communications Service. |

When satisfactory two-way communication has been established, and provided that it will not be confusing, the name of the location or the call-sign suffix may be omitted. The basic rule is that the full call-signs of both stations must be used on the first transmission. For example:

Aircraft: 'Southend Tower GABCD.'
ATC: 'GABCD Southend Tower pass your message.'

Aircraft call-signs may take various forms, but they must remain the same throughout the flight. However, if aircraft on the same frequency have similar call-signs, ATC may instruct them to alter the format temporarily to avoid confusion. One other point is that aircraft in the heavy wake turbulence category must include the word 'heavy' immediately after the call-sign in the initial call. This is to remind the controller that increased separation may be necessary for following aircraft.

Aircraft are identified by one of the following types of call-signs:

(a) the registration of the aircraft, eg GBFRM, N753DA

(b) the registration of the aircraft preceded by the approved telephony designator of the operating company, eg Speedbird GBGDC

(c) the flight identification or trip number, eg Manx 501.

Once satisfactory two-way communication with an aircraft has been established, controllers are permitted to abbreviate the call-sign but only to the extent shown in the table below.

| Full call-sign | Abbreviation |
|---|---|
| GBFRM | GRM |
| Speedbird GBGDC | Speedbird DC |
| N31029 | N029 |
| N753DA | N3DA |
| Cherokee GBGTR | Cherokee TR |
| Manx 501 | No abbreviation |

In practice other variations are to be heard, some pilots using their company three-letter designator and flight number rather than the normal company name and flight number, eg RDK 232 for Irish Tours 232. Either is correct and it is quite common for controllers, faced with an unfamiliar company designator on a flight progress strip, or simply forgetting what it stands for, to revert to the three-letter prefix.

The aim is to prevent incidents and potential accidents caused by call-sign ambiguities, but they still occur in sufficient numbers to cause concern. Regular bulletins of Mandatory Occurrence Reports (MORs) are circulated among pilots and controllers, and they often contain reports of aircraft with similar call-signs taking instructions meant for each other by mistake.

Private aircraft normally use the aircraft registration letters or numbers as a call-sign, as do some taxi and executive aircraft, as well as some airliners on training or empty positioning flights. Otherwise, commercial operators use their company designator and flight number as in (c) above. Intensive use of flight numbers often leads to call-sign confusion when two aircraft with the same flight number are on frequency together, for example Air France 532 and Air Malta 532. The problem is under constant scrutiny and a possible solution is the use of alpha-numerics. The late-lamented Dan-Air ran a trial in the 1980s, a typical call-sign being Dan-Air Bravo Six Foxtrot Echo, but the scheme failed to secure international agreement and was shelved. Further confusion has been caused by call-signs resembling flight levels or headings, so operators have agreed, as far as possible, not to allocate flight numbers that end in zero or five; in practice, this means figures below 500.

## Glossary of aviation terms heard on radio

See also Abbreviations and lists on pages 20, 21 and 47.

| | |
|---|---|
| *Abeam* | Passing a specified point at 90 degrees to the left or right |
| *Abort* | Abandon take-off or return prematurely |
| *Active* | The runway in use |
| *Actual* | Current weather conditions |
| *Air Pilot* | UK Aeronautical Information Publication |
| *Airprox* | Official term for a near-miss |
| *Alternate* | Alternate airfield if unable to land at destination |
| *Approach plate* | Alternative term for approach chart |
| *Approach sequence* | Position in traffic on to final approach |
| *Approved Departure Time* | See pages 61 and 93 |
| *Avgas* | Aviation gasoline |
| *Backtrack* | Taxi back along the runway |
| *Bandboxed* | Two or more frequencies when monitored by one controller during quiet periods |
| *Base check* | Periodic training flight to check the competency of commercial flight crew |
| *Base turn* | Turn on to final from an instrument approach when it is not a reciprocal of the outbound track |
| *The Bell* | Colloquial term for Belfast VOR |
| *Blind transmission* | Transmission from one station to another when two-way communication |

| | |
|---|---|
| | cannot be established, but where it is believed that the called station is able to receive the transmission |
| The Boundary | That between Flight Information Regions, or the edge of a Control Zone |
| Box | Radio, Box One being the main set and Box Two the stand-by |
| Breakthrough | Transmissions on one frequency breaking through on to another |
| Build-ups | Cumulo-nimbus clouds |
| CB | Cumulo-nimbus clouds (also referred to as 'Charlie Bravo') |
| Centrefix Approach | Self-positioning to final approach using the aircraft Flight Management System |
| Charlie | That is correct (common HF usage) |
| Chopping to approach | Military term for changing frequency |
| Clearance limit | Specified point to which an ATC clearance remains effective |
| Coasting in/out | Crossing the coast inbound/outbound |
| The company | As in 'Follow the company', ie an aircraft belonging to the same operator as the subject |
| Conflict Alert | See page 39 |
| Conflicting traffic | Other aircraft in the vicinity that may prove a hazard |
| The Cross | Colloquial term for Dean Cross VOR |
| Crosswind component | Strength of wind from the side on final approach |
| The Data | Temperature, QNH, runway in use, etc |
| Detail | Intentions during a particular training flight |
| Direct | Flying from one beacon or geographical point straight to another |
| Discrete | Separate frequency usually devoted to one aircraft for PAR talk-down, etc |

| | |
|---|---|
| Div Arrival | Arrival message sent to destination and other agencies when an aircraft diverts en route |
| Dover Tour | Standard 'sight-seeing' route conducted by Manston Radar for visiting military aircraft |
| Drift | Effect of wind on an aircraft (see page 17) |
| En route | As in 'Report going en route', ie changing to another frequency |
| Established | Aligned or 'locked on' with the ILS |
| Expected Approach Time | See pages 48 and 49 |
| Fanstop | Practice engine failure |
| Flag | Warning flag on a cockpit instrument that the ILS or other ground-based aid has failed or is not being received correctly |
| Fod | Jargon word for airfield debris, derived from the abbreviation of 'foreign object damage' |
| Free call | Call to a ground station without prior co-ordination by landline between this and the previous ATC unit with which the aircraft was in contact |
| Glide path | Final descent path to the runway on an ILS approach |
| Go around | Overshoot runway and rejoin the circuit or carry out a missed approach procedure |
| Good rate | Unofficial abbreviation for a good rate of climb or descent |
| The Gow | Colloquial term for Glasgow VOR |
| Guard frequency | International Distress Frequency that is monitored continuously by aircraft flying long-distance routes |

| | | | |
|---|---|---|---|
| *Heading* | Direction in which an aircraft is pointing (see also Track) | *Radial* | Magnetic bearing line from or to a VOR |
| *Heavy* | See page 21 | *Released* | Control of a particular aircraft handed over from airways controller to approach |
| *Intentions* | Course of action after a missed approach, etc | | |
| *IR Test* | Instrument Rating Test | *Recovery* | Military jargon for 'land back at base' |
| *Jet A-1* | Turbine fuel | | |
| *Land after* | See pages 56 and 57 | *Regional* | QNH for a defined area (see page 32) |
| *Localiser* | See page 36 | | |
| *Mach* | Speed expressed as a ratio of the speed of sound (Mach 1) | *Rejected take-off* | Abandoned take-off procedure that is often practised during pilot check-outs |
| *Navex* | Navigational Exercise | | |
| *No ATC speed* | Unofficial abbreviation for 'no ATC speed restriction' | *Resume own navigation* | Revert to self-navigation after a period of radar vectoring |
| *Off blocks* | Time the aircraft commenced taxiing | | |
| *On blocks* | Time on parking stand | *Runway heading* | Climb straight ahead after take-off |
| *On task* | Aircraft reporting on scene or job | *Sector* | Each leg of a series of (usually) scheduled flights; also the sub-division of an area control service |
| *Orbit* | Circle, usually over a specified point | | |
| *The Park* | Colloquial term for Brookmans Park VOR | *Securité* | Prefix to RAF flight safety message |
| *Pattern* | American equivalent of circuit | *Selcal* | Selective Calling (see page 75) |
| *Pax* | Passengers | | |
| *The Pole* | Colloquial term for Pole Hill VOR | *Sigmet* | Significant Meteorological Conditions |
| *Pop-up traffic* | Traffic that suddenly appears on radar, perhaps because it has just climbed into coverage | *Slot time* | See page 61 |
| | | *Snoclo* | Airfield closed during snow-clearing operations |
| | | *Snowtam* | See page 85 |
| *Powerback* | Reversing out of an apron stand under the aircraft's own power | *Special flight* | Police, photographic survey or other flight for which special permission has been granted by the CAA |
| *Practice asymmetric* | Engine failure simulation on a multi-engined aircraft | *Speed Limit Point* | Position before which an inbound aircraft entering a TMA must have slowed to the speed limit (normally 250kt), and after which the speed limit is lifted for a departing aircraft |
| *Procedure turn* | Similar to Base turn except that the aircraft retraces its steps on an exact reciprocal of the outbound leg | | |
| *Pushback* | Reversing out of an apron stand with the aid of a ground tractor | *Squawk* | SSR code (see page 63) |
| | | *Stand* | Numbered parking position on apron |
| *Radar heading* | Heading imposed by a radar controller | | |
| *Radar overhead* | Radar blind spot above aerial | *Standard Missed Approach* | Procedure followed if an aircraft is unable to land from an instrument approach |
| *Radar vectoring* | Specified headings given by radar (see page 49) | | |

| | |
|---|---|
| *Stepdown fix* | Defined point on the final approach track indicating that a critical obstacle has been safely overflown and descent to the next specified level may be commenced |
| *Stratus* | Low-lying cloud layer |
| *Stud* | Military pre-set frequency |
| *Teardrop* | 180° turn to land back on the runway from which the aircraft has just departed; often used by circuit training aircraft when the runway-in-use is changed |
| *Tech stop* | En route diversion for technical reasons |
| *Three greens* | Indication that the wheels are down and locked |
| *Track* | Path of an aircraft over the ground |
| *Traffic* | Other aircraft known to be in the vicinity |
| *U/s* | Unserviceable |
| *Volmet* | See page 86 |
| *Vortex wake* | See pages 91, 92 and 93 |
| *Wake turbulence* | Alternative form of vortex wake |
| *Waypoint* | Pre-selected geographical position used with a Flight Management System |
| *Wind shear* | See page 85 |

Moving on from call-sign presentation, there are certain other basic R/T rules with which pilots must comply. Aircraft flying in controlled airspace must obtain permission from the controlling authority before they can change frequency to another station. They should not, for example, call the tower until approach instructs them to do so. Pilots sometimes take instructions intended for other aircraft, particularly if the call-signs are similar. Controllers need to be constantly vigilant to the possibility of such mistakes.

Another important point is that an ATC route clearance is not an instruction to take off or enter an active runway. The term 'take-off' is used only when an aircraft is cleared for take-off; at all other times the word 'departure' is used. The disaster at Tenerife in 1977 was caused mainly by a flight crew interpreting a route clearance as also implying a take-off clearance. They must have known better, but there were pressing distractions and the fatal error was made.

There is also a stringent requirement to read back route (or airways) clearances because of the possible seriousness of a misunderstanding in the transmission and receipt of these messages. If the controller does not receive a read-back, the pilot will be asked to give one. Similarly, the pilot is expected to request that instructions be repeated or clarified if any are not fully understood.

The following ATC instructions should be read back in full by the pilot: level, heading and speed instructions; airways or route clearances; runway-in-use; clearance to enter, land on, take off on, backtrack, hold short of, or cross an active runway; Secondary Surveillance Radar operating instructions; altimeter settings; VDF information; frequency changes; and type of radar service. For example:

ATC: 'GBFVM cleared to cross Bravo 1 at Ottringham Flight Level 180.'
Aircraft: 'Cleared to cross Bravo 1 at Ottringham Flight Level 180, GVM.'

ATC: 'GTE contact East Midlands Approach 119.65.'
Aircraft: '119.65 GTE.'

Levels may be reported as altitude, height or Flight Level, according to the phase of flight and the altimeter setting, but a standard form of reporting is adhered to. In ATC instructions an aircraft climbs, descends, maintains, passes, leaves or reaches a level. For example:

'Shamrock 920 climb FL190.'
'Midland 581 maintain altitude 3,500ft.'
'Speedbird 58 report passing FL160.'
'Swissair 842 report reaching FL190.'

Aircraft: 'Manx 501 request descent.'

ATC: 'Manx 501 descend FL60.'
Aircraft: 'Manx 501 leaving FL90 for FL60.'

Sometimes a changing traffic situation may necessitate an intermediate halt to a descent or climb, for example: 'Shamrock 920 stop descent FL150.' Or perhaps for traffic reasons a higher than normal rate of climb or descent may be requested to avoid eroding separation: 'Shamrock 920 climb to FL190, expedite passing FL150.' The non-approved phrase 'good rate' can often be heard, verbal shorthand for a good rate of climb or descent.

## Separations

The rules for separation of IFR traffic, particularly when radar is not available, are quite complicated and probably of little interest to the layman. Suffice it to say that the basic radar separations are 5 miles laterally (but 3 and up to 10 in certain

cases) and/or 1,000ft vertically up to FL290. Above this level 2,000ft vertical separation is applied, and above FL450 for supersonic aircraft 4,000ft is the norm.

For aircraft departing from an airport the minimum separation is 1 minute, provided that the aircraft fly on tracks diverging by 45° or more immediately after take-off. Where aircraft are going the same way, and provided that the first has filed a True Air Speed (TAS) 40kt or faster than the second, the separation is 2 minutes. With a TAS of 20kt or more faster than the second aircraft, it becomes 5 minutes, and in all other cases it is 10 minutes. Radar may reduce some of these times, and they are also affected by the demands of vortex wake separation and local procedures.

## Categories of priority

Requests for clearances are normally dealt with in the order in which they are

*The Approach Radar Room at Leeds-Bradford Airport* (Andy Rackham, Air Supply).

received, and are issued according to the traffic situation. However, certain aircraft are given priority over others in the following descending order:

**Category A**   Aircraft in an emergency, and ambulance/medical aircraft when the safety of life is involved
Aircraft that have declared a 'Police Emergency'

**Category B**   Search and Rescue and post-accident flight checks of navigation aids

**Category C**   Royal Flights

**Category D**   Certain flights carrying Heads of Government or very senior government officials

**Category E**   Flight check aircraft engaged in, or in transit to, time- or weather-critical calibration flights

**Normal Flights**   Those that have filed a flight plan in the normal way and are conforming with normal route procedures
Initial instrument flight tests conducted by CAA (call-sign 'Exam')

**Category Z**   Non-standard and other flights, particularly training

# Chapter 3

# *Types of airspace*

## Flight Information Regions (FIRs)

The United Kingdom is divided into two FIRs, the London and the Scottish, the boundary between them being latitude line 55°N. Above 24,500ft these areas are known as Upper Flight Information Regions, abbreviated to UIR. The London FIR comes under the London Area and Terminal Air Traffic Control Centre at West Drayton, close to Heathrow, and the Scottish FIR under the Scottish Area Control Centre at Atlantic House near Prestwick. Southern Ireland comes under the jurisdiction of the ACCs at Shannon and Dublin, the stretches of the Atlantic to north and south being controlled by Reykjavik and Shanwick Oceanic Controls respectively. At Manchester Airport there is an ACC that controls traffic below FL195 over the North of England and the Irish Sea.

In November 1991 the UK adopted a new ICAO system, which aims to classify airspace internationally so that it is perfectly clear to users from anywhere in the world which flight rules apply and what air traffic services they can expect within a particular airspace. Actual procedures remain unaffected, the main change being one of terminology. The seven different categories of airspace are represented by the letters A to G, although Class C has yet to be adopted in the UK.

## Class A

This consists mainly of airways that are normally 10 miles wide (5 miles on each side of the centreline) and generally have a base of between 3,000ft and FL55. With some exceptions they extend vertically to FL245, the base of upper airspace in Britain. Aircraft flying in them are required to operate under IFR and are separated positively by ATC, using radar or procedural methods. 'Westbound' flights, which could in practice also be on north-west or south-west headings, fly at even numbered flight levels, and 'eastbound' flights at odd numbers. Some airways are activated for peak periods only, usually weekends and national holidays.

Other Class A airspace includes the London Control Zone and Control Area, the Daventry, Worthing and Cotswold Control Areas, and the Shanwick Oceanic Control Area.

## Class B

This consists of upper airspace extending from FL245 up to FL660, and is designated a Control Area. The Upper Air Routes lie within it, the majority of them following the line of the normal airway below, hence Bravo One and Upper Bravo One. However, fuel-saving requirements in the last decade or so have led to an increasing tendency for aircraft to fly direct routes between radio beacons sometimes several hundred miles apart. Some of these *ad hoc* routeings have resulted in the establishment of UARs to regulate their use and also 'DT' or Direct Track routes.

The whole of the upper airspace is covered by joint civil and military radar units to co-ordinate the large number of flights within it. The standard vertical separation above FL245 is increased to 2,000ft so that aircraft flying in opposite directions are that distance apart. Link Routes in the upper airspace connect the oceanic boundaries with UK and Continental domestic routes. Concordes have special Supersonic Link Routes.

## Class D
In general, these are Control Zones and Control Areas around airports.

## Class E
This comprises Scottish TMA airspace below 6,000ft (above 6,000ft is Class D), Belfast TMA and the Scottish Control Zone outside Glasgow and Prestwick Control Zones.

## Class F
This is reserved for Advisory Routes, normally referred to as ADRs, which have been established where public transport aircraft use certain routes but not in sufficient quantity to justify the full protection of an airway. To distinguish them from airways, the suffix 'Delta', eg Whiskey Two Delta, is used. Most of the ADRs are to be found in Scotland and Northern England with only one – Green Four Delta – in the south. A few have become busy enough to achieve airway status, one of them being Bravo Two, formerly Delta Blue 22, between the Scottish TMA and Aberdeen. In contrast to airways, the quadrantal rule is applied for level allocation (see page 18).

## Class G
This is unregulated airspace in the open FIR within which aircraft are allowed to fly as they wish without hindrance or radio calls. In instrument conditions pilots are expected to conform to a simple procedure called the quadrantal rule, which regulates altitude according to the aircraft's heading.

# Special zones and areas
## Aerodrome Traffic Zones
The dimensions of ATZs relate to the midpoint of the longest runway and its length. For example, if the longest runway is greater than 1,850 metres, the boundary of the ATZ will be a circle of 2$^1$/2 nautical miles radius from the midpoint of that runway. Aerodromes with shorter runways have smaller ATZs, but the vertical limit remains at 2,000ft above aerodrome level. Both within or outside controlled airspace, pilots must either avoid the ATZ or obtain permission to fly through it.

## Military Aerodrome Traffic Zones
The purpose of a MATZ is to provide a volume of airspace within which increased protection may be given to aircraft in the critical stages of circuit, approach and climb-out. It normally comprises the airspace within 5 nautical miles of the airfield from the surface up to 3,000ft. In addition, a 'stub' out to 5 miles protects the final approach path of the most used runway. Although it is not mandatory for civil pilots to request permission to penetrate a MATZ, it is obviously highly desirable for them to do so.

## Helicopter Main Routes and Protected Zones
The concentration of offshore oil and gas installations in the North Sea and, increasingly, the Irish Sea, with their busy helicopter support operations, has resulted in the introduction of protected airspace. Helicopter Main Routes (HMRs) and Overland Corridors have been established when helicopters operate on a regular basis from and to the mainland or between platforms.

A Helicopter Protected Zone (HPZ) is sometimes established around two or more installations, and a Helicopter Flight Information Service may also be provided. Apart from the East Shetland Basin, in which procedural separation is provided, the airspace is uncontrolled but its dimensions are published and military and civil pilots must obtain clearance to penetrate an HPZ and keep a good look-out when in the proximity of an HMR.

*Upper Airspace Routes, South Sheet* (CAA).

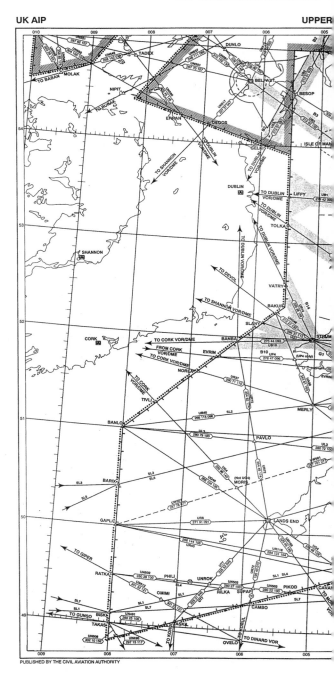

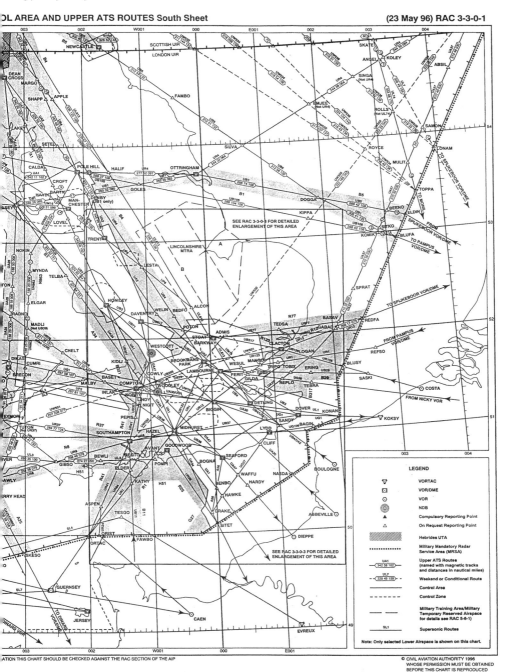

## ALTIMETER SETTING REGIONS

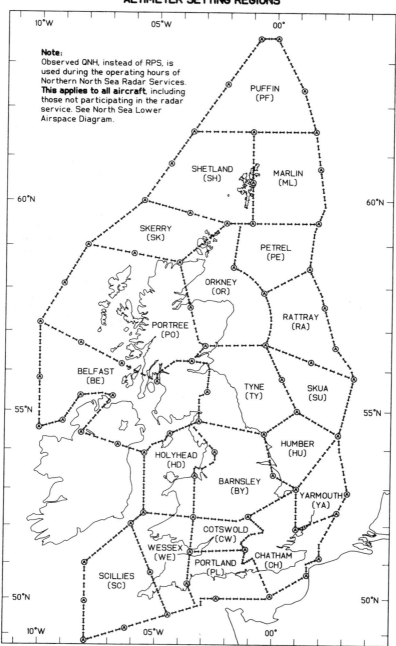

**Note:**
Observed QNH, instead of RPS, is used during the operating hours of Northern North Sea Radar Services. **This applies to all aircraft**, including those not participating in the radar service. See North Sea Lower Airspace Diagram.

*United Kingdom Altimeter Setting Regions (CAA).*

## Military Training Areas and Temporary Reserved Airspace

The North Wales MTA is a defined area of upper airspace, within which intense military flying takes place during weekdays and occasionally, with prior notification, at weekends. Certain airways, including Upper Alpha 25 and Upper Bravo 39, are affected when the MTA is active. The Lincolnshire Military Temporary Reserved Airspace is a similar operation, but is only active when required, thus allowing transit by civil aircraft on an opportunity basis.

## Aerial Tactics Areas and Air-to-Air Fuelling Areas

ATAs are used for air-to-air combat training over the North Sea. Lakenheath ATA is situated off Cromer, and The Wash ATA is off the Humber Estuary. Within The Wash ATA is NSAR, the North Sea ACMI (Air Combat Manoeuvring Instrumentation Range), otherwise known as 'Playground'. Fixed sensor towers monitor activity and send information by datalink to the mainland for subsequent analysis and debrief of aircrew.

There are 12 Air-to-Air Fuelling Areas (note that the 're' prefix is no longer used), mostly over the North Sea, with others over the West Country and the Scottish Highlands. Tankers orbit in the AFA to allow the receiving aircraft to home on to them. When 'on boom', the operation begins along a specific track within the AFA.

## Danger Areas

The most common Danger Areas are weapons ranges, but the term also embraces parachuting and other activities potentially hazardous to aircraft. Radar crossing services are available for some of them.

## Prohibited and Restricted Areas

Most Restricted Areas are centred on nuclear power stations, over-flight being prohibited below 2,000ft above ground level within a radius of 2 miles. The Highlands Restricted Area covers most of northern Scotland from the surface up to 5,000ft and enables military pilots to train at low level in all weather conditions. A number of sensitive places in Northern Ireland are defined as Prohibited Areas, with varying dimensions.

# Chapter 4

# *Navigational aids*

Radio navigational aids, or 'navaids', assist a pilot in threading his way through the airways, letting down at destination and then, if an Instrument Landing System is installed, following its beam down to the runway. The main types of navaid in the United Kingdom are described briefly below; more details of such aids as the Global Positioning System can be found in *International Air Band Radio Handbook* (Patrick Stephens Ltd).

## Non-Directional Beacon (NDB)

The commonest and one of the simplest of aids is the Non-Directional Beacon. It is used to mark airways, when its useful range may be up to 100 miles, and as an approach and landing aid, sometimes referred to as a Locator Beacon, when its range will be about 15 miles. It consists merely of a radio transmitter in the medium frequency band that sends out a continuous steady note in all directions. A call-sign of three letters in morse code (two for airport locator beacons) is superimposed at regular intervals as a check that the desired beacon has been selected. The Automatic Direction Finder (ADF), or radio compass, fitted in an aircraft will, when tuned to the appropriate frequency, indicate the relative position of the transmission source by means of a needle on a dial.

The great disadvantage of the NDB is that it is very prone to interference. For example, a thunderstorm cell in the area will often cause the cockpit needle to point to it in preference to the beacon, not a happy state of affairs!

## VHF Omni-Directional Range (VOR)

VORs also broadcast their signals in all directions, but the signals vary around the compass in such a way that each direction has its own signal, which cannot be confused with that of any other direction. If an aircraft receiver can pick up and decode the signal from a VOR, it can tell the bearing (or 'radial' as it is termed) from the station. As a convenience the receiver can add 180 to the 'From' determination and instruct the pilot which way to fly 'To' the station. A 'To/From' flag on the instrument display tells the pilot in which mode it is operating.

## Distance Measuring Equipment

While VOR gives accurate, specific directional information, it cannot make explicit distance measurements. The answer is to use DME, which is associated closely with VOR, the combination providing an accurate position fix. A special transmitter in the aircraft sends out pulses in all directions and these are received at the DME station on the ground. As each pulse is received an answering pulse is transmitted automatically and this is picked up in the aircraft. It is in fact reverse of secondary radar (qv).

**Right** *An ILS DME Chart for Runway 27L at London/Heathrow (CAA).*

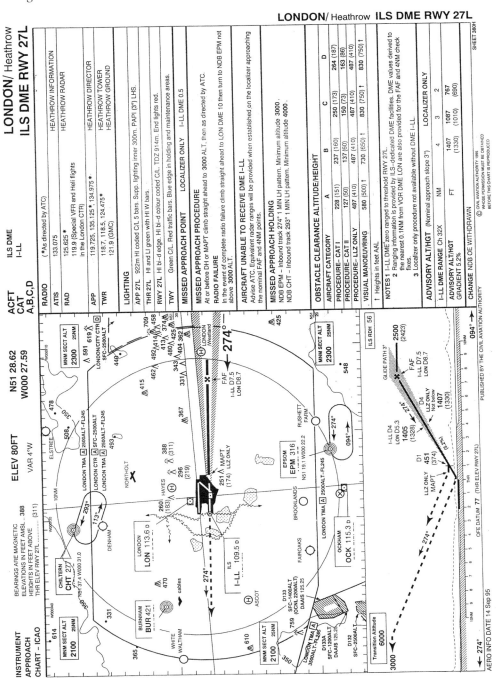

LONDON/ Heathrow **ILS DME RWY 27L**

As the speed of radio waves is constant at 186,000 miles per second, a computer in the aircraft, measuring the time interval between the transmission of the pulse and the receipt of the response, can convert the interval into a distance and display it to the pilot in nautical miles. The presentation is either by means of a mechanical meter or more often nowadays by a computer display. In both cases the distance is in miles and tenths of a mile. With some equipment, the 'time to go' to the beacon will also be displayed.

It should be noted, incidentally, that the height of the aircraft affects the distance measurement; when directly above the station at 36,000ft the instrument will show the aircraft as still being 6 miles from it. This is because the DME measures slant range rather than ground distance, but it is of little importance except when very close to the station.

DMEs are normally co-located with VORs and the frequencies of the two installations are 'paired'. For example, the VOR frequency of 112.7MHz is always matched by a DME on Channel 74, a VOR on 114.9 by a DME on Channel 96, and so on. This means that aircraft equipment can be arranged so that the selection of a particular VOR frequency means that the related DME channel is selected at the same time.

## Instrument Landing System (ILS)

ILS is a pilot-interpreted aid that gives a continuous indication of whether the aircraft is left or right of the final approach track, and also its position in relation to an ideal glide path to the runway. The latter is a standard 3°, giving an approximate rate of descent of 300ft per minute. Certain airfields may have greater angles owing to high ground on the approach or other local considerations.

This information is augmented by marker beacons on the ground showing range, the outer marker at about 4 miles from touchdown and a middle marker at around 3,500ft. As the aircraft passes over them they give an audible signal. The outer marker transmits low-toned dashes and the middle marker alternates dots and dashes on a medium tone. These markers cannot only be heard, they also light up lamps on the instrument panel. The outer marker illuminates a blue lamp and the middle an amber, each flashing in time with the codes and transmitted on a standard 75MHz. Increased use of airport-sited DME is slowly phasing out the markers because the pilot now has a continuous read-out of his range from touchdown.

A transmitter with a large aerial system known as the Localiser is sited at the far end of the runway, transmitting its signals on either side of its centreline and approach. These signals, called blue on the right of the approach path and yellow on the left, overlap in a beam about 5° wide exactly along the approach centreline.

A second unit, the glide path transmitter, is sited at the nearer end and slightly to one side of the runway. Aboard the aircraft there is an instrument with two needles, one that pivots from the top of its case, moving like a windscreen wiper and actuated by the signals from the Localiser, and one that pivots on the left-hand side of the case, moving up and down and operated by the transmissions from the glide path aerial. When the two needles cross at right angles, the aircraft is lined up perfectly for a landing. Any deviation can rapidly be corrected by an experienced pilot. ILS Localiser/DME systems dispense with the glide path beam, but the DME ranges enable the pilot to monitor his rate of descent.

Initial approach on to the ILS is normally achieved by Approach Radar, the aim being to place the aircraft on a closing heading of about 30° to the final approach at a range of between 7 and 9 miles. The aircraft should be at an appropriate altitude so that the glide path can be intercepted from below rather than attempting to 'chase' it from above. The final turn-on can be done by radar direction, but these days it is usually done automatically by coupling the ILS with the FMS or autopilot. Where no radar is available, a procedural ILS is flown, similar to an NDB approach with the exception that the procedure turn will intercept the ILS and enable the pilot to establish himself on it.

ILSs are divided into three categories as follows:

Category 1: Operation down to 60m decision height with Runway Visual Range in excess of 800m.

Category 2: Operation down to 60m decision height with RVR in excess of 400m.

Category 3: Operation with no height limitation to and along the surface of the runway with external visual reference during the final phase of landing with RVR of 200m.

Sub-divisions are Category 3b, with RVR of 45m, and a planned Category 3c, with RVR of zero. They both require guidance along the runway and for the latter also to the parking bay. Special ground lighting is required for Category 2 and 3 ILSs, together with safeguarded areas around the sensitive aerial systems to avoid fluctuations caused by vehicles or taxying aircraft. Localiser/DME ILSs are non-precision and therefore uncategorised.

## Microwave Landing System (MLS)

The MLS is so-called because it works in the much higher frequency microwave band, as opposed to the VHF band used by ILS. This creates a number of advantages, not least of which is a high accuracy, which means Category 3 for all installations. In addition, non-standard offset or curved approaches can be made to avoid obstacles or noise-sensitive areas, and the glide path is adaptable to high-angle approaches by STOL aircraft or helicopters.

The CAA is currently evaluating MLS equipment at Heathrow (Runway 27R) to gain the technical and operational experience necessary for the approval of future installations in the UK. ICAO once planned that MLS would replace ILS by 1998, but the decision has been deferred because of pending developments in satellite navigation. The datalink from the test MLS at Heathrow is being used to uplink Differential Global Positioning System (DGPS) corrections to a specially equipped British Airways Boeing 767 in order to demonstrate the feasibility of this concept. This integration of MLS and DGPS would enable precision approaches to be made and provide a cost saving of around 50% on each MLS installation because of the elimination of certain functions such as Precision DME and departure guidance. Both of these can be provided by DGPS.

## Decca

The Decca Navigator provides a position-fixing ability over an area up to 300 miles around its transmitter by use of a group (or chain) of special long-wave transmitters about 70 to 100 miles apart that radiate in unison. The information thus received enables a pen on a moving map display to trace the path of the aircraft over the ground.

## Doppler

The Doppler navigation system is self-contained and produces the desired information on position through a measurement of aircraft velocity by means of Doppler radar, and measurement of direction by means of a sensor such as a gyro or magnetic compass. The two sets of information are then processed in a computer.

## Inertial Navigation System (INS)

INS operates independently of ground stations, being based on a computer aboard the aircraft that derives its input from gyroscopic accelerometers. A predetermined journey can be programmed in, the output of which will direct the autopilot or FMS to fly the required tracks. This enables aircraft to fly direct routeings without reference to radio beacons if first requested from, and approved by, ATC.

## LORAN-C

A ground-based long-range radio navigation system that is interpreted by a cockpit computer.

## Omega

A long-range area navigation system that uses VLF (Very Low Frequency) signals from eight ground stations located to provide near worldwide coverage.

## Satellite Navigation (GLONASS and GPS)

Currently there are two systems of satellite navigation: GLONASS, the GLobal Orbiting NAvigation Satellite System developed by the former USSR; and the American GPS, Global Positioning System. A joint system combining the GLONASS and GPS satellites is planned so that worldwide coverage will be increased significantly and a greater measure of redundancy introduced to guard against satellite failure. Global positioning is the most accurate form of navigation technology under development and it will play a major role in increasing airspace capacity as well as improving safety. However, before it does, a serious problem will have to be resolved. GPS was devised originally by the USA for military purposes and it reserves the right to 'adjust' its accuracy during time of war or international tension. Obviously certain guarantees will have to be made before its universal adoption.

Currently under evaluation is the concept of Differential GPS, whereby the integrity of the satellite-derived position information is constantly verified and corrected if necessary by a ground station using Mode S datalink to the aircraft. When perfected the system could enable precision

approaches to be made in association with ILS or MLS. GPS operates in the band 1559–1610MHz.

## Transponder

The transponder is not a navigational aid in the true sense, but its use certainly improves the service that ATC is able to give. A small airborne transmitter waits until a radar pulse strikes its antenna, then instantly broadcasts, at a different frequency, a radar reply of its own – a strong synthetic echo. Since ordinary 'skin return' (the reflection of the ground radar pulse from the aircraft structure) is sometimes quite weak, especially at great distances or with small aircraft, the transponder helps the radar operator to track targets that might return an echo too weak to display.

The transponder is simple in concept but in practice is a complex, sophisticated device. It is triggered into either of two modes of reply by the nature of the ground radar pulse. Without delving too deeply into the technicalities, Mode A is employed for identification and Mode C for altitude information. Mode B is in military use only and Mode S (Selective) is a datalink for the exchange of operational information. At the UK Control Centres, radar replies are channelled into a computer that decodes the pulses, converts them into a letter and number display, and places a label alongside the appropriate target on the radar screen. The information includes the call-sign and altitude of the aircraft.

Secondary Surveillance Radar (SSR) has many advantages. One of the most important is that aircraft identification is easy to achieve and eliminates the necessity of requesting a turn of at least 30° from the original heading to confirm which blip is which on the screen. R/T loading is reduced considerably because altitude information is presented continuously to the controller, and the pilot no longer needs to make constant checks.

When the Traffic Alert and Collision Avoidance System (TCAS) is fitted to aircraft, the equipment reacts to the transponders of other aircraft in the vicinity to determine whether or not there is the potential for a collision. TCAS is currently under worldwide evaluation and is already mandatory for public transport aircraft in the USA. Since many foreign and British-registered aircraft operating in UK airspace are fitted with TCAS, there is increasing reference to it on R/T.

Warnings are given in two steps. Typically 40 seconds before the assumed collision, a Traffic Advisory (TA) warning indicates where the pilot must look for the traffic, then between 20 and 30 seconds before the assumed collision a Resolution Advisory (RA) gives the pilot advice to climb, descend or remain level. The two warnings, TA followed by RA, can only be received if the conflicting aircraft is transponding on Mode C or Mode S. Where both aircraft in an encounter are fitted with TCAS Mode S, the transponders will communicate with each other to agree which aircraft is to pass below and which above the other.

Mode S is a datalink system that has a number of potential applications in ATC, one being the eventual replacement of many routine radio messages, such as route clearances and weather information. Warnings appear on a small cockpit display indicating the relative positions of the conflicting aircraft in plan view and elevation, together with an aural warning spoken by a synthetic voice.

Secondary radar differs from primary radar in that the 'echo' returned to the ground station is augmented by a signal triggered from the aircraft's transponder equipment. Interference from weather and other causes is virtually eliminated. This is not the case with primary radar, which is not quite the magic eye the layman would believe; it suffers from all sorts of interference. Depending on the wavelength of a particular radar, weather clutter can swamp the screen with returns from rain and snow. There are ways of removing, or at least reducing, this clutter, but the aircraft echo can be lost too, especially if it

is a smaller type. It is not uncommon therefore to hear a controller say that he is unable to give a radar approach due to rain clutter and offer an alternative, such as an ILS approach.

## Ground Proximity Warning System (GPWS)

GPWS is not a navigational aid, but provides an audible warning to the pilot if an aircraft experiences any of the following conditions:

(a) Excessive sink rate
(b) Excessive terrain closure rate
(c) Altitude loss after take-off or overshoot
(d) Proximity to terrain when not in the landing configuration
(e) Deviation below the glide slope

In the first four conditions the warning consists of an audible tone and a spoken warning over a cockpit loudspeaker: 'Whoop, whoop. Pull up'. For the last condition the warning 'Glide slope, glide slope' is used. The warning is repeated as long as the conditions exist.

Aircraft flight manuals instruct pilots to climb immediately to a level where the warning is no longer being received. If a pilot gets a 'pull up' warning, his recovery action is to establish the power setting and attitude that will produce the maximum climb gradient consistent with the aircraft configuration. If a 'glide slope' warning is received, recovery action is to apply power to regain the ILS glide slope.

Unfortunately GPWS is an extremely sensitive piece of equipment and spurious warnings can be caused by several factors. One of these is a sudden variation in terrain, even though it is well below the aircraft. GPWS incidents can occasionally be heard being discussed on air band frequencies.

## Flight Checks

Some of the navaids, particularly ILS, require regular flight checks to ensure that their performance remains consistent. These checks, normally flown by the CAA Calibration Unit's HS748 or Fieldair's Navajo aircraft, call-signs 'Calibrator' and 'Checker' respectively, are not as intensive as those made when the equipment was first installed at a specific location, but they are still quite time-consuming. The CAA's Aerodrome Standards 2 department is responsible for the flight checking of visual lighting aids, call-sign 'Standards'.

# Chapter 5

# Area or Airways Control

Since messages between the Area Control Centres (ACCs) and aircraft on the UK airways system are those that are most easily monitored from all parts of the country, this seems a logical point at which to begin. There are three Centres, London, Manchester and Scottish (note that London is now known as the London Area and Terminal Control Centre). The dividing line between London and Scottish is latitude 55°N (roughly the Scottish border), and Manchester handles traffic below FL195 on the airways around Manchester and over the Irish Sea.

Transmitter/receiver stations are sited at various strategic positions around Britain and linked to the ACCs by land line. The aim is to achieve a balanced coverage over the whole area with no 'dead' spots. Similarly, the radar stations are 'remoted' on high ground, where possible, to improve range. London ATCC (LATCC) is served by radar heads at Heathrow, Ash near Canterbury, Ventnor on the Isle of Wight, Clee Hill in Shropshire, Burrington in Devon, and St Annes near Blackpool. Additional service is provided on a Eurocontrol agency basis from Mount Gabriel in Eire, a station that extends SSR cover out to 15°W in the south-west approaches.

More information on SSR will be found in a separate section of this book, but briefly while the main function of primary radar is to provide aircraft position, secondary radar, or SSR, depends for its operation on a transponder carried in the aircraft, which, on receipt of pulses from a ground interrogator, will transmit coded reply pulses back to the ground. When these are decoded by the display equipment, they give the Flight Level of the aircraft together with a four-figure identifying number known as a 'squawk'. The primary and secondary information received by the radar stations is processed in a common 'plot extractor', converting the base radar data into digital form and automatically sending the information to the ACCs over land lines.

At the ACC, display processing equipment employing modern computer technology is used to decode the combined radar information from several antenna, and displays either a manually selected radar station or a composite area mosaic picture. The SSR squawk is paired with the aircraft call-sign in the computer and this call-sign label is displayed on the screen instead of the code. This enables the controller to match the radar picture with the strips on his flight progress board.

When the mosaic picture is selected at LATCC, the computer divides the London FIR into 16-mile squares, each of which has radar cover from a 'preferred' radar and a 'supplementary' radar. This avoids the blind spots possible if only one radar were in operation. Should the preferred radar fail, the supplementary will take over automatically, information from a third radar head being upgraded in turn to supplement it.

All incoming primary and secondary digital data is continuously recorded, and the tapes are kept for 30 days before being erased and reused. The same applies to all ATC radio messages, whether they be Area,

*Remote Radio and Radar Sites*

## London Area and Terminal Control Centre and London Military Remote Transmitter Sites and their frequencies

Chedburgh, Suffolk: 118.475, 121.325, 127.1, 128.125, 128.7, 129.6, 132.6, 133.325, 133.45, 136.55, 233.8
Clee Hill, Shropshire: 124.2, 124.75, 125.1, 126.875, 128.7, 133.6, 133.9, 134.75, 135.15, 135.425, 275.35, 275.475
Daventry, Northamptonshire: 127.1, 127.875, 129.2, 131.125, 275.35
Davidstow Moor, Cornwall: 124.75, 126.075, 127.7, 129.375, 132.95, 133.3, 133.6, 135.15, 275.475
Grantham, Lincolnshire: 120.025, 124.6, 136.2, 260.025
Great Dunfell, Cumbria: 125.475, 299.975
Greenford, Middlesex: 127.875, 128.25, 129.2, 129.425, 275.35
Kelsall, Cheshire: 124.2, 125.1, 126.65, 129.1, 133.05, 133.4, 134.425, 134.925, 135.575, 231.625
Mount Gabriel, Eire: 132.95
Preston, Lancashire: 127.45, 129.1, 131.125, 134.425, 135.575, 231.625
Rothwell, Humberside: 126.775, 131.225, 135.075, 135.275, 135.625, 135.925, 299.975
Snaefell, Isle of Man: 125.475, 126.875
Swingfield, Kent: 118.475, 120.025, 128.25, 128.425, 129.6, 132.45, 133.45, 134.45, 134.9, 135.425, 136.55, 136.6, 230.05
Trimmingham, Lincolnshire: 121.325, 124.6, 125.475, 126.775, 128.125, 133.575, 299.975
Ventnor, Isle of Wight: 124.75, 126.075, 129.425, 132.3, 133.3, 135.05, 135.25, 135.325, 136.6, 235.05
Warlingham, Surrey: 124.6, 127.425, 128.425, 132.45, 132.6, 134.45, 134.9, 135.05, 135.325, 135.575, 251.225
Winstone, Gloucestershire: 120.025, 126.075, 127.425, 127.7, 129.375, 133.9, 134.75, 135.25, 235.05

Note that some frequencies may be offset up or down by 2.5, 5 or 7.5kHz (see page 120)

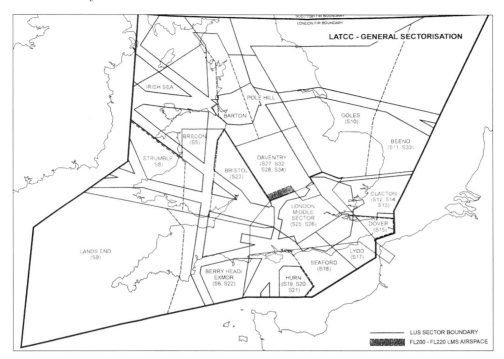

*LATCC Sectors.*

Tower or Approach. The purpose of these recordings is to help an investigating authority to build up a picture of the events surrounding an accident or incident.

To facilitate traffic handling, LATCC's airspace is broken up into sectors, each with its own radio frequencies, a primary and several 'as directed' channels to enable the sector to be split during busy periods. Aircraft are passed from one sector to the next with co-ordination between the Controllers concerned. From mid-evening as traffic decreases, sectors are 'closed down', the frequencies being 'bandboxed', to use the jargon. Hence nothing may be heard on what is in daytime a busy airways frequency. By the early hours the whole FIR may be controlled by only two frequencies. When the morning shift comes on duty the sectors are activated again to meet the new traffic flow.

Before computers came on the scene in British ATC in the 1970s, flight progress strips at the ACCs were hand-written in vast quantities. Today the system is automated, apart from a shut-off period for computer maintenance in the small hours of the morning, and it would be advantageous to describe briefly what happens when a particular flight leaves Leeds, for example, for Heathrow.

If the flight is a scheduled one, it will be on a 'stored plan' in the LATCC computer's bulk store file; if not it will be input on a teleprinter at Manchester ACC. At the appropriate time as programmed into the computer, usually about 40 minutes before Estimated Time of Departure (ETD), warning strips will be printed by flight strip printers at Manchester and at any location at LATCC where advance information of the flight is required.

When Manchester receives the actual time of departure from Leeds, via a direct

telephone link, an activation message will be input to the computer via a keyboard. This will generate an update message for the sectors at the Sub-Centre, and those sectors at London that have warning strips. Additionally 'live strips' will be printed at any sector or location concerned with the flight that did not have a warning strip. In all cases the computer will have calculated and printed times for en route reporting points based upon the airborne time input at Manchester. The forecast winds at various levels will have been programmed in and thus automatically taken into account.

The flight of an aircraft from Heathrow to Manchester serves as a good example of how traffic is fed through the airways system. When the departing aircraft comes on to the LATCC Departure Radar Controller's frequency and has complied with the minimum noise routeing element of its Standard Instrument Departure, it is started on its climb to cruising level, using radar separation where necessary between it and other arriving, departing or transitting traffic. To ease the task of the Departure Controller in regard to co-ordination with other sectors concerned with the airspace, there is an internal procedure that permits him to climb the aircraft to an arbitrary level without reference to other sectors.

However, before it reaches this Flight Level or, alternatively, when the aircraft is approaching the airspace for which the next Sector Controller is responsible, prior co-ordination is carried out. When this has been done, the aircraft is instructed to contact the new sector (still with the same 'London Control' call-sign).

Clearance is given for the aircraft's climb to its cruising level, once again using radar to resolve any conflict with other traffic. By this time it is also possible to check the computer on the elapsed time between reporting points and, if these deviate by 3 minutes or more, the estimates for the rest of the flight are revised and a new ETA is passed to Manchester.

As the flight nears the Manchester TMA boundary, co-ordination takes place between the sector and the TMA Controller. Descent instructions dependent upon the Manchester traffic situation are then issued and the aircraft transferred to the Manchester Control frequency. The Manchester TMA Controller has a radar display similar to that used by the London controller and, as the aircraft descends into his airspace, its call-sign and level will be visible on his screen. He will also have displayed in front of him the flight progress strips generated by the computer, which have been updated by any revised estimates. The descent will be continued until the aircraft comes under the jurisdiction of the Manchester Approach Controller (call-sign 'Manchester Director') and positioned on the ILS as described in the next chapter.

Ideally, traffic is given an uninterrupted climb to cruising level and, from a convenient point, a continuous descent to final approach. In practice, however, the presence of other traffic rarely makes this possible. Traffic climbing to, say, FL180 may be given an initial limit of FL120 against conflicting traffic at FL130. By the time it is approaching FL120, the other aircraft may be well out of the way and the controller will be able to instruct the pilot to continue his climb to the required level. Before the days of SSR height read-outs, the Area Controller in this example would ask the pilot to report passing FL110, and would then assess the situation with regard to further climb.

The phraseology used in Area Control is mainly self-evident, and some, concerning level changes, has already been covered in an earlier chapter. Common phrases to be heard are as follows:

Aircraft: 'Speedbird 345 request descent.'
ATC: 'Speedbird 345 maintain FL110 expect descent after Lichfield.'

ATC: 'Air France 045 descend to cross

**Left** *Part of the London Area and Terminal Control Centre* (Siemens Plessey Systems).

Honiley FL170 or above. After Honiley descend to FL130.'

The standard airways position report is a little gem of brevity dating back decades to when procedural airways control was first developed. A typical example might be as follows:

Aircraft: 'Loganair 123 Dean Cross 45 FL90 Pole Hill 10.'

This means that the aircraft was over the Dean Cross VOR, near Carlisle, at time 45, maintaining FL90 and estimating over the Pole Hill VOR, west of Leeds, at 10 minutes past the next hour.

Nowadays, with comprehensive radar coverage of the airways system, a pilot may be instructed to omit position reports when flying in certain areas, his progress being monitored by the SSR read-out. This reduces the R/T loading considerably.

Certain phrases concerning the operation of transponders are listed below. Since SSR in the United Kingdom is confined mainly to the ACCs, they will most commonly be heard on airways' frequencies. Few Approach Control units have SSR capability as yet, but the number is slowly increasing. The use of the word 'squawk', by the way, seems to have been inspired by the wartime instruction to operate IFF (Identification, Friend or Foe), 'Make your cockerel crow', and the pilot's confirmation that the IFF equipment was switched off after landing, 'Cockerel strangled'.

| Phrase | Meaning |
|---|---|
| *Squawk (code)* | Set the code as instructed |
| *Confirm squawk* | Confirm the code set on the transponder |
| *Recycle* | Reselect assigned code |
| *Squawk ident* | Operate the special position identification feature |
| *Squawk low* | Select 'low sensitivity' feature |
| *Squawk normal* | Select normal feature |
| *Squawk stand-by* | Select the stand-by feature |
| *Squawk Charlie* | Select altitude reporting feature |
| *Stop squawk Charlie* | Deselect altitude feature |
| *Verify your level* | Check and confirm your level (used to verify the accuracy of the Mode C derived level information displayed to the controller) |

# Chapter 6

# Approach Control

An arriving aircraft is transferred from Area to Approach Control at a specified release point. This is not obvious from R/T transmissions because it is passed by land line between controllers shortly before the aircraft comes on to the approach frequency. It may be a position, time or level – the transfer of control is made deliberately flexible to react to differences in the flow of traffic. For example, if the release is 'Leaving FL50' the Approach Controller may not alter the heading of the aircraft until he has received a 'passing FL50' report. The reason for this is that Area Control may have been separating the inbound aircraft from other traffic above FL50.

Ideally, the arriving aircraft should be released in plenty of time to enable it to carry out a straight-in approach and at the same time to lose height. However, should a busy traffic situation exist, it might be necessary to put it into a holding pattern based upon a radio beacon. The release would then be at a specified level in the holding stack. The holding patterns are a standard oval 'racetrack', the direction of turn and headings being published in navigational charts or approach plates.

At airfields without radar, traffic is separated by procedural methods, the first aircraft making an instrument approach from, say, 3,000ft, other aircraft continuing to hold above at 1,000ft vertical intervals. As soon as the first aircraft reports visual with the ground or approach lights, and there is a reasonable likelihood of a successful landing, a second aircraft is cleared for the approach and so on. If the aircraft carries out a missed approach prior to becoming visual, it must climb to the safe terrain clearance altitude, in this instance 3,000ft. Hence it is not hard to see why this altitude is left vacant at the beacon until the first aircraft breaks cloud.

The Decision Height is the level at which the pilot on a precision approach must carry out a missed approach if he fails to achieve the required visual reference to continue the approach to a landing. A precision approach is defined as being provided by an ILS, MLS or PAR facility. All other procedures, including SRAs and Localiser/DME approaches, are non-precision and the term Minimum Descent Height is used instead.

Obstacle Clearance Height is the minimum safe height to which an aircraft may descend either on an instrument approach or in the event of a missed approach. The OCH is published on the approach charts for each airfield, aircraft being divided into five speed-related categories, resulting in a reduction of the OCH for the more manoeuvrable types.

The obstacle clearance criteria are, of course, tied in with company minima for visibility and cloud base, below which a public transport flight is not allowed even to attempt an approach. So far, there are no such statutory provisions for non-public transport flights. However, recommended minima are published for the approach aids at each airfield for the guidance of pilots, and these will be passed on R/T when conditions demand.

The term Expected Approach Time is often heard at non-radar-equipped airports.

This indicates to a pilot that if he has a radio failure he must not commence an instrument approach until this specific time, in order to allow preceding aircraft to descend and land. 'No delay expected' means that a pilot can begin his approach as soon as he reaches the beacon.

A standard 7 minutes is assumed to complete the let-down procedure; if the pilot's estimate for the beacon is 12, the next aircraft's EAT will be 19, the third's 26 and so on. Three minutes will be added to this if an aircraft arrives from certain points of the compass and has to realign itself in the correct direction for the descent. The controller will calculate the figures and update them as necessary. Note that EATs are not issued in busy TMAs when the delay is likely to be less than 20 minutes. If it is likely to be more, inbound aircraft are given a general statement about anticipated delay, and EATs are issued as necessary. Pilots' interpretations of instrument let-downs vary enormously, the 7-minute standard ranging from 5 to 10 or more, depending upon wind strength, aircraft performance and other factors.

One other phrase used in connection with EATs is the rarely heard 'delay not determined'. This is used to meet certain eventualities, such as a blocked runway, when it is not known how long an aircraft may have to hold.

Where Approach Radar is in use, as well as giving a release the ACC also transfers radar identity in what is called a 'handover' (a 'handoff' to the Americans). The Approach Controller is thus certain that the aircraft he is directing is the correct blip. The object is to pass headings (vectors) to the pilot to enable him to lock on to the ILS beam by the shortest practicable route commensurate with losing height. If there is no ILS, a Surveillance Radar Approach (SRA) will be given, or, when the weather is suitable, radar positioning to a visual final.

In effect a radar-directed circuit is flown, the terms 'downwind', 'base leg' and 'final' (see page 57) all being used where necessary, although the area of sky covered is far bigger than in the normal visual traffic pattern. A closing heading of about 30° is recommended so that when the aircraft intercepts the ILS only a gentle turn is necessary to lock on. The aim is to intercept the standard 3° glide path at approximately 7 to 8 miles out on the extended centreline of the runway. As a 3° glide path is roughly equal to 300ft of descent per mile, the aircraft should be between 2,000ft and 2,500ft at this point.

Subsequent landing aircraft are vectored not less than 5 miles behind, or further depending upon the vortex wake category of the preceding traffic (see Chapter 13). Bigger gaps may also be built in to give space for departing traffic at single-runway airports. At certain locations, Heathrow for example, reduction of the separation to 3 miles is authorised to ensure maximum utilisation of the arrival runway; the vortex rules still apply, of course. It requires great skill to arrange traffic in line astern with the correct spacing, particularly at Heathrow where four holding stacks serve the airport. Speed control is also used extensively to even out the flow, a minimum of 170kt being permissible for jets and 160kt for large propeller-driven aircraft. Within the TMAs during the intermediate stages of the approach, a speed limit of 250kt is imposed on all traffic to make the radar controller's task a little easier. The same speed limit applies to outbound traffic, but the controller can lift it by using the phrase 'No ATC speed restriction', often abbreviated to 'No ATC speed'. (I once heard a Shorts 360 pilot respond with 'Would that it made any difference!')

Other examples of phraseology relating to speed are: 'Report airspeed/Mach number.' 'Maintain present speed.' 'Maintain X knots.' 'Maintain X knots or greater.' 'Do not exceed X knots.' 'Increase/reduce speed to Mach X.' 'Increase/reduce speed to X knots.' 'Maintain X knots until 4-mile final/outer marker.' 'Resume normal speed.'

The Approach Controller passes an 8-mile check on intercom to his colleague in the tower who will already have details of the arriving aircraft. If there are no pending

## STARs via BIGGIN — LONDON/Heathrow

**GENERAL INFORMATION**
1 Standard Routes may be varied at the discretion of ATC.
2 Cross SLPs or 3 min before holding facility at 250kts IAS or less.
3 When BIG VOR is out of service the routing will be SANDY-DET. (For aircraft on AWY A2 the routing will be WEALD. Designators will become WEALD 2A (WLD 2A), 2B, 2C, 2D & 1E. WEALD). Designators will become WEALD 2A (WLD 2A), 2B, 2C, 2D & 1E.
4 As lowest level in BIG/WEALD holding stack (7000') is above transition altitude, aircraft will be instructed by ATC to fly at the appropriate flight level.
5 The routes shown also apply to aircraft inbound to Northolt.
6 STARs BIG 2D and BIG 1E are NOT to be used for flight planning purposes. Use only when instructed by ATC.

TRANSITION LEVEL - ATC
TRANSITION ALT 6000'
NOT TO SCALE

HOLDING SPEEDS
Holding speed in the LTMA up to and including FL140 is 220kts IAS. At FL150 and above standard ICAO holding speeds apply.

DESCENT PLANNING - ATC REQUIREMENTS
Pilots should plan for possible descent clearance as follows:
BIG 2A — FL 150 by TIGER
BIG 2B — FL 150 by BIG 025
BIG 2C — FL 140 by LYD VOR
BIG 2D — FL 140 by LYD VOR
BIG 1E — FL 150 by SABER
As directed by ATC
N.B. ACTUAL DESCENT CLEARANCE WILL BE AS DIRECTED BY ATC.

LONDON LON 113·6D
LAMBOURNE LAM 115·6D N51 38·7 E000 09·2
BIGGIN BIG 115·1D N51 19·8 E000 02·2
BOVINGDON BNN 113·75D
DETLING DET 117·3D N51 18·2 E000 35·9
LYD LYD 114·05D N50 59·9 E000 52·8
SANDY N51 03·9 E001 04·0 DET 023
HILLY N51 20·0 E000 14·7 LAM D19
TIGER N51 03·9 E000 26·6 BIG D22
CLIFF N50 52·7 E000 43·6
SABER N51 44·90 E001 38·48
LOGAN N51 44·90 E001 38·48

| STAR DESIGNATOR | VIA | ROUTE |
|---|---|---|
| BIGGIN 2A (BIG 2A) | A20 | CLIFF-BIG |
| BIGGIN 2B (BIG 2B) | A2 | SANDY-BIG |
| BIGGIN 2C (BIG 2C) | A30 | LYD-BIG |
| BIGGIN 2D (BIG 2D) | R1/UR1/R126/UA37 | LOGAN-LAM-HILLY-BIG (Below FL155) |
| BIGGIN 1E (BIG1E) | R1/UR1/R126/UA37 | LOGAN-DET-BIG (Above FL155) |

CHANGE BIG 1D REDESIGNATED 2D WITH ROUTEING VIA HILLY. RADIALS UPDATED.
AERO INF DATE 7 Dec 95
500

## STARs via BOVINGDON — LONDON/Heathrow

**GENERAL INFORMATION**
1 Standard Routes may be varied at the discretion of ATC.
2 Cross SLPs or 3 min before holding facility at 250kts IAS or less.
3 When BNN VOR is out of service route to BOVVA. Designators become BOVVA 1A (BVA 1A), 1B, 1C, 1D & 1E.
4 As lowest level in BNN holding stack (7000') is above transition altitude, aircraft will be instructed by ATC to fly at the appropriate flight level.
5 The routes shown also apply to aircraft inbound to Northolt.
6 STARs BNN 1D and BNN 1E are NOT to be used for flight planning purposes. Use only when instructed by ATC.

TRANSITION LEVEL - ATC
TRANSITION ALT 6000'
NOT TO SCALE

HOLDING SPEEDS
Holding speed in the LTMA up to and including FL140 is 220kts IAS. At FL150 and above standard ICAO holding speeds apply.

DESCENT PLANNING - ATC REQUIREMENTS
Pilots should plan for possible descent clearance to FL150 by BNN 025.
ACTUAL DESCENT CLEARANCE WILL BE AS DIRECTED BY ATC.

MANCHESTER MCT 113·55D N53 21·4 W002 15·6
DAVENTRY DTY 116·4D N52 10·8 W001 06·7
HONLEY HON 113·65D N52 21·4 W001 39·7
WESTCOTT WCO 335 N51 15·1 W000 57·6
BOVINGDON BNN 113·75D N51 43·5 W000 32·9
LAMBOURNE LAM 115·6D N51 38·7 E000 09·2
LONDON LON 113·6D
DONNA N51 42·0 W000 27·3 LAM D33
KENET N51 31·2 W001 27·3
BVA 1E
BOVVA N51 45·5 W000 32·9 BIG D32

| STAR DESIGNATOR | VIA | ROUTE |
|---|---|---|
| BOVINGDON 1A (BNN 1A) | A1/B3 | HON-WCO-BNN |
| BOVINGDON 1B (BNN 1B) | A1 | MCT R157-WCO-BNN |
| BOVINGDON 1C (BNN 1C) | A47 | DTY-WCO-BNN |
| BOVINGDON 1D (BNN 1D) | G1 | KENET-BNN |
| BOVINGDON 1E (BNN 1E) | UA37/R1/UR1/R126 | LAM-DONNA-BNN |

CHANGE EDITORIAL
AERO INF DATE 7 Dec 95
501

**Left** *Standard Terminal Arrival Charts for London/Heathrow* (CAA).

departures at the runway holding point, a landing clearance may be given at this point, but it is more usual to give it at the 4-mile range. Alternatively, once the pilot reports that he is established on the ILS, Approach may tell him to contact the tower, who will give landing clearance when available.

Pilots expect to receive a landing clearance at around 4 miles on final approach, but this is not always possible owing to departing traffic or a previous landing aircraft being slow to clear the runway. Because a go-around is a fairly major operation, 2 miles is the absolute minimum for large transport aircraft. The phrase 'expect late landing clearance' is sometimes heard because light aircraft in a busy circuit may, of necessity, only receive one on very short final. They may even be told to go around if they get too close to the aircraft in front.

For a runway not equipped with ILS the radar controller is normally able to offer a Surveillance Radar Approach. If the weather is poor this can be down to half a mile from touchdown, assuming that the radar is approved for this purpose. With certain types of radar, approaches to 2 miles only may be allowed. This ensures a reasonable chance of seeing the approach lights and making a successful landing in all but the worst weather.

Where only one Approach Controller is on duty and the ILS fails, he may be unable to offer a half-mile SRA because of the necessity for continuous transmissions during the last 4 miles of the approach. This of course means that any other traffic cannot communicate with him until the talkdown is complete. If a second controller is available, the first can do a half-mile SRA on a discrete frequency while his colleague continues to sequence traffic on to long final for handover as soon as the preceding aircraft has completed its approach.

SRAs to 2 miles, however, do not require continuous transmissions, and the controller can talk to other traffic as necessary, although he must time his calls so that range checks and the associated advisory heights are passed at the correct intervals. The advisory heights are based upon a glide path of $3°$, so at $6^1/2$ miles the aircraft should be at a height of 2,000ft (as already mentioned, descent on a $3°$ glide path is equivalent to about 300ft per mile). Some airfields have non-standard glide path angles because of local obstructions and other considerations, the advisory heights being adjusted accordingly. It is assumed that the aircraft is flying on QFE, but if the pilot advises that he is using QNH the runway threshold elevation is added to the advisory heights and rounded up to the next 25ft, the term 'altitude' being used in place of 'height'.

# Phraseology for Surveillance Radar Approaches

## During the Intermediate Procedure

'This will be a Surveillance Radar Approach, terminating at X miles from touchdown. Check your minima, stepdown fixes and missed approach point. Check wheels.'

## Azimuth information

'Turn left/right X degrees, heading XXX. Closing (final approach) track from the left/right. Heading of XXX is good. On track. Slightly left/right of track.'

## Descent information

'Approaching X miles from touchdown – commence descent now to maintain a X degree glide path. X miles from touchdown – height should be X feet. Do not reply to further instructions. Check minimum descent height.'

## Completion

'Approach completed, out. Continue visually or go around [missed approach or further instructions].'

## Breaking off

'Turn left/right X degrees, heading XXX,

climb to X feet [further instructions], acknowledge. Climb immediately, I say again climb immediately on heading XXX to altitude X feet [further instructions], acknowledge.'

## General Approach Control Phraseology

Since all major airports now use radar to direct their traffic, I shall deal with this aspect first. An aircraft must be identified before it can receive a radar control or advisory service; in other words, the controller must be sure that one particular blip on his screen is the aircraft he is directing. This is simple with a radar handover from another ATC unit or by means of SSR, but at airfields outside controlled airspace, where aircraft may approach from random directions with no prior notification, a standard procedure is observed.

ATC: 'GVM report heading and level.'
Aircraft: 'GVM heading 140 at 2,500ft.'
ATC: 'GVM for identification turn left heading 110.'

The identification turn must be at least 30° different from the original heading. When the pilot reports steady on the new heading, and the controller is sure that he has related a specific blip on his screen to the aircraft, he transmits: 'GVM identified 12 miles south of X (airfield)'.

The service to be given is then added.

ATC: 'Vectoring for an ILS approach runway X.'

The weather and pressure settings are then passed as a separate transmission.

If in the initial call the aircraft makes the turn requested and is still not observed on radar, perhaps because it is out of range, in weather clutter, or below cover, the controller will say 'GVM not identified. Resume own navigation'. D/F will then be used to home the aircraft towards the airfield for eventual radar

pick-up. When identified, the aircraft will be vectored, that is given headings to steer to fit it into the approach sequence or, if traffic is light, direct to final approach. Outside controlled airspace the aircraft may be vectored around unidentified traffic. Information will be given by the use of the 12-hour clock, 12 o'clock being straight ahead, 3 o'clock over the pilot's right shoulder, and so on. The distance and relative direction of movement is also given, together with any information on speed, type of aircraft if known, etc. Typical traffic information is passed in this form: 'ABC123 unknown traffic 10 o'clock, 5 miles crossing left to right, fast moving.'

If the pilot does not have the traffic in sight he may request avoiding action. This may, in any case, be initiated by the controller if he considers it necessary. Sometimes rapid action is required to avert the risk of collision: 'ABC123 avoiding action turn left immediately heading 110.' A few incidents have occurred where, by using a too relaxed tone of voice, the controller has failed to convey to the pilot the urgency of the required action and the pilot's more leisurely response has led to an awkward situation that might have been averted. The CAA eventually instructed all controllers to ensure that their tone of voice does not lull pilots into a false sense of security on these occasions!

At locations with no radar, procedural methods are used. The same applies when radar is normally available but unserviceable or seriously affected by weather clutter, or if the pilot wishes to carry out a procedural approach for training purposes. On transfer from the ACC, the first call will go something like this:

Aircraft: 'Inverness Approach GBC descending to FL60, estimating INS at 42.'
ATC: 'GBC cleared for VOR/DME approach Runway 06 descend to altitude 3,500ft QNH 1021. Report beacon outbound.'

Subsequent reports will be made when 'base turn complete' and, if the beacon is several miles out on final approach, a 'beacon inbound call' will be made as well. These standard calls help the tower controller to plan his traffic, bearing in mind that there may be no radar to give him ranges from touchdown.

Where the airport is equipped with ILS, permission to make a procedural approach is given thus: 'GMB cleared for ILS approach Runway 27, report beacon outbound QFE 1008.' Subsequent exchanges would be:

Aircraft: 'GMB beacon outbound.'
ATC: 'GMB report established inbound.'
    (The phrase 'Report procedure turn
    complete' may be substituted.)
Aircraft: 'GMB established ILS inbound.'
ATC: 'GMB report outer marker' (or
    'Report 4 DME').
Aircraft: 'GMB outer marker' (or '4 DME').
ATC: 'GMB contact Tower 118.1.'

In good weather, by day or night, even though nominally flying IFR, a pilot may request permission to make a visual approach. This may be granted subject to certain provisos, the most important of which is that the pilot must have visual reference to the surface, ie the ground or water, and a reasonable assurance exists that he will be able to complete the landing visually. Standard separation continues to be applied between this aircraft and other arriving and departing traffic unless the pilot states that he can see an aircraft ahead in the approach sequence and can follow it down to the runway. During daylight hours only, IFR flights may be cleared to approach maintaining VMC and their own separation, if reports indicate that this is possible.

Inbound VFR traffic will be cleared into a control zone via a Visual Reference Point (VRP), which ensures that it remains well away from the flight paths of arriving and departing IFR traffic. An altitude restriction will also be imposed for the same reason, as well as a clearance limit in the vicinity of the airfield. This will be an easily identifiable ground feature over which the aircraft can orbit until it can be fitted into the traffic pattern.

Mention should be made of QGH, a military procedure that is only available at a handful of civil airfields, usually where a University Air Squadron is based. The QGH dates back to the Second World War, but is nevertheless highly effective in bringing aircraft safely down to a position from which an approach can be continued visually. This particular Q-Code means 'Controlled descent through cloud', and uses a cathode ray tube VDF to home the aircraft to the overhead at a safe altitude. Subsequent bearings bring it down a safety lane on to final approach. During the procedure, the pilot's replies are used to obtain D/F bearings, and additional transmissions may be requested using the words 'Transmit for D/F'. Immediately the aircraft has passed over the VDF aerial, turn instructions are given to get it on to the outbound track:

ATC: 'V91 D/F indicates that you have
    passed overhead. Turn left heading 120.
    Report steady.'

On completion of the overhead turn and when bearings indicate that the aircraft is outbound, heading corrections derived from a series of bearings are given by the controller as required to make good the outbound track. Descent instructions and the appropriate pressure are also given at this point: 'V91 descend to 1,000ft QFE 1006, report level.' The controller times the outbound leg with a stop watch (usually 3 minutes), then gives the aircraft a turn on to a heading to intercept the final approach track. Further D/F checks ensure that it remains within the safety lane and the pilot is told to continue down to Minimum Descent Height and report airfield in sight.

The civilian counterpart of the QGH is the VDF Approach, which is virtually the direct opposite, in that the pilot interprets the QDM information rather than the controller. VDF approaches are uncommon these days, reflecting the greater availability of radar and ILS. Apart from this they require a lot of practice by the pilot to perfect them, and were never very popular! QDMs, by the way, are passed as three digits, eg 355. The class of accuracy is passed with the initial bearing, depending on the CAA's approval of the equipment in use, and also with any subsequent bearings that show unusual fluctuations: Class A is accurate to within ±2°; B to within ±5°; C to within ±10°; and D represents an accuracy worse than Class C.

# Chapter 7

# *Aerodrome Control*

The Aerodrome Controller's function is defined as the issuing of information and instructions to aircraft to achieve a safe, orderly and expeditious flow of traffic and to assist pilots in preventing collisions between:

(a) aircraft in flight in the vicinity of the aerodrome traffic zone
(b) aircraft taking off or landing
(c) aircraft moving on the apron
(d) aircraft and vehicles, obstructions and other aircraft on the manoeuvring area (ie the runways and taxiways)

The apron may also come under the jurisdiction of the marshaller, who makes sure that aircraft are parked in the required places. This is particularly important at airports where all or part of the apron is out of sight of the tower. At larger airports, self-manoeuvring markings are painted on the tarmac to guide pilots to the stand that has been allocated on R/T, thus obviating the need for 'the man with the bats'. Some major airports have docking guidance systems using lights and symbols.

It would, however, be impossible to control all the service vehicles moving about the apron, so these are confined, as far as possible, to lanes outlined in white paint. Airfield fire and maintenance vehicles that need to go on the runways and taxiways are controlled on a UHF domestic frequency; these are not published but can be found in the range 455–461MHz (NFM). Most operate on a split frequency where the base station transmits on, for example, 455.6375 and the

mobile on 460.9375. Sometimes the VHF tower or GMC frequency is re-broadcast on the UHF channel (at Manchester, for example) so that vehicle drivers can be aware of aircraft movement. At some airfields the tower VHF frequency is used for controlling vehicles. Standard phraseology is used (aircraft 'taxi', vehicles 'proceed' or 'tow') and vehicles have self-explanatory call-signs such as 'Sweeper One', 'Works Two', 'Fire Five', etc.

To smooth the running of the larger airports, it may be necessary to split the duties of Aerodrome Control into Air Control and Ground Movement Control (referred to as GMC). The latter's responsibility covers aircraft moving on the apron and aircraft and vehicles on the manoeuvring area, except on runways and their access points. Major airports have a Surface Monitoring Radar to follow aircraft and vehicle movements in bad visibility. R/T loading at some locations, notably Heathrow, Gatwick and Manchester necessitates a further sub-division of GMC known as Ground Movement Planning (GMP), call-sign 'Delivery', on which start-up and route clearances are passed.

Until recently the Tower Controller had few aids apart from the 'Mark 1 eyeball' and a pair of binoculars. Now many Visual Control Rooms (VCRs) are equipped with an Air Traffic Monitor (ATM). This is a daylight-viewing, colour radar showing the local area out to a radius of about 10 miles. At airports with only one runway and a high movement rate – Manchester and Gatwick for example – it is invaluable in judging whether there is sufficient room to

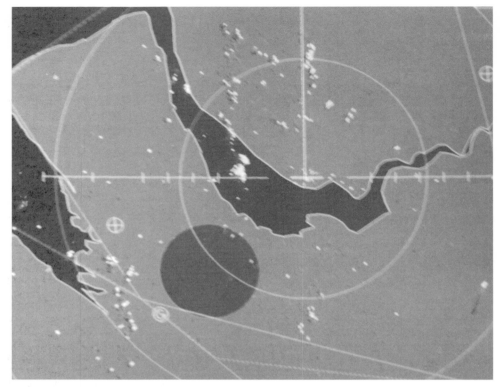

*Liverpool's Air Traffic Monitor display showing the 10-mile radius, coastline, runway centrelines, range marks, etc. An inbound aircraft can be seen on the far right, near the bottom.*

clear a departing aircraft to take off or to give priority to an aircraft on final approach. It also serves to confirm the turn on to track of a preceding aircraft so that a second aircraft can be permitted to depart. The Radar Controller is required to give 8-mile and 4-mile checks for traffic on final approach to his colleague in the tower. The aim is to confirm landing clearance at about 4 miles, but certainly at not less than 2 miles.

Runway occupancy is governed by the following rules:

(a) An aircraft shall not be permitted to begin take-off until the preceding departing aircraft is seen to be airborne or has reported 'airborne' by R/T and all preceding landing aircraft are clear of the runway in use.

(b) A landing aircraft will not be permitted to cross the beginning of the runway on its final approach until a preceding departing aircraft is airborne.

There is, however, a phrase 'land after', which seems to puzzle some private pilots who probably think it is a place in Wales! Its purpose is to increase runway utilisation by permitting a landing aircraft to touch down before a preceding landing aircraft is clear of the runway. The onus for ensuring adequate separation is transferred from controller to pilot, and the provisos are:

(a) The runway is long enough to allow safe

separation between the two aircraft and there is no evidence to indicate that braking may be adversely affected.

(b) It is during daylight hours.

(c) The controller is satisfied that the landing aircraft will be able to see the preceding landing aircraft clearly and continuously until it is clear of the runway.

(d) The pilot of the following aircraft is warned.

There is one other runway procedure that is authorised only at Heathrow and Gatwick, where arriving aircraft are 'cleared to land after' (this phrase also being unique). Certain conditions must be met and the procedure is also allowed behind departing traffic. The aim is to achieve an increase in runway capacity.

At some airfields the Tower and Approach function may be combined on one frequency. This is perfectly satisfactory with light to medium traffic flows, but on busy weekends the R/T congestion can be serious.

Airfields outside controlled airspace possess an Aerodrome Traffic Zone, through which flight is prohibited without a clearance. The circuit direction is a standard left hand, although this may vary for different runways to avoid overflying built-up areas, hospitals and the like. The reason for the left-hand pattern is said to date back to the First World War when aircraft like the Sopwith Camel turned much more easily to the left than the right, owing to the torque effect of the rotary engine. When larger aircraft with side-by-side seating were introduced, the pilot sat on the left and this has become traditional. In helicopters, however, this is reversed!

Circuit height is normally 1,000ft above ground level, but at airfields such as Manchester-Barton it is 800ft, which sometimes leads to confusion when trainee pilots land elsewhere. These days some pilots tend to fly enormous 'bomber circuits', much to the annoyance of ATC and other aircraft in the circuit.

The circuit is divided into four legs: crosswind, downwind, base and final approach. The first aircraft to report downwind will be told to 'report final' ('number one' may be added to this). The second will be told 'Number two, follow the Cherokee on base', and so on. If the circuit is very busy the tower may instruct a trainee pilot to 'report before turning base, four aircraft ahead'. When the pilot does

*Critical positions in the aerodrome traffic circuit.*

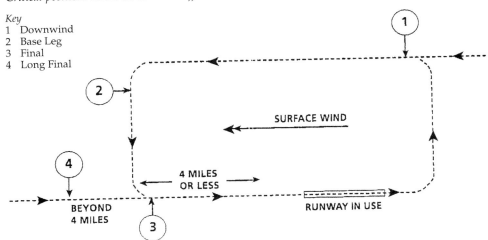

Key
1   Downwind
2   Base Leg
3   Final
4   Long Final

this he will be given an update on his position in traffic, there perhaps being only two ahead by that time.

The standard circuit-joining procedure is to arrive overhead the field at 2,000ft, descend on the dead side, ie the one opposite the live downwind leg, and let down to 1,000ft. While watching for departing traffic, the trainee pilot then joins the crosswind leg over the upwind end of the active runway. (Wags may be interested to know that there is a cemetery under the dead side at Cambridge Airport.) This should ensure that a joining aircraft does not conflict with one just airborne, there having been numerous cases in the past of collisions because of careless rejoins a mile or so off the end of the runway. Of course a high-performance aircraft can easily be at 1,000ft by the time it reaches the end of a longish runway, so it is up to the tower to make sure that a joining aircraft does not cross its path. At many controlled airports the standard join is not used, aircraft being authorised to join directly on to final, base or downwind.

Scheduled and other large aircraft are usually fed straight into the final approach, which can sometimes be tricky. One way to achieve this safely if there is circuit traffic is to instruct the trainer to continue downwind until he has the arriving aircraft in sight, then follow it. The other solution is an orbit – a 360° turn – always away from the final approach, to be continued until the traffic is sighted. The first method has the disadvantage that a strong tailwind may carry the aircraft into the next county, with perhaps an inexperienced pilot losing sight of the aerodrome. An orbit may be impracticable because of following traffic in the circuit. There is a limit to the number of aeroplanes you can orbit safely in a circuit!

If things are particularly congested and large aircraft are expected, trainers can always be told to land and taxi back to the holding point to await further take-off clearance. Another complication is vortex wake, a phenomenon once referred to as slipstream or propwash, but now known to be a rapidly revolving cylinder of air from each wingtip. This can be so violent that it can overcome the control forces of a following aircraft and invert it. Aircraft in the United Kingdom are placed in four categories depending upon maximum total weight at take-off: Heavy, Medium, Small and Light. More details will be found on page 91.

Helicopter operations are less of a problem than might be imagined, the main difficulty being the crossing of an active runway. However, they can clear it quickly and can thus be slotted between arriving and departing aircraft, remaining below 500ft until clear of the traffic zone. The same applies to their arrival, although at places like Liverpool with an adjacent wide river, pilots are understandably reluctant to approach or depart at low level. In this case, the normal procedure is to change the direction of the circuit traffic away from the helicopter.

Overflying helicopters are treated like any other crossing traffic, either cleared overhead above 2,000ft if the circuit is busy, or asked to report a few miles away and given traffic information so that they can fly through the pattern without conflict.

The Aerodrome Controller is, of course, pre-warned of arriving traffic by Approach, or at some places he handles both functions on the same frequency. Similarly, for departing IFR traffic he will have the flight progress strips on his pending board, made up when the flight plan was filed with ATC.

At certain busy airports pilots on VFR flights, local, landing away or circuits, are required to 'book out' over the telephone with ATC, giving brief details. This is particularly important with circuit training as the tower controller may refuse to accept more than a certain number, dependent upon weather conditions, scheduled traffic, existing congestion and other factors. At smaller airfields, pilots merely call for taxi clearance from the parking area stating their requirements. Training flights are

**Right** *Aerodrome Chart for Manchester* (CAA).

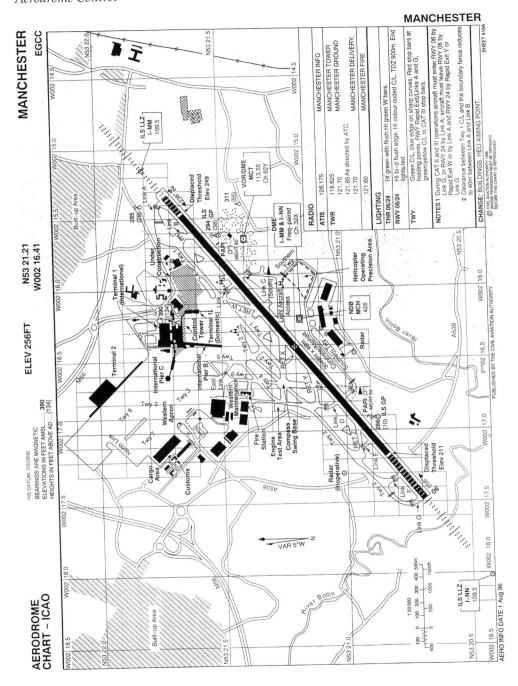

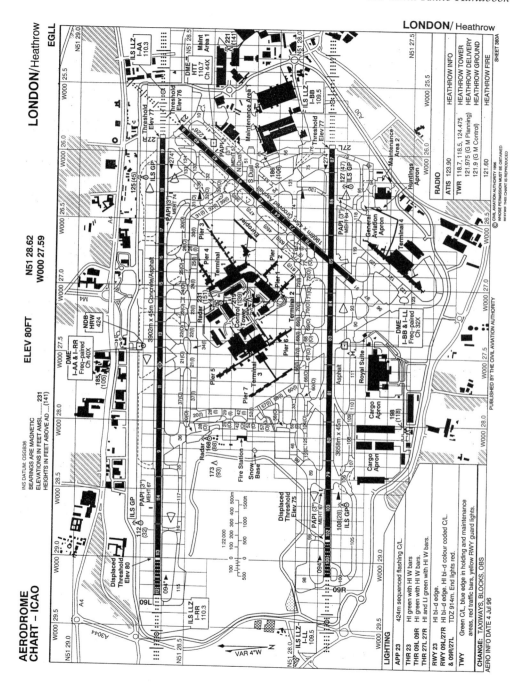

**Left** *Aerodrome Chart for London/Heathrow* (CAA).

often referred to by the word 'detail' as in 'Coventry Tower GAXVW request taxi clearance, two on board circuit detail'. This is a throwback to military jargon, as is the term 'fanstop' for a practice engine failure after take-off.

Aircraft on IFR flight plans should first request permission to start engines so that ATC can warn of any likely delays and thus minimise fuel wastage. If there is no delay, 'Start-up approved' is passed, together with the outside air temperature in degrees Celsius. The QNH, QFE, runway in use and wind information may also be given in the same transmission, although this is optional. The alternative is to pass them when taxi clearance is given. In practice, pilots often call in advance for this 'airfield data', acknowledge it and say 'call you again for start'.

Traffic on the congested holiday routes to the Mediterranean and other parts of Europe is subject to complex rules known as Departure Flow Regulation (DFR). These require the aircraft to take off at a specified time, ATC being allowed 5 minutes before and 10 after this to cover any taxying delays or short waits for landing traffic. These Approved Departure Times (ADTs) were formerly known as 'slot times', and this terminology is still heard occasionally on R/T. Further details will be found on page 93.

For example, a system known as Passive Slot Allocation is used for scheduled airline flights into London's airports from various British cities. Since the flight data is already stored in Brussels' computer it is a simple matter to allocate the ADTs well in advance by means of a telex to the operator and local ATC.

Other domestic traffic within the UK is also regulated at peak periods. For example, the Channel Islands airports become very busy during the summer and flow control is employed to reduce congestion. On occasion, routes over the Irish Sea and Scotland are also subject to

flow management. A time band normally of 10 minutes, within which an aircraft must cross a specified point en route, is used as an alternative to an ADT.

If there are no problems, taxi instructions will be given to the appropriate runway. In the meantime, ATC will have obtained an airways clearance from the parent ACC by land line, and this is passed to the aircraft at a convenient moment. Local procedures vary from one airport to another, and it may be necessary to contact the ACC again as the subject nears the runway for permission to let it take off. Sometimes a restriction may be applied to separate it from overflying traffic, such as: 'Not above altitude 2,500ft until further cleared by Manchester Control.'

On occasion, the ACC may allow the aircraft to take off with the condition that Approach Radar will separate it from inbound conflicting traffic. It will then be given a suitable radar heading to fly after departure and/or a level restriction. As soon as it is airborne the aircraft will be transferred to the Approach frequency and it will only be handed over to the ACC when the conflict has been resolved ('clean' in ATC slang).

Where no local restrictions are applied the tower will put the aircraft over to the ACC immediately after take-off. The departure time is also passed to the ACC by telephone to be fed into the computer. At the busiest UK airports, including Heathrow, Gatwick and Manchester, the flow of arrivals and departures is designed so that the two do not conflict. The ideal is a 'conveyor belt' system, but although in practice this is virtually impossible to achieve, it comes quite near. Of necessity the other lesser airfields in a TMA, for example Liverpool in the case of Manchester, are somewhat subservient. Their traffic flows are very much subject to those of their busier neighbours although, on the credit side, sometimes more flexible.

Often, if the weather is good, pilots on IFR flight plans may elect to go VFR. This saves en route navigation charges and it is also a way to avoid delays at busy periods

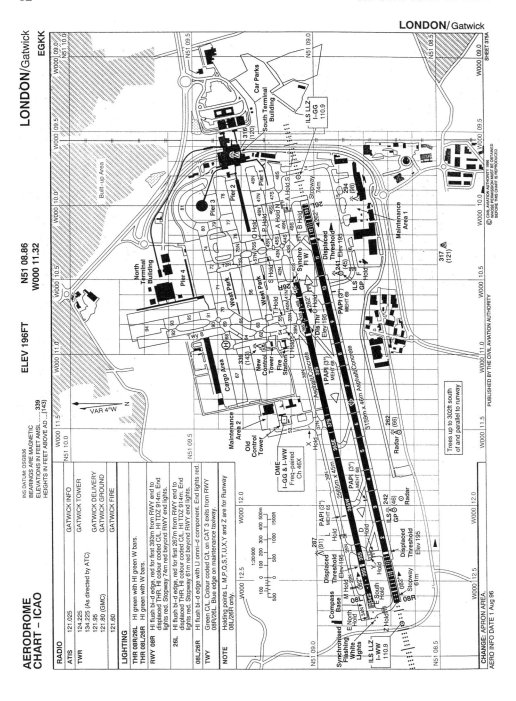

**Left** *Aerodrome Chart for London/Gatwick* (CAA).

when an airways clearance is not immediately forthcoming from the ACC. However, pilots who try to beat the system and rejoin controlled airspace further down the airway will not get much sympathy and are likely to suffer further delay as a result! A typical ATC acknowledgment of a request to go VFR is: 'Atlantic 991 roger, IFR flight plan cancelled at 36'.

The SSR code, or 'squawk' as it is known, is allocated according to a predetermined system. The UK participates in the internationally agreed Originating Region Code Assignment Method (ORCAM), developed by Eurocontrol and endorsed by ICAO. Since there are insufficient code blocks to develop a worldwide system it has been necessary to group certain countries into Participating Areas. The ICAO EUR region is divided into five of these areas, the United Kingdom falling into PA West.

ORCAM is designed to reduce R/T and cockpit workload by allocating an SSR code that will be retained by the aircraft from take-off to touchdown. This helps controllers in forward planning, particularly in areas of radar data processing. Each ACC is allocated two blocks of codes, one for internal flights (Domestic) and the other (ORCAM) for international flights. The ACC with jurisdiction over the airspace first entered by an aircraft will assign a discrete code from one of its blocks. This code will depend on the destination and will be retained throughout the flight within the Participating Area, being transferred from centre to centre along the route (see Appendix 7). SSR Mode S will solve the problem of the very limited number of codes available (4,064). Mode S transponders employ a unique 'address' for each individual aircraft, 16 million being available worldwide. Unfortunately the ground interrogator system has its own limitations at present, which severely offset the airborne advantages.

Approach Control units with SSR capability have their own small block of codes that they can allocate to traffic crossing their area, provided of course that the aircraft is transponder-equipped. Fortunately nowadays most private aircraft can comply with this. Mention of the special 'squawk' 7000 is often made on R/T. Pilots flying outside controlled airspace and Aerodrome Traffic Zones and who are not receiving a radar service are advised to set 7000, the conspicuity code, on the transponder. As the name implies, this makes the aircraft show up better on radar as well as indicating its altitude. Above FL100, 7000 is mandatory.

## Aerodrome Control Phraseology

Aircraft: 'Luton Tower Britannia 835A request start-up.'
ATC: 'Britannia 835A start-up approved, temperature plus 8.'

These start-up requests should always be made by aircraft that intend to fly airways, as there may be unexpected delays; far better to postpone starting for a few minutes than waste fuel at the holding point. The phrase 'Start-up at your discretion', together with an expected departure time, may be used so that the onus is on the crew to start engines at a convenient time. Note that the words 'at your discretion' are used by controllers to imply that any traffic delays, getting stuck in soft ground and other misfortunes will henceforth be the pilot's fault! Controllers have very definite responsibilities and are understandably reluctant to take on more.

Aircraft: 'Heathrow Ground Alitalia 235 Stand Echo 3 request pushback.'
ATC: 'Alitalia 235 pushback approved.'

Many airports have nose-in parking at the terminal to save apron space and to facilitate passenger handling. Aircraft therefore have to be pushed backwards by a tractor into a position from which they

**Left** *Leeds-Bradford Tower* (Ken Cothliff, Air Supply).

can taxi for departure. A variation is the 'powerback', in which a turboprop aircraft reverses under its own power.

Aircraft: 'Liverpool Tower GBGTR at Alpha request taxi for local.'

ATC: 'GTR taxi Charlie hold Runway 09, wind 100 degrees 10 knots, QNH 1008.'

Taxi instructions must always specify a clearance limit, which is the point at which an aircraft must halt and ask for further permission to proceed. The limit is normally the holding point of the runway in use, but it may also be an intermediate position, perhaps short of another runway that is in intermittent use. To maintain a smooth operation, controllers try to anticipate calls from taxying aircraft so that they do not actually have to stop at intermediate points. Some UK airports have quite complex taxiway systems and each significant section is given a number or a descriptive name such as North West Taxiway, Eastern Link and Inner Loop. At Edinburgh a short-cut is aptly known as the Lazy Lane! Holding points are allocated a letter from Alpha onwards.

The ideal is to establish a circular flow of taxying aircraft so that those just landed do not get in the way of those moving towards the holding point. Alas, many airports have inadequate taxiway systems with two-way flows and bottlenecks, perhaps in the worst cases, as at Coventry, having runway access at only one end. A refusal to give crossing clearance of an active runway is passed in the form: 'GVW hold short Runway 23.' Permission to continue is: 'GVW cross Runway 23, report vacated.'

When ready for take-off, permission is sought from the tower. If the runway is occupied by traffic that has just landed, the aircraft will be told to 'line up and wait'. The American phrase 'taxi into position' is sometimes tried when a foreign pilot seems to have difficulty in understanding what is meant. (Controllers always have something

up their sleeves to break the language barrier, and often have to resort to plain speech to convey a meaning to some uncomprehending student pilot!)

If there is traffic on final, the aircraft at the holding point may be told: 'After the Cherokee on short final, line up.' Care must be taken that there is no possibility of confusion with another aircraft that may have just landed. Where a preceding aircraft is beginning its take-off roll, the second aircraft may be told: 'After the departing Cessna, line up and wait.' The use of the words 'cleared immediate take-off' means that the aircraft must go without delay to leave the runway free for landing traffic. It is only to be used where there is actual urgency so that its specific meaning is not debased.

The circuit-joining procedure has already been covered, so a few examples of phraseology will suffice.

Aircraft: 'Coventry Tower GAYMN at Ansty for landing.'

ATC: 'GMN join right-hand downwind Runway 05, QFE 1004', or 'GMN cleared straight-in approach Runway 23, QFE 1004.'

Aircraft: 'GMN downwind.'

ATC: 'GMN number two, follow the Cessna 150 on base.'

Aircraft: 'GMN number two, traffic in sight.'

Alternatively:

ATC: 'GMN extend downwind, number two to a Cessna 150 4 miles final on radar approach.'

Aircraft: 'GMN wilco.'

Having already explained the criteria for issuing landing and take-off clearances, mention should be made of a few extra points. Aircraft on what used to be known as 'circuits and bumps' may wish to do a 'touch and go' landing; in other words, the aircraft lands, continues rolling and takes off again without a pause. The wording 'cleared touch and go' is the only one approved officially, but pilots may ask for a 'roller', the military equivalent. (A pilot was once heard to read back 'cleared for a hit and run', but such levity is not encouraged!) Instructions to carry out a missed approach may be given to avert an unsafe situation, such as when one aircraft is too close behind another on final: 'GTE go around, I say again, go around. Acknowledge.'

Depending on local procedures, a departing aircraft will be retained on the tower frequency until it is clear of the circuit or changed to Approach immediately. Airways flights will of course be transferred to the ACC just after take-off or as soon as they have been separated from any conflicting traffic. When the landing roll is complete, the arriving aircraft will be told to clear the runway in the following manner:

ATC: 'GMN vacate left', or 'GMN taxi to the end, report runway vacated', or 'GMN take next right. When vacated contact Ground 121.7.'

The appropriate taxying instructions are then passed. Airborne and landing times may be passed by the tower, although there is no official requirement for this.

Interestingly enough, controllers are not responsible for reminding pilots to put their wheels down on final, except when a radar approach is being provided. However, if an aircraft were to land wheels-up in broad daylight, the controller would no doubt suffer some criticism, apart from the dent to his professional pride! Fortunately it is a rare occurrence these days, but I once earned a pint from a Cessna 337 pilot whom I reminded just in time (cheap at the price – the saving in repairs would have paid my year's salary!).

One last point is defined as 'Essential Aerodrome Information', and refers to any obstruction or unserviceability that is likely to affect operations. It is always prefixed with the word 'caution', examples being 'Caution work in progress ahead north side of the taxiway', 'Caution PAPI Runway 27 unserviceable', or 'Caution large flock of birds north of Runway 27 threshold'.

Where water is present on a runway, it will be described as Damp, Wet, Water Patches or Flooded.

# Chapter 8

# ATC at London's airports

Because of its intensity, traffic in the London TMA is handled rather differently from that of other British airports. London ATCC's Combined Control Function (CCF) is designed to maximise traffic flows. The TMA is divided into sectors, each sector controller being responsible for a defined segment. Traffic flows predominantly in the same direction to minimise points of conflict, and the need for co-ordination between controllers is kept to a minimum. Approach Control services for Heathrow, Gatwick and Stanstead have been moved to a new operations room at LATCC, West Drayton. The CCF's airspace extends up to FL155, above which is LATCC 'en route' airspace, and from FL300 upwards (FL260 in its centre) is the London Upper Sector, which allows more effective handling of high-level overflying traffic.

Aircraft inbound to Heathrow are directed by LATCC to one of four VORs located at Bovingdon, Lambourne, Biggin and Ockham. If traffic is light they may not actually route overhead these beacons but are vectored by radar directly to intercept the ILS for the runway in use. As the traffic flow increases, aircraft may arrive at the beacons faster than the runway is able to receive them, allowing for the requisite separation on approach. Hence the term 'stacking' (in ATC more usually referred to as 'holding'). When these inner holds are full, perhaps because fog is persisting, inbound transatlantic traffic may be held at high level at en route beacons as far away as the Wallasey VOR in North West England.

During 1995 Heathrow handled a total of 434,082 aircraft movements. At busy periods six controllers work as a team consisting of two Approach Controllers, two Intermediate Approach Directors, a Final Director and a Special VFR Controller. Each Approach Controller with his Intermediate Director controls the traffic from either Bovingdon and Lambourne in the north or from Ockham and Biggin in the south. As the aircraft nears one of these VOR beacons CCF releases it to Heathrow Approach. On contact the pilot is told to enter the hold or, if there is no delay, is vectored directly into the landing sequence. The frequencies in use are 119.725, 120.4, 134.975 and 125.625, but not all will be active during less busy periods. The Special VFR Controller operates on 119.9.

The Approach Controllers and Intermediate Directors work closely together, instructing pilots to adjust their height, speed and heading so that two orderly streams of aircraft, one from the north, the other from the south are brought on to the approach path. Aircraft in these two streams are then handed over to the Final Director so that he can integrate them into a single stream of aircraft approaching the runway.

At this stage a correct landing interval must be established and the Final Director ensures that all aircraft are correctly separated, depending on the prevailing weather conditions and types of aircraft involved. The vortex wake separations are explained in Chapter 13, but there are other considerations. For example, an MD-83 following a Shorts 360 will obviously have no problem with vortex wake, but will

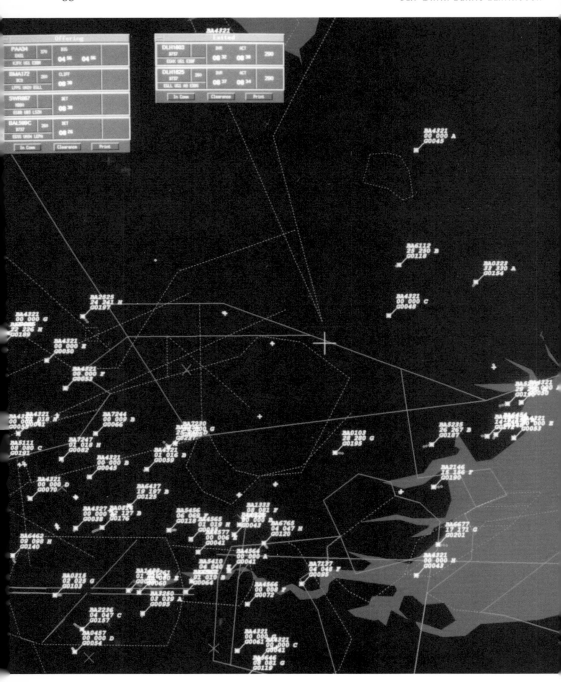

catch up rapidly if this is not allowed for. Similarly, if visibility is on limits an aircraft may be slow to clear the runway and the 'land after' procedure cannot be applied, resulting in a go-around if the next aircraft is too close behind.

The Special VFR Controller is responsible for helicopters and light aircraft that wish to land or merely transit the London Control Zone within the levels for which Heathrow Approach is responsible. Inbound aircraft are fitted into the approach pattern to cause as little inconvenience as possible to the main commercial traffic. Helicopters are required to follow special routes in the London area, designed where possible to keep them over the River Thames and the most thinly populated areas.

The usual destination is the Westland Heliport at Battersea. All inbound helicopters have to route via the Thames, initially routeing to Kew Bridge, Barnes or London Bridge, depending on the direction from which they are approaching. There are numerous compulsory and on request reporting points, and helicopters may be held at a number of positions to await onward clearance. They are all located at easily recognisable places such as Hampton Court, Sunbury Lock and Hanworth.

When the two streams of approaching aircraft are satisfactorily merged into one, and as each aircraft is established on the ILS at a distance of 6 to 8 miles from touchdown, control is transferred to Air Arrivals Control in the tower. Like any other tower controller he issues landing clearances, passes wind checks and details of surface conditions where appropriate. The frequency is 118.7.

After the aircraft has landed and left the runway it will be transferred to the Ground Movements Controller on 121.9 who directs it to the parking stand. He continues to monitor its progress and co-ordinates its movements with those of other aircraft and vehicles. All airports have their quota of service vehicles, but Heathrow inevitably has more than most. There is, for example, a full-time mobile bird control unit, radio call-sign 'Seagull'. 'Checker' is the airport surface and lighting inspection vehicle.

The maintenance of runways and taxiways and their associated lighting is one of the biggest problems for Ground Movement Control – it seems that there is almost always some part of the airport being dug up or resurfaced. Each controller has an airport plan on which he notes the current unserviceable areas before taking over watch in the tower. For easy reference Heathrow is divided up into numbered blocks.

To help things run smoothly at night or in poor visibility equipment known as Surface Movement Radar (SMR) is used to monitor aircraft and vehicle movements. Its aerial is mounted on top of the tower and scans the airport at very high speed so that the radar picture is continuously renewed. Runways and taxiways show up clearly in plan view on the display, as do the aircraft and vehicles that need to be tracked. Current development will tag the call-sign to the aircraft on the display and include 'windows' listing pending departures and arrivals. At night the aircraft are assisted by green centreline and red stop bar lights set flush with the taxiways. These can be illuminated in sections to ensure that no two aircraft are in or crossing the same section at any one time. This complex lighting system is operated by an ATC assistant on instructions from the Ground Movement Controller. The lighting control panel is a mimic diagram, ie it is designed in the form of an airport plan with switches that directly operate the lighting in the corresponding section of the airport.

When an aircraft is ready for departure, the pilot, having noted the data on the continuous broadcast on the ATIS, calls the Ground Movement Planner on 121.975 (call-sign 'Delivery') for permission to start engines. This may be granted at once or a start time given to minimise ground delays and thus save fuel. Also taken into

## COMPTON SIDs      LONDON/Heathrow

**GENERAL INFORMATION**
1 SIDs reflect Noise Preferential Routeings.
2 Initial climb straight ahead to 580' QNH (500' QFE).
3 Cross Noise Monitoring Points not below 1080' QNH (1000' QFE) thereafter maintain minimum climb gradient of 4% to 4000' to comply with Noise Abatement requirements.

| Grid Speed | kt | 75 | 100 | 150 | 200 | 250 | 300 |
|---|---|---|---|---|---|---|---|
| 4%(244' per nm) | ft/min | 305 | 407 | 610 | 813 | 1017 | 1220 |

4 Callsign for RTF frequency use when instructed after take-off 'London Control'.
5 Callsign for frequency marked* will be 'Heathrow Director'.
6 En-route cruising level will be issued after take-off by London Control.
7 Max IAS 250kts below FL100 unless otherwise authorised.

**TRANSITION ALT 6000'**

**COMPTON CPT 114·35D** N51 29·5 W001 13·1

**WOODLEY WOD 352·** N51 27·2 W000 52·7

**LONDON LON 113·6D**

NOT TO SCALE

**AREA MNM ALT 25NM**

| 21 | 23 |
|---|---|
| 21 | 23 |

| | AVERAGE TRACK MILEAGE TO WOD | AIRWAY ROUTE |
|---|---|---|
| CPT 2F/2G | 15 | Via CPT G1-Westbound |
| CPT 2H | 16 | |
| CPT 4J | 21 | |
| CPT 3K | 22 | |

| SID | RWY | ROUTEING (incl. Noise Preferential Routeing) | ALTITUDES |
|---|---|---|---|
| CPT 2F 129·075 | 27R | Straight ahead to intercept **LON VOR** R260 until **LON** D7, then turn right onto QDM 273° to **WOD NDB** (**LON** D16), then to **CPT VOR**. | Cross **LON** D12 above 3000' **WOD NDB** (**LON** D16) above 4000' **CPT** D8·3 above 5000' **CPT VOR** at 6000' |
| CPT 2G 129·075 | 27L | Straight ahead to intercept **LON VOR** R260 until **LON** D7, then turn right onto QDM 273° to **WOD NDB** (**LON** D16), then to **CPT VOR**. | |
| CPT 2H 129·075 | 23 | Straight ahead to **LON** D2, then turn right onto QDM 278° to **WOD NDB** (**LON** D16), then to **CPT VOR**. | |
| CPT 4J *134·975 | 09R | Straight ahead to **LON** D2, then turn right onto QDM 285° to **WOD NDB** (**LON** D16), then to **CPT VOR**. | |
| CPT 3K *134·975 | 09L | Straight ahead to **LON** D1·5, then turn right onto QDM 285° to **WOD NDB** (**LON** D16), then to **CPT VOR**. | |
| **CHANGE** | | CPT 4J/3K INITIAL TURNING POINTS. SID DESIGNATORS. EDITORIAL. | |

AERO INF DATE 28 Mar 96

506

---

## MIDHURST SIDs      LONDON/Heathrow

**GENERAL INFORMATION**
1 SIDs reflect Noise Preferential Routeings.
2 Initial climb straight ahead to 580' QNH (500' QFE).
3 Cross Noise Monitoring Points not below 1080' QNH (1000' QFE) thereafter maintain minimum climb gradient of 4% to 4000' to comply with Noise Abatement requirements.

| Grid Speed | kt | 75 | 100 | 150 | 200 | 250 | 300 |
|---|---|---|---|---|---|---|---|
| 4%(244' per nm) | ft/min | 305 | 407 | 610 | 813 | 1017 | 1220 |

4 Callsign for RTF frequency use when instructed after take-off 'London Control'.
5 En-route cruising level will be issued after take-off by London Control.
6 Max IAS 250kts below FL100 unless otherwise authorised.

**TRANSITION ALT 6000'**

**OCKHAM OCK 115·3D**

**LONDON LON 113·6D**

**BURNHAM BUR 421**

**MIDHURST MID 114·0D** N51 03·2 W000 37·4

NOT TO SCALE

**AREA MNM ALT 25NM**

| 21 | 23 |
|---|---|
| 21 | 23 |

| | AVERAGE TRACK MILEAGE TO MID | AIRWAY ROUTE |
|---|---|---|
| MID 3F/3G | 30 | Via A34 A1(via BOGNA-HARDY join A47) South-bound. |
| MID 3H | 28 | |
| MID 2J/2K | 29 | |

| SID | RWY | ROUTEING (incl. Noise Preferential Routeing) | ALTITUDES |
|---|---|---|---|
| MID 3F 120·475 | 27R | Straight ahead to intercept **LON VOR** R244 until **LON** D5·5, then turn left onto **BUR NDB** QDR 166°· At **LON** D5·5, then turn right onto **MID VOR** R022 to **MID VOR**. | Cross **LON** D8 above 4000' **LON** D12 above 4000' **LON** D17 (**MID** D10) above 5000' **MID VOR** at 6000' |
| MID 3G 120·475 | 27L | Straight ahead to intercept **LON VOR** R244 until **LON** D5·5, then turn left onto **BUR NDB** QDR 166°· At **LON** D12 turn right onto **MID VOR** R022 to **MID VOR**. | |
| MID 3H 120·475 | 23 | Straight ahead to intercept **BUR NDB** QDR 166°· At **LON** D12 turn right to **MID VOR** R022 to **MID VOR**. | |
| MID 2J 120·475 | 09R | Straight ahead to **LON** D2, then turn right onto **LON VOR** R030 to **MID VOR**. | Cross **MID** D16 (Abm OCK) above 3000' **MID VOR** R030/D12 above 4000' **MID VOR** R030/D8 above 5000' **MID VOR** at 6000' |
| MID 2K 120·475 | 09L | Straight ahead to **LON** D1·5, then turn right onto **LON VOR** R129 until **LON** D3·5, then turn right onto **MID VOR** R030 to **MID VOR**. | |
| **CHANGE** | | MID 2J/2K INITIAL TURNING POINTS. SID DESIGNATORS. EDITORIAL. | |

AERO INF DATE 28 Mar 96

507

**Left** *Standard Instrument Departure (SID) Charts for London/Heathrow* (CAA).

consideration are the number of other aircraft that have already started, air route congestion and ADTs issued by the Central Flow Management Unit.

Once start-up clearance is given, the pilot is told to contact GMC when ready to taxi. The latter is responsible for issuing 'pushback' clearance from the stand by means of a tractor. Guidance is then given to the runway in use, and as this is approached the aircraft is handed over to the Air Departures Controller on 118.5 who arranges the aircraft in a departure sequence to achieve the maximum use of the runway. A large pan at the holding point, as well as several runway access points, provide sufficient space to 'shuffle' the order of departures. As a matter of interest, repeats of the tower and ground frequencies are broadcast in the band 453–456MHz (NFM) for the benefit of airfield vehicles. A number of other ground services can be heard in this band.

The basic rule of thumb is to alternate the departures between straight ahead, left and right. For example, when two aircraft of a similar type are departing in succession, one for a destination to the north followed by one to the south, they are allowed to leave 1 minute apart. However, due to the variety of aircraft types using Heathrow, this time interval may have to be increased depending on vortex wake categories and specific departure route. To minimise runway occupancy time, on receipt of line-up clearance pilots are expected to line up on the runway as soon as the preceding aircraft has started its take-off roll. Again, once receiving take-off clearance, they are required to roll immediately.

As soon as it is airborne the aircraft is transferred to London Control and fitted into the airways system. The pair of westerly (27) runways tends to be used most frequently because of prevailing winds. One is normally used for landings and the other for departures, but a local agreement ensures a change from one to the other at around 1500 hours local time each day in order to spread the noise more evenly. When the tailwind component is no greater than 5 knots on Runways 27 Right and Left, they will be used in preference to Runways 09 Right and Left, provided the runway surface is dry. When the crosswind component on these main runways exceeds 20 knots Runway 23 will normally be made available for landings if there is a lesser crosswind component affecting it. Departures from Runway 23 are confined to propeller-driven aircraft of 24 tonnes maximum take-off weight, and then only with the prior permission of the Airport Duty Ops Manager. Its opposite direction, Runway 05, is no longer used for either take-offs or landings.

ATC at Gatwick is somewhat less complex because of the single runway operation and the two, rather than four, holding stacks known as WILLO and Eastwood. The parallel Runway 08 Left/26 Right is a non-instrument runway and is used only when 08 Right/26 Left is temporarily non-operational by reason of maintenance or accident. Simultaneous operations are not permitted as the runways are too close together. Traffic from and to London/City Airport is handled by a facility known as Thames Radar, which is co-located with Heathrow Approach. Because of its proximity to London/City, Biggin Hill's IFR traffic is also co-ordinated by Thames Radar.

Traffic at Stansted, currently with just one holding stack, continues to grow and its airspace and Approach Control are now incorporated in the CCF.

At the time of writing, it seems likely that executive and commuter aircraft will be encouraged to use RAF Northolt in an effort to ease the pressure on Heathrow.

# London TMA Frequencies

| | |
|---|---|
| 120.175 | Inbounds via LUMBA, TIMBA |
| 120.475 | Inbounds via WILLO and departures via Midhurst and Worthing |

| | | | |
|---|---|---|---|
| 129.075 | Inbounds via Ockham and departures via Compton and Southampton | 133.975/ 134.125 | Biggin Hill, Southend |
| 121.225 | Inbounds via Lambourne | 119.775 | Departures via Bovingdon |
| 121.275/ 129.275 | Inbounds via Bovingdon | 118.825 | Departures via Brookmans Park |
| 133.175 | Inbounds to London/City, | 120.525 | Departures via Detling |

# Chapter 9

# Oceanic Control and HF listening

Although traffic over the North Atlantic communicates with ATC by means of the HF radio band, VHF being too restricted in range, aircraft requesting clearance to enter the Shanwick Oceanic Control Area from overhead the United Kingdom can be heard on certain VHF frequencies. ATC in the Shanwick OCA is provided by the Oceanic ACC at Prestwick, supported by the communications station at Ballygireen just north of Shannon Airport in Eire, hence the composite call-sign Shanwick Oceanic. Jet aircraft are required to request oceanic clearance while east of 2°W (roughly Manchester–Bournemouth) or as early as possible if departing from a point west of 2°W, so it is easy to intercept their transmissions in much of the United Kingdom.

For subsonic aircraft over the Atlantic there is a procedure known as the Organised Track System (OTS). As a result of passenger demands, time zone differences and airport noise restrictions, much of the North Atlantic air traffic is contained in two flows – westbound in the morning and eastbound in the evening. Because of the concentration of the flows and the limited vertical height band that is economical for jet operations, the airspace is comparatively congested. The track system is thus designed to accommodate as many aircraft as possible on the most suitable flight paths, taking advantage of any pressure systems to provide a tailwind where possible.

Prestwick OACC is responsible for the day track system and Gander for that at night. In each case, planners on both sides of the Atlantic consult with one another and co-ordinate as necessary with adjacent OACCs, as well as with domestic ATC agencies, to ensure that the system provides sufficient tracks and Flight Levels to satisfy anticipated traffic demands.

On completion of negotiations the OTS is sent out from the OACC concerned by signal to all interested parties in Europe and North America. The daytime system is usually published by Prestwick between midnight and 01:00 hours. In addition, the track co-ordinates are broadcast on frequency 133.8 and this can be heard in many parts of the United Kingdom on a normal air band radio. The tracks are known as Alpha, Bravo, Charlie and on to Mike, the most northerly being Alpha. For night use the tracks are designated Zulu for the most southerly, Yankee for the adjacent one to the north, ending at November. Letters India and Oscar are not used. For aircraft not equipped with HF radio there are several routes, known as 'Blue Spruce', which follow short hops between Iceland, Greenland and Canada within VHF coverage.

Military colour-coded routes are another special case. Intended for transatlantic tactical fighter deployments with mid-air refuelling, they include Blue Route, which terminates at waypoint QQ1 (the same position as the old Machrihanish TACAN); Red Route, terminating at Lands End VOR; Gold Hi East, terminating at 56°N 10°W; and its reverse, Gold Hi West, starting at the same point. Brown and Yellow Routes are further south into Spanish airspace. Another series of colour routes was developed primarily for USAF transport aircraft to facilitate the activation of short-notice altitude reservations over the Atlantic. Black Route feeds into the UK military TACAN Route system (see page 111) overhead RAF Leuchars, then Coltishall. Orange and Purple Routes enter France and Spain respectively.

Each oceanic flight plan received from the departure airport includes the track, Flight Level and cruise Mach number requested. When the pilot requests an oceanic clearance, the Planning Controller attempts to fit the flight into the planned slot according to the aircraft's requested level, Mach number and boundary estimate.

Once the clearance is accepted by the pilot, the information is relayed to the relevant ACC and, where necessary, to adjacent OACCs. The clearance is then fed into Prestwick's computer, which prints the appropriate en route flight strips and passes the information to Gander's computer. These flight strips give all relevant flight details and computed times of arrival at specific reporting points along the track, normally at intervals of 10° of longitude. The controller uses them to monitor the progress of the flight through the OCA. He is assisted in his task by the use of the Flight Data Processing System (FDPS), which carries out conflict prediction and detection, automatic update of flight profiles and data transfer to on-line adjacent ATC units.

Compared with the brief content of domestic airways clearances, these oceanic clearances are fairly long-winded because of the need to specify a large number of latitude and longitude positions, although in certain circumstances they can be abbreviated. It is useful for the air band listener to record these messages on tape for subsequent analysis; the same applies to other ATC transmissions when an air band radio is being used for the first time.

Most flights across the North Atlantic are handled in this way, but some aircraft may wish to operate outside the organised track system, for example on flights between Europe and the Caribbean, or between Europe and the West Coast of the USA. These so-called random tracks are also handled by Shanwick, as are transatlantic flights by Concorde. The latter operate along fixed tracks, normally between 50,000ft and 60,000ft. Because of the extremely small number of aircraft flying within this height band it is usually possible for the OACC to issue a clearance before take-off. This allows Concorde to operate on a supersonic 'cruise climb profile', which is the best in terms of fuel economy.

Unique to oceanic control is the method by which aircraft request clearances. Irrespective of geographical location, an aircraft will always use one of two frequencies, either 123.95 or 127.65MHz. Aircraft registered west of 30°W use the first, those registered east of 30°W the second. In practice this generally means that British airlines use 127.65 and American, Australian and Canadian airlines use 123.95. 135.525 is used as a stand-by.

Concorde flying over the Atlantic is a special case because an idealised flight profile would commence with an uninterrupted climb to supersonic cruise, followed by an uninterrupted descent to destination. Sonic boom considerations and the presence of other traffic obviously render this impossible, so in order to avoid supersonic flight over the UK land mass, a typical flight to the USA via the Woodley and Lyneham beacons climbs initially to around FL260 and maintains Mach .95 until the 'nominal acceleration point' after crossing the coastline south of Brecon VOR. The final tactical consideration for clearance for transonic acceleration along the Bristol Channel is made by the Radar Controller at LATCC. Likewise, on the return trip the transonic deceleration is completed over the sea prior to crossing the coast.

Concorde has special, unvarying oceanic tracks, known as 'Sierra Mike' when westbound and 'Sierra November' when eastbound. 'Sierra Oscar' is a reserve track in both directions. Air France Concorde flights to North America depart from Paris Charles de Gaulle and enter the London UIR south-west of Lands End. They then route to the same oceanic entry point at 50°N 08°W. Supersonic Link Routes numbers SL1 to SL7 connect the oceanic tracks with domestic airspace.

Outside VHF range, aircraft crossing the Atlantic communicate with ATC by means of HF radio. The same applies to any ocean or underdeveloped land mass where the short range of VHF radio waves would prove useless. An average of 800 commercial, military and general aviation flights overfly the North Atlantic each day, all being handled by Shanwick. Thus the ownership of an HF receiver opens up a whole new area of interest for the enthusiast.

In Britain there are a wide variety of listening possibilities, principally the civil stations (nets) controlling traffic over the Atlantic from Polar regions to the Equator, the US Air Force's extensive network, and those of the RAF and airline operators. There are nearly 140 ATC centres operating on HF around the world and, depending on the performance of one's receiver and other factors, many of them can be monitored. During the transatlantic slack periods (ie between the late morning/early afternoon westbound flights and the eastbound flights in the early hours of the morning) one can listen in to other parts of the world. For example, aircraft in the Far East can be monitored in the late afternoon, Africa in the evening, then for an hour or so either side of midnight the Caribbean and the eastern seaboard of the USA are very busy.

HF stations use a block of radio frequencies to circumvent the effects of atmospheric conditions. HF transmissions 'bounce off' the ionising layers that lie above the earth, but since the layers are affected by day and night conditions, a suitable range of daytime frequencies might suffer severe interference at night and vice versa. Although having very long range, HF lacks the clarity of the VHF channels, and the atmospheric noises and constant chatter make it very tiring for crews to maintain a continuous listening watch.

The answer is SelCal, short for Selective Calling. By this method, crews need not monitor the frequency, but when the ground station wishes to communicate with them a tone is sent and decoded by the cockpit equipment. A 'bing-bong' sound can be heard on the radio, and on the flight deck a chime or light signal alerts the pilots to respond by R/T. Each aircraft with SelCal capability is allocated a four-letter code by ARINC (Aeronautical Radio Inc), an American company that acts as agent to ICAO to perform this function.

On the first contact with the controller the SelCal will normally be checked, and this is where the interest lies for the aircraft registration collector. The SelCal code remains with the aircraft as long as the 'box' does, despite changes of ownership. ARINC does not make public the registration/SelCal tie-ups, but painstaking detective work by enthusiasts has tracked down most of them. The Aviation Society in Manchester publishes an extensive list in *High in the Sky*, which is available from them or specialist bookshops. The Society's magazine and that of LAAS International (see pages 189 and 190) list new allocations.

Over the Atlantic, position reports are passed in a similar fashion to those on VHF, ie the present position and a forward estimate for the next one. The positions are given in terms of latitude and longitude, '56 North 10 West' being an example, or as a reporting point or beacon when nearing a land mass. Approximately one aircraft per hour is requested by the Oceanic Control Centre to 'Send Met', and they will also include weather information with each position report. This consists of outside air temperature, wind speed and direction derived from INS equipment, plus any other relevant observations. A typical position report might be: 'Position Swissair 100 56N 20W 1235 Flight Level 330 estimate 56N 30W 1310, next 56N 40W.'

The airspace between 27,500ft and 40,000ft over most of the North Atlantic is known as MNPS (Minimum Navigation Performance Specification) airspace. Aircraft flying within it are required to carry a certain scale of navigation equipment so that they can be flown accurately within the parameters of the ATC clearance. In this congested area, mostly unmonitored by radar, any deviation could be dangerous.

This is reflected in the fairly large lateral separation between flights, vertical separation being the same as that described on page 26. Aircraft that do not meet the MNPS requirements are separated laterally by 120 nautical miles, which is reduced to 90 miles in certain designated airspace. A spacing of 60 miles is allowed for aircraft that meet the MNPS.

The same applies to supersonic aircraft operating at or above FL275. The rules for longitudinal spacing, ie one aircraft following another on the same track, are too complicated to list here, but vary from 15 minutes to 10 minutes, and sometimes less. It all depends upon speed, which is expressed as a Mach number. Satellite navigation, coupled with the replacement of HF by VHF satellite communications, is likely to reduce separations considerably over the next few years.

The Oceanic Controllers at Prestwick do not talk to the aircraft directly, but teletype their instructions to specialised, usually ex-marine, radio operators at Ballygireen. The latter talk to the aircraft and teletype the responses back to Prestwick. This is not as inefficient as it sounds because HF communications can be so distorted that experienced radio operators do better than the controllers themselves, and the short delay in reply is insignificant with such long distances between aircraft.

Single Side Band (SSB) signals are used by 99.9% of short wave aircraft communications. Without going into too many technicalities, the AM (Audio Modulation) method employed by VHF transmissions is built up of three components: a Lower Side Band, a carrier, and an Upper Side Band. By removing the carrier and one of the side bands, the power of the signal is compressed into a smaller band width, which boosts reception at long range and reduces interference. However, an ordinary shortwave receiver that may have the necessary frequency bands (2–28MHz) will pick up SSB as something that has been described as 'sounding like Donald Duck'. To make the signal intelligible, the carrier has to be reintroduced, and this can only be done if a Beat Frequency Oscillator (BFO) or crystal-controlled carrier oscillator is fitted. Beware of shortwave sets that receive only broadcast bands or else have no SSB capability. Advertisements are often misleading on these vital points, implying that the product will receive everything.

Unfortunately, a basic HF set with SSB costs considerably more than the equivalent simple VHF radio. However, for about £130 the Sangean ATS803A will do the job admirably. It has digital tuning, which is highly desirable with HF as there are so many operational frequencies and it obviously helps to identify them precisely for future reference. The built-in aerial is only useful for strong local signals like Shanwick, and for wider coverage one needs a long wire aerial. The longer (10 to 30 yards) and higher the better, orientated as near horizontal as you can and if possible at right angles to the direction of the station you most want to listen to, for example north–south for Atlantic traffic. Beware of short circuits in the rain from whatever tree or pole you have attached it to, not to mention lightning strikes! An aerial tuning unit (ATU) is a good investment. It tunes the aerial length electronically and matches it to the receiver to produce a peak signal.

If you are rich enough to move up-market for higher performance, the Lowe HF150 and HF225 at around £330 and £430 respectively are said to have the performance of much more expensive receivers. The Kenwood range includes the R-5000, retailing at around £900, and somewhat cheaper is the AOR AR-3030 at £700. Ideally, the enthusiast needs a scanner that can monitor VHF and UHF air band as well as HF air communications, but it is only recently that modern electronics have made this possible in a convenient package. Many scanners now feature HF SSB as well as VHF and UHF air band. Unfortunately these so-called wideband receivers are inevitably a compromise between the demands of different sections of the frequency bands – a dedicated HF receiver will almost always outperform them. Of course, with this sort of equipment you are getting far more than the air bands. The radios mentioned above and others, including the Icom and Yaesu ranges, are communications receivers in the fullest sense of the word. The AR3000A at around £950 spans virtually the entire radio spectrum from long wave broadcasts up to the limits of current usage.

We now move on to an outline of what can be heard on HF in Britain. Do not expect the quality of VHF air band and be warned that you may have to work very hard and try a lot of frequencies before you intercept anything. HF propagation conditions can fluctuate enormously. The AERAD Supplements (see page 127) and amateur radio magazines publish HF propagation forecast graphs, which are very useful in narrowing down the possibilities.

The North Atlantic HF network is divided into six 'families' of frequencies to obtain a balanced loading of communications on the oceanic track system, and these are designated NAT-A to NAT-F. Each uses a primary frequency with a secondary one for use when reception is poor. The frequencies are shared by several OACCs, including Shanwick, which serves aircraft between 45 North and 61 North and between 10 West and 30 West. The Iceland OACC at Reykjavik is responsible for traffic north of 61 North, and Gander works aircraft to the west of 30 West.

Santa Maria in the Azores looks after traffic south of Shanwick's area and from 15 West to 40 West. New York OCC controls flights over a large proportion of the south-west of the North Atlantic, and with favourable reception conditions those from the Caribbean and South America can be heard as well. San Juan in Puerto Rico is responsible for aircraft south of New York's area, using the same frequencies.

Long Distance Operational Control Facilities (LDOCF) are operated by or on behalf of many airlines throughout the world for company messages similar to those heard on VHF air band. Some of these stations are equipped to provide direct voice communications between flight crews and their company operations using phone patch techniques. Alternatively, the ground radio operator will accept messages for relay over the normal telephone or telex circuits. British Airways handles its own aircraft by HF from Heathrow, along with those of many other companies subscribing to the service. Portishead Radio is operated by British Telecom for phone patches into the international public system. A similar service is provided by Berna Radio in Switzerland, Stockholm Radio in Sweden, Rainbow Radio in Newfoundland and ARINC in the USA. Of course, many of the messages may not be in English! More information on company messages will be found in Chapter 14.

Military aircraft use HF frequencies within broadly the same range as civil aircraft, so you can listen to both with the same radio, unlike VHF/UHF. Military radio traffic is, however, a lot more varied and much less predictable than civil. It is also difficult to find out enough background information to understand some of the things to be heard, which is perhaps just as well! Further information can be found in Chapter 17.

A fairly simple way of expanding the capabilities of an HF receiver is to use it to monitor Radio Teletype, known as 'Ritty' from its initials RTTY. A personal computer is required, or alternatively a RTTY module. The radio's speaker extension is connected by lead into the PC or module and the read-out is displayed on screen and printed out if desired. The Aeradio stations around the world churn out masses of information, much of it weather reports and forecasts, but the interesting items for enthusiasts are the flight plans, which are also sent by this method.

RTTY is a very specialised branch of air band listening, and these notes are included merely to alert readers to the possibilities. There are several frequency and reference guides available, a good source being *Short Wave Magazine*'s Book Service. Suppliers of RTTY reception equipment advertise regularly in this magazine and a regular column 'Decode' covers the subject in detail. Aeronautical information is of course only a small fraction of the data sent worldwide in RTTY mode.

Also of great interest is a new computer program called Airtrak. Devised by John Standen of JHS Software, Pickering, North Yorkshire, it is intended for worldwide tracking of aircraft reporting their positions by HF radio. A digitised world map data base containing some 178,000 latitude and longitude points is included. For an acceptable-looking map with not too many long, straight lines, the scale needs to be 1:5,000,000 plus. The minimum area that looks reasonable is 4 degrees of latitude by 8 degrees of longitude, ie about 240 miles square, although the programme plots on to a blank screen down to about 3 miles by 4 miles. A blank screen can be overlaid with airways and TMAs, but small areas have not been extensively tested as Airtrak is really intended for use in trans-oceanic plotting.

For example, the North Atlantic area can be displayed on the screen complete with adjacent land masses and an overlaid grid of latitude and longitude. As an aircraft makes a position report and gives a forward estimate for the next reporting position on HF to Shanwick or Gander Oceanic, the details are input via the keyboard and displayed on screen. An aircraft can thus be tracked right across the Atlantic in real time. The program also contains a number of useful options, including the ability to enter a complete oceanic clearance, match many thousands of aircraft registrations with SelCal codes, and identify a very large number of operators from their two- and three-letter call-sign prefixes. HF frequencies for all the main oceanic areas are also available for display. Future upgrades in the development stage will gather data from the Internet and ACARS (Aircraft Communications Addressing and Reporting System) decoders (see page 99). The program requires a mere 640K RAM and 5Mb hard drive space. It is bound to prove popular with the many enthusiasts who specialise in monitoring HF communications. Time and dedication are required, but these devotees tend to have plenty of both!

## A selection of HF frequencies

The Civil Air Route Regions (ICAO), frequencies and major ground stations involved are listed below. Do not expect to hear the distant ones routinely. Virtually all frequencies listed are USB.

AFI = African; CAR = Caribbean; CEP = Central East Pacific; CWP = Central West Pacific; EUR = European; MID = Middle East; NP = North Pacific; SAM = South America; SAT = South Atlantic; SEA = South East Asia; SP = South Pacific.

| | | |
|---|---|---|
| NAT-A (southern tracks) | 3.016 5.598 8.906 13.306 17.946 | New York, Gander, Shanwick, Santa Maria |
| NAT-B (N/S Am-regd a/c) | 2.899 5.616 8.864 13.291 17.946 | Gander, Shanwick, New York |
| NAT-C (Eur/ Asia-regd a/c) | 2.872 5.649 8.879 11.336 13.306 17.946 | Gander, Shanwick, New York |
| NAT-D (polar routes) | 2.971 4.675 8.891 11.279 13.291 17.946 | Gander, Shanwick, Iceland |
| NAT-E (south) | 2.962 6.628 8.825 11.309 13.354 17.946 | |
| NAT-F (Mid-Atlantic) | 3.476 6.622 8.831 13.291 | New York, Santa Maria tracks |

| EUR-A | 3.479 5.661 6.598 10.084 13.288 17.961 | Berlin, Malta |
|-------|------|------|
| CAR-A | 2.287 5.550 6.577 8.846 8.918 11.396 13.297 17.907 | New York, Paramaribo, San Juan, Panama |
| MID-1 | 2.992 5.667 8.918 13.312 | Ankara, Baghdad, Beirut, Damascus, Kuwait, Bahrain, Cairo, Jeddah |
| MID-2 | 3.467 5.601 5.658 10.018 13.288 | Bahrain, Karachi, Bombay, Lahore, Delhi, Calcutta |
| SEA-1 | 3.470 6.556 10.066 13.318 17.907 | Calcutta, Dhaka, Madras, Colombo, Male, Cocos, Kuala Lumpur |
| SEA-2 | 3.485 5.655 8.942 11.396 13.309 | Hong Kong, Manila, Kuala Lumpur |
| SEA-3 | 3.470 6.556 11.396 13.318 13.297 | Manila, Singapore, Jakarta, Darwin, Sydney, Perth |
| AFI-1 | 3.452 6.535 6.673 8.861 13.357 17.955 | Casablanca, Canaries, Dakar, Abidjan, Roberts |
| AFI-2 | 3.419 5.652 8.894 13.273 13.294 17.961 | Algiers, Tripoli, Niamey, Kano |
| AFI-3 | 3.467 5.658 11.300 13.288 17.961 | Lagos, Brazzaville, Luanda, Windhoek, Johannesburg, Lusaka |
| AFI-5/INO-1 | 3.476 5.634 8.879 13.806 17.961 | Seychelles, Johannesburg, Lusaka, Mauritius, Colombo, Perth |
| CEP-5 | 2.869 3.413 5.547 5.574 8.843 11.282 13.261 13.354 17.904 | Honolulu, San Francisco |
| CWP-1/2 | 2.998 4.666 6.532 6.562 8.903 11.384 13.300 17.904 21.985 | Hong Kong, Manila, Guam, Tokyo, Honolulu, Port Moresby |
| NP-3/4 | 2.932 5.628 6.655 10.048 11.330 13.273 13.294 17.904 | Tokyo, Cold Bay, Anchorage, Honolulu |
| SP-6/7 | 3.467 5.643 8.867 13.273 13.300 17.904 | Sydney, Auckland, Nandi, Tahiti, Honolulu, Pascua |
| SW/SAM-8 | 2.944 4.669 6.649 10.024 11.360 17.907 | Pascua (Easter Island) |
| SAM-1 | 2.944 4.669 6.649 10.024 11.360 17.907 | Pascua, Panama, Lima, Santiago, Cordoba, Punta Arenas |
| SAM-2 | 3.479 5.526 8.855 10.096 13.297 17.907 | Manaus, Belem, Recife, Brasilia, Rio, Montevideo, La Pas, Leticia |
| SAT-1 | 3.452 6.535 8.861 13.357 17.955 | Recife, Salvador, Brasilia |
| SAT-2 | 2.854 5.565 11.291 13.315 17.955 | Paramaribo, Cayenne, Dakar, Canaries |

## Base Stations

Portishead 4.807 *5.610* 6.634 8.170 8.960 10.291 *11.306* 12.133 14.890 15.964 16.273 17.335 18.210 19.510 20.065 23.142; Berna 4.654 6.643 8.936 *10.069* 13.205 15.046 18.023 21.988 23.285 25.500; Stockholm 3.494 5.541 8.930 11.345 13.342 17.916 23.210; ARINC (USA) 6.640 10.075 11.342 17.925 21.964; Rainbow Radio 5.604 8.819 13.285

## Company frequencies (may be used by other carriers as well)

Aero Lloyd 13.327; Air France 6.637; Air India 8.930 10.072; American Trans-Air 13.333; Britannia 5.535 6.556 8.921 10.072 13.333; Cathay Pacific 13.333; Cyprus 11.363; Lufthansa 13.327; El Al 13.04; Gulf Air 5.38; Hapag Lloyd 10.69; Iberia 5.529 13.327; KLM 13.336; Balkan-Bulgarian 11.382; LTU 10.030 13.324 13.327; MEA

13.330; PIA 8.930; Qantas 6.637 13.342;
Royal Jordanian 13.255; Tarom 10.021;
South African 8.933 13.330; Saudia 5.544
11.288; United 5.604; British Airways
(Speedbird London) 5.535 8.921 10.072
13.333 17.922 21.946

## Volmet
RAF 4.722 11.200; Shannon 3.413 5.505
8.957 13.264; Gander/New York 3.485 6.604
10.051 13.270; St John's 6.753 15.035

## Rescue
5.680 (primary) 3.023 3.085 5.695 8.364
(International Distress)

## RAF STCICS ('Architect')
2.591 4.540 *4.742* 5.713 6.738 8.190 9.032
11.204 *11.234* 13.257 15.031 18.018 23.220

## UK Air Defence Region Sector Operations Control (call-sign 'Buchan'/'Boulmer'/'Neatishead')
3.916 4.707 4.710 4.739 5.178 6.734 6.748
8.992

## US GHFS (call-sign 'Croughton'/'Ascension'/'Incirlik'/ 'Lajes', etc)
*11.176* 3.067 4.725 5.703 6.738 *6.750 6.757*
8.967 8.993 13.201 14.615 15.015 15.036
17.975

## Royal Canadian Air Force
St John's Military 3.092 4.704 5.718 6.705
9.006 11.233 13.231 13.257 15.031 17.995
18.012

## NASA
14.925 21.395 (re-broadcast of space shuttle
commentary, but rarely heard in UK)

Frequencies in *italics* are those most
commonly used. The decimal point is
normally omitted when frequencies are
referred to during communications.

*Chapter 10*

# Flight Information Services

An ATC service can be provided only by licensed controllers, but at certain small airfields an Aerodrome Flight Information Service is in operation. The FIS Officers, or FISOs for short, are also required to be licensed, and many of them are flying instructors doing this ground job on a part-time basis. Air band listeners will notice certain differences in the R/T phraseology used by FISOs, reflecting the fact that their instructions are of an advisory nature only. For example, where a licensed controller would say 'cleared take-off', a FISO would say 'take off at your discretion'.

The aerodrome air/ground service (A/G) is a rudimentary one, for which no qualifications are required, although persons providing it must possess a CAA 'Authority to Operate'. It is often encountered at club and privately owned aerodromes, Wigtown in southern Scotland, Bourn in Cambridgeshire and Hethel in Norfolk being examples. Basic information is passed to the pilots, covering such essentials as the wind direction and whether the runway is clear. The call-signs for AFIS and A/G are 'Information' and 'Radio' respectively.

The Flight Information Service provided by licensed controllers at ACCs on a 24-hour basis is somewhat different and requires further explanation. The London FIR outside controlled airspace is divided into three with a separate radio frequency for each, as is the Scottish FIR. The FIR controller is able to offer the following services: weather information, changes of serviceability of radio navigation aids, aerodrome conditions, proximity warnings, and any other information pertinent to safety. Because of the multiplicity of possible reporting points in the FIR,

*The 1930s vintage tower at Barton, a typical small airfield with air/ground service* (Adrian Thompson).

ranging from disused airfields to towns and coastal features, it is difficult to assess the possibility of collision and therefore no positive control or separation can be provided. The other problem is that of civil and military aircraft on random tracks and for whom there is no requirement to contact the FIR.

Outside controlled airspace a Radar Advisory Service is provided by certain ATC units, subject to the coverage of the radar equipment and the unit's workload. Where such a service is given by an airfield approach unit, it is usually limited to a range of 40km from the aerodrome traffic zone. Pilots are informed of the bearing, distance and, if known, the level of the conflicting traffic with advice on the action to be taken to maintain separation if the pilot does not have the traffic in sight. If the pilot decides to ignore the advice given, whether he has visual contact or not, he is responsible for any avoiding action that may subsequently prove necessary.

An alternative is the Radar Information Service, in which the participating pilot is warned of conflicting traffic. No avoiding action is offered and the pilot is wholly responsible for maintaining separation from other aircraft, whether or not the controller has passed traffic information. A pilot wishing to take advantage of an RAS or RIS must first establish verbal agreement with the controller (an 'accord'), no radar service being provided until this agreement has been reached. A request for an RAS to be upgraded to an RIS will be accepted subject to the controller's existing workload.

Since mid-1983 military ATC radar units have been providing a Lower Airspace Radar Advisory Service (LARS) to any aircraft outside controlled airspace that requests it. The lower limit is 3,000ft and the upper limit is, with certain exceptions, FL95, the service being given within about 30 miles of each participating unit. From FL100 up to FL245 a similar Middle Airspace Advisory Service is provided. Whenever possible aircraft will be handed over from one controller to the next and pilots told to contact the next unit.

## FIR Frequencies

London Information: 124.75 (west of Alpha One) 124.6 (east of Alpha One) 125.475 (north of Bravo 1)

Scottish Information: 131.3 (north and north-east) 127.275 (north-west) 119.875 (west and south)

# Chapter 11

# Weather and Air Traffic Control

Met observations at the larger airports are made every 30 minutes at 20 minutes past and 10 minutes to each hour. At the less busy airports they are made once in each hour. Special observations, known as SPECIs (pronounced 'Spessys') must be made within these times if certain changes are observed, for example at the onset or cessation of hail or thunderstorms. If there is a Met Office available, the observations will be done by met staff who are all employees of the Ministry of Defence. Otherwise they are made by ATC personnel who are required to hold a Met Observer's Certificate, gained after a short course at the Met College.

There is a standard format that is passed to aircraft, consisting of the wind direction in degrees True and its average speed in knots with a note of any significant gusts. This is, however, normally read by the controller in degrees Magnetic direct from the instruments in front of him so that it can be related by the pilot to the magnetic heading of the runway. The visibility is passed in metres and kilometres in increments of 100m when 5,000m or less, and in whole kilometres when greater than 5,000m. The distance is determined from the known ranges of conspicuous landmarks visible in the locality. The next item is the weather, for example drizzle, fog or rain.

Cloud base is measured by means of a cloud base recorder, which scans the sky overhead with a laser beam. Unfortunately it may give inaccurate low readings when haze, mist or smoke is present. At less-well-equipped airfields, cloud base is found by estimation, with experience a surprisingly accurate method. Pilot reports can be requested to confirm the base. At night estimation is difficult, so a vertical searchlight is often used. The angle of the 'spot' on the cloud can then be found by sighting with a simple instrument known as an alidade. Trigonometry from a pre-calculated table enables it to be converted quickly to cloud height.

Cloud amount is given in oktas, ie eighths, and height in feet up to and including 5,000ft. Cloud above this level is of academic interest only to aircrew in the UK, so is not reported. Not more than three layers are reported, the exception being when cumulo-nimbus cloud, known as CB or Charlie Bravo, is present. If necessary this can be reported as a fourth group. Cloud amounts are now referred to simply as Few (1–2 oktas), Scattered (3–4 oktas), Broken (5–7 oktas), or Overcast (8 oktas). For their own aircraft, RAF stations reduce the data to a simple colour code as shown in the table overleaf.

Air temperature is passed in degrees Celsius, together with the dew point if the two figures are significantly close, indicating that fog may be about to form. The QNH and QFE (Threshold QFE at certain airfields) is given in millibars. These units may one day become hectopascals in the United Kingdom and are already referred to as such in most European ATC systems. American aircraft occasionally ask for the pressure settings in inches of mercury, so a table is kept handy in the tower for a quick conversion.

Where the weather conditions meet particular criteria – visibility of 10km or

**MINIMUM WEATHER CONDITIONS**

| SURFACE VISIBILITY | | COLOUR | BASE OF LOWEST CLOUD LAYER |
|---|---|---|---|
| **RN/RAF Km (nm)** | USAFE★ Km (Stm) | | **RN/RAF - of ⅜ or more** USAFE★ - of ⅝ or more |
| **8(4·3)** | 8(5) | Blue | 2500ft AGL |
| **5(2·7)** | 5(3) | White | 1500ft AGL |
| **3·7(2)** | 3·7(2·3) | Green | 700ft AGL |
| **1·8(1)** | 1·6(1) | Yellow | 300ft AGL |
| **0·9(0·5)** | 0·8(0·5) | Amber | 200ft AGL |
| **Less than** **0·9(0·5)** | 0·8(0·5) | Red | Below 200ft AGL |
| Black A/D not usable for reasons other than cloud or visibility minima. Black will precede actual colour code. | | | |

★ Includes USAFE bases in UK and Canadian, Netherlands & West German bases in 2ATAF.

*RAF colour codes for aerodrome availability/weather state.*

more, no precipitation, no thunderstorm or shallow fog, no cloud below a level of 5,000ft above aerodrome elevation and no CB at any level – the visibility and cloud groups are omitted and the word 'CAVOK' ('Ceiling and Visibility OK', pronounced 'Cav okay') is passed.

At the busiest UK airports the current met observation is transmitted continuously on the appropriate Terminal VOR or Information frequency by means of a pre-recorded tape. A transcript of a typical broadcast for Newcastle, on the Newcastle VOR, is as follows:

'This is Newcastle Arrival Information Juliet. 13:20 weather, 300 at 15 knots, 8 kilometres recent rain, overcast at 1,500ft, temperature plus 8, dew point plus 7, QNH 1001 millibars. Landing Runway 33. Report Information Juliet received on first contact with Newcastle Approach.'

The significance of 'Juliet' is that each observation is given a code letter, beginning with Alpha and working through the alphabet, starting once more when Zulu is reached. The controller is thus sure that the pilot has copied the latest observation. These automatic transmissions are very useful in reducing R/T loading as crews can monitor them at their leisure and the controller does not have to pass repeated weather information.

Runway Visual Range, or RVR as it is normally referred to, makes available a more localised assessment of how far the pilot is likely to be able to see along the runway. Measurement only begins when the official met report gives a general visibility of 1,500m or less, and it is essential to enable the pilot to decide whether or not it is within the limits of what are known as 'company minima' for landing or take-off.

RVR is calculated by either the human observer method or by means of electronic equipment. The former requires a person, usually an airport fireman, to stand on a vehicle adjacent to the runway threshold at a specified height to simulate pilot eye-level. He then counts the number of lights that he can see down one side of the runway. The total is passed by radio to the tower and the RVR read off a pre-computed table.

The Instrumented RVR system, called IRVR, measures the opacity of the atmosphere and gives a constant read-out in the tower of the RVR at three fixed points along the runway, referred to as touchdown, mid-point and stop end, and can easily be switched manually to the opposite end if required.

The term 'Sigmet' ('Significant Meteorological Conditions') is sometimes heard on R/T, this being a warning of such hazardous phenomena as thunderstorms, severe turbulence and severe airframe icing. Another jargon word is 'Nosig', short for 'No Significant Change', and sometimes appended to aerodrome forecasts when passed on the radio. The term 'trend' is employed to indicate the way the weather is likely to go, codes like 'tempo' for a temporary change being added as appropriate.

A hazard that has always been with us but has only recently become recognised is that of wind shear, and pilots can often be heard reporting its presence to the tower so that following aircraft can be warned. Briefly, wind shear is a change of windspeed and/or direction between two points in the atmosphere. By such a definition it is almost always present and normally does not cause undue difficulty to the pilot. However, on take-off or landing what amounts to an instantaneous change in headwind can be dangerous. An instantaneous decrease in headwind on the approach will tend to increase the rate of descent and an instantaneous increase in headwind will tend to decrease it. In both cases the pilot is faced with a rapid change in airspeed, coupled with a departure from

the glide path, and either a 'hot and long' landing or an undershoot becomes likely.

Horizontal wind shears are generally outflows from the bases of CB clouds, or are caused by the passage of active weather fronts. Local topographical features, both natural and artificial, can also cause shear. Buildings and other large structures close to runways can spark off turbulence and rotor effects, with marked differences in wind direction. Since wind shear is obviously invisible, much experimental work is being carried out with acoustic Dopplers, Doppler radar and optical lasers to try to detect and measure it. Heathrow is unique in the United Kingdom in having a wind shear alerting service. Certain weather criteria are used to assess its possible presence and this is backed up by pilot reports. The alert message is inserted in the arrival and departure ATIS broadcasts.

Another major hazard to aircraft is fortunately easier to measure. This is braking action when the runway is icy, or if snow or slush is present. There are two methods of determining it: the simple Tapley Meter decelerometer, and the sophisticated (and expensive) device that has largely superseded it, the Mu Meter. The latter consists of a runway friction-measuring trailer towed by a vehicle travelling at 40 mph. It provides an automatic print-out of the mean co-efficient of friction at three equi-distant points along the runway. When manual mode is selected, further readings can be obtained as required. The lower the figure, the worse the braking action; for example, something like 0.25 would indicate a very icy surface, 0.85 would be a dry runway.

The word 'Snowtam' refers to an ingenious system of describing and tabulating runway conditions under snow, slush or ice, and the degree to which they are cleared or about to be cleared. Braking action as determined above is also included. A series of letters and figures, each referring to a specific detail, can easily be decoded on receipt by telex.

Finally, in many parts of the country it is

possible to pick up the broadcasts of the London and Scottish Volmet Services, the 'Vol' part of the title being derived from the French word for flight. Weather conditions in a standardised form are transmitted continuously every half-hour for the main UK and selected European airports. Pilots can thus monitor Volmet while en route and note the current conditions at their destination and suitable alternatives without having to make specific calls for the information. If their destination is a smaller airfield not on the Volmet, they can either call it direct or request the information via London or Scottish Flight Information, who will obtain it by telephone.

There are four separate broadcasts on different VHF frequencies:

London Volmet North, broadcast from Great Dun Fell in Cumbria on 126.6MHz, for Gatwick, Manchester, Isle of Man, East Midlands, Teesside, Liverpool, Blackpool, Newcastle and Leeds.

London Volmet South, broadcast simultaneously from Davidstow Moor in Cornwall, Ventnor on the Isle of Wight, and Warlingham, south of London on 128.6MHz, for Birmingham, Bristol, Luton, Bournemouth, Southampton, Norwich, Southend, Cardiff and Jersey.

London Volmet Main, also broadcast simultaneously from Davidstow Moor in Cornwall, Ventnor on the Isle of Wight, and Warlingham, south of London on 135.375MHz, for Heathrow, Gatwick, Stansted, Manchester, Glasgow, Amsterdam, Dublin, Brussels and Paris/Charles de Gaulle.

Scottish Volmet, broadcast on 125.725MHz for Aberdeen, Aldergrove, Edinburgh, Glasgow, Inverness, Heathrow, Prestwick, Stornoway and Sumburgh.

The rather mechanical speech is due to the fact that the message is made up from a store of individual words and short phrases on tape, which are selected by a computer and joined to form the required sentences. (ATIS is sometimes also broadcast in this form.)

The presentation of the information is as described above, but where significant changes are expected, one of the following will be heard:

| | |
|---|---|
| *Gradu* | The change is expected at a constant rate |
| *Rapid* | The change is expected in a short period of less than 30 minutes |
| *Tempo* | The change is expected to last for less than one hour |
| *Inter* | Frequent changes are expected, fluctuating almost constantly |
| *Trend* | A change is anticipated but it is expected to occur slowly throughout the period |

# Chapter 12

# Airfield visual aids

Airfield lighting ranges from the rudimentary edge lights found at many smaller locations to the complex and impressive systems to be seen at major airports. The paraffin flares from an earlier era, known as 'goosenecks', are still in use at a few places as emergency lighting, but are gradually being replaced by portable battery lamps, which although easier to handle are no more effective.

On certain instrument runways the caution zone, ie the last 600m, may have yellow rather than white lights. In addition the centreline is usually delineated by flush-fitting lights for the whole length. These are colour-coded to give an indication of the distance remaining in poor visibility. The lights are coloured red over the final 300m and alternately red and white between 900m and 300m from the runway end.

As well as centreline lighting, all runways that comply with Precision Approach Category 2 and 3 lighting standard are provided with Touchdown Zone lights (TDZs). These consist of many flush-fitting white lights set into each side of the centreline in the first 900m of the runway. A row of green threshold lights marks the beginning of the paved surface and a similar line of red ones marks the stop end.

Approach lighting is usually non-existent at small aerodromes, and at others varies in standard, depending upon the approach aids and type of traffic handled. The approach lights at major airports begin at an average distance of 300m out from the threshold and extend for a further 900m out on the approach. They consist of a centreline and up to five cross-bars in white lights. Where Category 2 and 3 lighting standard is required, red supplementary approach lighting is provided within the basic system for the inner 300m as an extra aid for landing in marginal weather conditions. All lighting is controlled in intensity from the tower, the criteria being laid down clearly for differing met conditions.

The lights are displayed all the time at busy airports, but the normal requirement for them to be on in daylight hours is whenever the visibility is less than 6km and/or the cloud base less than 700ft. At night, when traffic is light at some places, the lights are turned on 15 minutes before an ETA and left on until 15 minutes after an aircraft has departed.

Taxiway lights are standardised as green for the centreline and blue for the edges. The latter are used only to delineate apron edges and as an extra guide for bends in taxiways. The lights are 15m apart, reduced to 7.5m for Category 3 systems. Red stop bars mark holding points, especially those at runway entrances. There may also be traffic lights for airfield vehicles. Both can be operated from the tower and the stop bars normally have a short time delay so that they revert to red after an aircraft has passed. London Heathrow has a particularly elaborate system of lighting for the control of taxiways. At most airports they are designated by a letter of the alphabet, excluding Oscar, India and X-Ray. Where there are more taxiways than letters of the alphabet, double letters are used to designate some of them. Double letters may also be used to identify short taxiway stubs between a runway and parallel taxiway, or between a taxiway and adjacent runway.

Fast turn-offs, now known as rapid exit taxiways, only have their centreline lights lit from the runway direction. The lights in the opposite direction are blanked off to prevent inadvertent infringement of an active runway. This was yet another result of the enquiry into the Tenerife collision.

Runway guard lights, consisting of a pair of alternately flashing lights and known colloquially as 'wig-wags', may be located on both sides of holding positions. The purpose of these yellow lights is to improve the conspicuity of holding points and to warn pilots of the proximity of an active runway.

Once a pilot on approach is within sight of the runway, visual guidance is provided by the Precision Approach Path Indicator (PAPI). Four PAPI lights are placed in line to the left of the runway threshold in such a way that when the pilot is on the correct approach path two appear white and the other two are red. If a third light shows red, the pilot knows that he is getting slightly low; if all four are red he is significantly below the glide path. Conversely, four white indicators will tell him that he is too high. PAPI is effective out to a range of about 20km, compared with about 5km for the virtually obsolete Visual Approach Slope Indicator (VASI) described in previous editions of this book. It also performs better when the pilot is looking into bright sunlight. A number of smaller airfields have an installation called LITAS

*PAPI and how it is interpreted* (CAA).

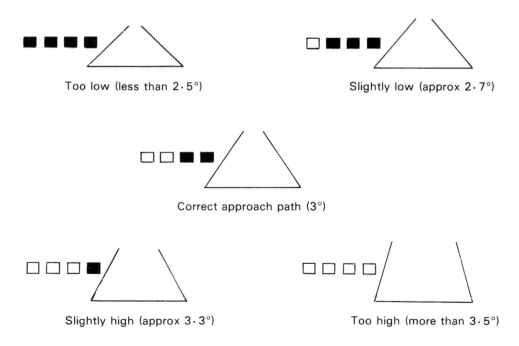

Too low (less than 2·5°)

Slightly low (approx 2·7°)

Correct approach path (3°)

Slightly high (approx 3·3°)

Too high (more than 3·5°)

Key ■ Red □ White

(Low Intensity Two-Colour Approach Slope). Although designed for use at night, the system has been found to give assistance by day in anything other than bright sunlight.

The other major visual aids at airports are the painted markings on the manoeuvring area. All runways in regular use will have centreline and threshold markings, the latter varying from the designator number alone to separate 'piano keys' and designator, depending upon the importance of the runway and its associated instrument aids. While threshold markings are usually at the end of the runway, they sometimes need to be displaced upwind if, for example, there are obstacles like a public road on the approach. Arrows then indicate that the first portion of the runway is sterile for landing.

All runways more than 1,600m long without VASI or PAPI, and all precision instrument runways, will have an additional symbol 300m from the landing threshold known as the 'fixed distance marker'. The apparent distance between this and the threshold marking, seen from the approach, should aid pilots in judging their angle of descent, and the two markings also bracket the optimum Touchdown Zone on the runway.

Touchdown Zone markings, extending for a distance of at least 600m from the threshold, will be provided on precision approach runways with such aids as ILS. These are intended to give added texture by day and, except in fog, added texture by night in the light of landing lamps. Yellow lines delineate the centres of taxiways, and at certain airports self-manoeuvring stand markings enable aircraft to be taxied to the correct parking position without the aid of a marshaller.

At airports that accept non-radio-equipped aircraft, ground signals will be displayed for guidance. They are normally to be found in front of the Control Tower, but not always, which gives rise to a funny story. One day a pilot who had suffered a radio failure landed at Blackpool. On

*Standard runway markings* (CAA).

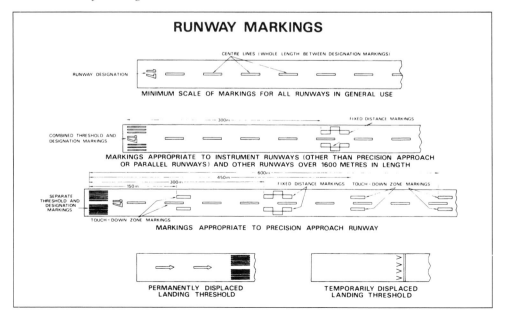

reporting to the tower he complained that he could not make any sense from the ground signals. Further conversation revealed that he had been trying to interpret the strange shapes on the Crazy Golf Course adjacent to the airport's public enclosure!

The following ground signals cover all those to be seen at UK civil locations, but obviously not all of them can be seen at any one airfield. The list does not include signs peculiar to military airfields.

*Large white 'T'*
Aircraft land or take off in a direction parallel to the 'T' and towards the cross-arm. A white disc above the cross-arm of the 'T' indicates that the direction of landing and take-off do not necessarily coincide.

*White 'dumb-bell'*
Aircraft movement on the airfield is confined to paved surfaces only. A black strip across each disc of the dumb-bell at right angles to the shaft signifies that aircraft taking off and landing shall do so on a runway, but that ground movement is not confined to paved surfaces. A red letter 'L' superimposed on the dumb-bell signifies that light aircraft are permitted to take off and land either on a runway or on the area designated by a further 'L' (painted white) elsewhere on the aerodrome.

*Red and yellow striped arrow*
A right-hand circuit is in force. This can also be shown by a rectangular green flag flown from a mast.

*Red square with one yellow diagonal bar*
This warns that the state of the manoeuvring area is poor and pilots must exercise special care.

*Red square with a yellow cross superimposed along the diagonals*
Airfield is unsafe for the movement of aircraft and landing is prohibited. (Usually found at grass airfields that are water-logged in the winter months!)

*White letter 'H'*
Helicopter landing area.

*Double white cross*
Glider flying is in progress. (A yellow cross indicates the tow-rope dropping area on the runway.)

*Red and yellow checkered flag or board*
Aerodrome Control is in operation (aircraft may only move on the manoeuvring area with ATC permission). A black letter 'C' on a yellow board indicates the position at which a pilot can report to the ATC unit or to the person in charge of the aerodrome.

*Triangular orange and white markers, alternating with orange and white flags*
Areas of 'bad ground' on grass aerodromes. Similar coloured markers outline the aerodrome boundary.

# Chapter 13

# Airport operations and procedures

## Vortex wake

Behind each wingtip of an aircraft and behind the tip of each rotor blade of a helicopter in flight, a trailing cylinder of rapidly rotating air is created, known as a vortex. The heavier the aircraft, the more intense the effect, which is quite capable of rolling a following aircraft on to its back if it gets too close. These hazardous wake vortices begin to be generated when the nose-wheel lifts off the runway on take-off and continue until it touches down on landing. To minimise the danger controllers apply a system of spacing, which is outlined below.

In the United Kingdom aircraft are divided into four vortex wake categories according to their maximum total weight at take-off:

| | |
|---|---|
| *Heavy* | 136,000kg or greater |
| *Medium* | Less than 136,000kg and more than 40,000kg |
| *Small* | Less than 40,000kg and more than 17,000kg |
| *Light* | Less than 17,000kg |

There are, however, a few exceptions to this. Helicopters generate more intense vortices from their rotors than fixed-wing aircraft of the same weight, therefore Sikorsky S61Ns and larger types are included in the Small category. Several aircraft types have been grouped into vortex categories that do not conform to those listed above. For example, the Boeing 707, DC-8, VC-10 and IL-62 series have been classified as Medium, as experience has shown that the characteristics of these types conform more to that group. Similarly, it has been decided to place the BAe 146 in the Small category.

The Medium category embraces aircraft in the BAC 111/Boeing 737/MD-83 class, together with propeller aircraft like the Hercules and Electra. The Small category includes the Viscount, Fokker 50 and Herald, and Light anything from executive jets downwards.

## Arriving flights

Where flights are operating visually (IFR flights operating under the reduced minima in the vicinity of aerodromes, VFR flights, or a mixture of the two), pilots are informed of the recommended spacing.

For other flights, the spacing listed below is applied between successive aircraft on final approach.

| *Leading aircraft* | *Following aircraft* | *Minimum distance* |
|---|---|---|
| Heavy | Heavy | 4 miles |
| | Medium | 5 miles |
| | Small | 6 miles |
| | Light | 8 miles |
| Medium | Medium | 3 miles* |
| | Small | 4 miles |
| | Light | 6 miles |
| Small | Medium or Small | 3 miles |
| | Light | 4 miles |

* Where the leading aircraft is a 757, the minimum distance is increased to 4 miles

# Aerodrome operations

The minimum spacing listed below is applied between successive aircraft on both IFR and VFR flights.

(a) Aircraft departing from the same runway or from parallel runways less than 760m apart (including grass strips):

| Leading aircraft | Following aircraft | | Minimum spacing at time aircraft are airborne |
|---|---|---|---|
| Heavy | Medium, Small and Light | departing from the same take-off position | 2 minutes |
| Medium or Small | Light | departing from the same take-off position | 2 minutes |
| Heavy (full-length take-off) | Medium, Small and Light | departing from an intermediate take-off point | 3 minutes |
| Medium or Small | Light | departing from an intermediate take-off point | 3 minutes |

(b) Operations on a runway with a displaced landing threshold if the projected flight paths are expected to cross:

| Leading aircraft | Following aircraft | Minimum spacing at time aircraft are airborne or have touched down |
|---|---|---|
| Heavy arrival | Medium, Small and Light departure | 2 minutes |
| Heavy departure | Medium, Small and Light arrival | 2 minutes |

(c) Operations on crossing and diverging runways or on parallel runways greater than 760m apart. The following spacings are to be applied whenever the projected flight paths of the aircraft cross:

| Leading aircraft | Aircraft crossing behind | Minimum distance | Time equivalent |
|---|---|---|---|
| Heavy | Heavy | 4 miles | 2 minutes |
| | Medium | 5 miles | 3 minutes |
| | Small | 6 miles | 3 minutes |
| | Light | 8 miles | 4 minutes |
| Medium | Medium | 3 miles | 2 minutes |
| | Small | 4 miles | 2 minutes |
| | Light | 6 miles | 3 minutes |
| Small | Medium or Small | 3 miles | 2 minutes |
| | Light | 4 miles | 2 minutes |

(d) Opposite direction runway operations. A minimum spacing of 2 minutes is provided from the time a Heavy aircraft making a low or missed approach crosses over the take-off position of a Medium, Small or Light aircraft departing from the opposite direction runway.

# En route and intermediate approach

No special longitudinal spacings based on time are required. When a Medium, Small or Light aircraft is positioned by radar to cross behind or follow the same track as a Heavy aircraft, the minimum spacing is 5 miles.

# Departure Flow Regulation

At airports handling international traffic one will hear frequent references on the Tower or Ground Movement frequencies to Approved Departure Times. These were known previously as 'slot times' and this term is sometimes also heard. During the peak summer months some countries are, for a number of reasons, unable to cope with the extra traffic. For instance, more than 50 European and 27 UK airports are currently sending aircraft to the Mediterranean. Spain has about nine airports to receive the majority of them, with Palma the most popular destination. When the number of aircraft wishing to fly outstrips the capacity of the foreign ATC systems, the flow of traffic has to be regulated to ensure safe separation both nationally and internationally. This means that aircraft have to be held on the ground at the departure airports until such time as they can be accepted.

Europe's Central Flow Management Unit (CFMU) is located at Brussels and provides departure times about 2 hours ahead for every aircraft flying on a regulated route. This ensures an organised system of queuing for all flights as well as enabling airlines to plan aircraft and crew utilisation. When the ATC system in any part of Europe is in danger of being overloaded, a queue starts to form as a result of delaying departure times; a list of airways with DFR restrictions is therefore published in a NOTAM well in advance of the summer season. That at least is the theory, but as we all know there are so many variable factors that the aims are often impossible to achieve.

A NOTAM (Notice to Airmen) is defined as 'a notice containing information concerning the establishment, condition or change of any facility, service, procedure or hazard, the timely knowledge of which is essential for the safe and efficient operation of aircraft.' Urgent NOTAMS are sent out by telex, those of lesser importance as Supplements to the UK Air Information Publication.

Complications arise from different airways having different restrictions depending on destination, Flight Level or routeing, and countries overflown. If the system becomes overloaded, the flow of traffic has to be reduced, and the CFMU thus has the responsibility of allocating the correct number of aircraft at the intervals prescribed for a particular airway, route, Flight Level or destination.

The Traffic Orientation Scheme (TOS) forms the basis for the routeing of aircraft on the major traffic flows during the summer peak season. The aim is to balance the demand on Europe's air route system by confining traffic for a specified destination to a particular route with an alternative in the event of unforeseen en route congestion. Tied in with TOS is the Contingency Routeing Scheme designed to avoid airspace over the former Yugoslavia. For this reason a flight from Manchester to Rhodes usually routes over Germany, Austria, Hungary, Romania and Bulgaria.

An aircraft's ADT stipulates that it must not be airborne before a specified time, but an allowance is added to this to cover taxiing delays or holding for landing traffic. This can cause the GMC or Tower Controller something of a headache, as extra-careful planning is often necessary to make sure that the aircraft gets away on time. The situation is not helped by pilots who taxi excruciatingly slowly or arrive at the runway threshold long before the ADT!

# Noise abatement

In an effort to minimise noise nuisance to local residents, most airports have their own noise abatement procedures. These are devised by the aerodrome operating authority in conjunction with airlines and local airport consultative committees. Over built-up areas Noise Preferential Routes (NPRs) have been defined, which carefully route aircraft away from the more densely populated areas. Engine climb power is also reduced for the period when the aircraft must fly over certain conurbations.

At Heathrow different parallel runways are used for take-off and landing, and these are alternated regularly so that noise is spread more equitably over the areas beneath the flight paths. Runways 27 Left and 27 Right are the preferred ones, provided the tailwind component does not exceed a certain figure; in addition, flights are severely restricted at night. At Manchester the direction of approach is changed at regular intervals, and at both locations noise levels are monitored. Operators whose aircraft exceed the permitted values are penalised.

NPRs are integrated with the lower end of Standard Instrument Departures, which are themselves designed to cause the least disturbance to those living below. Similarly, Continuous Descent Approaches (CDAs) have been brought into operation, particularly at Heathrow, to reduce noise and, as a bonus, to speed up the arrival rate. Headings and Flight Levels at which aircraft are to leave the holding pattern are passed by ATC. On receipt of descent clearance the pilot descends at the rate he judges to be best suited to achieve continuous descent. The object is to join the glide path at the appropriate height for the distance without recourse to level flight.

The procedure requires that aircraft fly at 210kt during the intermediate approach phase. ATC may request speed reductions to between 160kt and 180kt on, or shortly before, the closing heading to the ILS, and 160kt when established on the ILS. Aircraft unable to confirm to these speeds are expected to inform ATC and state which speeds they are able to use. Since wheels and flaps remain retracted until the final stages, less engine power is needed, which results in a much quieter approach.

## Standard Instrument Departures (SIDs) and Standard Terminal Arrival Routes (STARs)

SIDs have been developed for the main runways of major airports, the routes terminating at an airway, advisory route or at a radio navigational fix. Noise Preferential Routeing is also built in. All aircraft departing from an airport under IFR are required to follow the appropriate SID, unless and until authorised to do otherwise by the relevant ATC unit. Each SID has a designator that incorporates the name of the radio beacon on which it is based. An example is the Wallasey Two Tango from Runway 27 at Liverpool, for traffic joining Bravo One or Bravo Three westbound. Subsequent changes to SIDs result in a new number up to Nine, then back to One again. The suffix letter indicates the runway.

STARs are virtually the reverse of SIDs, an example being the WILLO 1B for Gatwick traffic arriving from Golf One or Alpha One, which is Midhurst VOR-HOLLY-WILLO.

Aircraft are expected to cross Speed Limit Points (SLPs) at or below 250kts indicated air speed.

## VOR/DME holding procedures

An example of these is DAYNE, south of Manchester Airport, an 'offset' holding pattern for traffic inbound to Manchester and Woodford. Its axis is aligned on Trent VOR Radial 315, and its position is between Trent DME 13 and 17 miles. The pilot flies towards the VOR/DME on this designated inbound radial, and on reaching the holding fix position carries out a procedure turn on to the reciprocal outbound track. This outbound track is flown until the limiting DME is attained and the pilot then turns the aircraft to intercept the inbound

**Right** *Standard Instrument Departure (SID) Charts for Glasgow (CAA).*

## NEW GALLOWAY SIDs — GLASGOW

JET AIRCRAFT ONLY

GENERAL INFORMATION
1 Initial climb straight ahead to 526' QNH (500' QFE).
2 To comply with Obstacle Clearance Requirements, Minimum Climb Gradients of 4.5% for RWY 05, and 3.8% for RWY 23 departures are necessary.

| Grd Speed | kt | 75 | 100 | 150 | 200 | 250 | 300 |
|---|---|---|---|---|---|---|---|
| 3.8%(231'per nm) | ft/min | 289 | 385 | 577 | 770 | 962 | 1155 |
| 4.5%(274'per nm) | ft/min | 342 | 456 | 685 | 913 | 1141 | 1370 |

To comply with ATC and Airspace Restrictions the following Climb Gradients apply: NGY 1H 7% to 6000', NGY 1J 8% to 6000'. (See para 5.2 for climb table).
3 En-route cruising levels will be issued after take-off by 'Scottish Control'.
4 Max IAS 250kts below FL100 unless otherwise authorised.

TRANSITION ALT 6000'

NOT TO SCALE

AREA MNM ALT 25NM
45 45 / 39 30

NEW GALLOWAY NGY 399 N55 10·6 W004 10·0
TURNBERRY TRN 117·5P
NORBO N55 35·8 W004 45·6 TRN 017
GLASGOW GLG 350 N55 55·5 W004 20·1
GLASGOW GOW 115·4P N55 52·2 W004 26·7
GLASGOW AC 325 N55 48·8 W004 32·5

| SID | RWY | ROUTEING (incl. Noise Preferential Routeing) | OBSTACLE CLEARANCE REQUIREMENTS | ALTITUDES | AIRWAY ROUTE |
|---|---|---|---|---|---|
| NGY 1H Jet A/C Only | 23 | Climb ahead via AC NDB onto GOW VOR R234. At GOW 014 turn left onto TRN VOR R009. At NORBO (TRN R009 017) turn left onto NGY NDB. QDM 146° to NGY NDB. | Maintain mnm 3·8% climb to 1200'. | Cross GOW 012 above 5000'. GOW 014 at 6000'. NGY NDB at 6000'. | A1 A2 A25 |
| NGY 1J Jet A/C Only | 05 | Straight ahead to GLG NDB. Turn left onto PTH VOR R240. At TRN VOR R013 turn left onto TRN VOR R009. At NORBO (TRN R009 017) turn left onto NGY NDB QDM 146° to NGY NDB. | Maintain mnm 4·5% climb to 1500'. | Cross GLG NDB above 2000'. TRN VOR R020 at 6000'. NGY NDB at 6000'. | |

AVERAGE TRACK MILEAGE TO NGY: NGY 1H 53, NGY 1J 74

| CHANGE | LEVEL ACCELERATION INFO DELETED | 154 |

AERO INF DATE 29 Sep 94

## TALLA SIDs — GLASGOW

JET AIRCRAFT ONLY

GENERAL INFORMATION
1 Initial climb straight ahead to 526' QNH (500' QFE).
2 To comply with Obstacle Clearance Requirements, Minimum Climb Gradients of 4.5% for RWY 05, and 3.8% for RWY 23 departures are necessary.

| Grd Speed | kt | 75 | 100 | 150 | 200 | 250 | 300 |
|---|---|---|---|---|---|---|---|
| 3.8%(231'per nm) | ft/min | 289 | 385 | 577 | 770 | 962 | 1155 |
| 4.5%(274'per nm) | ft/min | 342 | 456 | 685 | 913 | 1141 | 1370 |

To comply with ATC and Airspace Restrictions the following Climb Gradients apply: TLA 1H 7% to 6000', TLA 1J 8% to 6000' unless otherwise authorised.
3 En-route cruising levels will be issued after take-off by 'Scottish Control'.
4 Max IAS 250kts below FL100 unless otherwise authorised.

TRANSITION ALT 6000'

NOT TO SCALE

AREA MNM ALT 25NM
45 45 / 39 30

TALLA TLA 113·8P N55 29·9 W003 21·1
TURNBERRY TRN 117·5P
NORBO N55 35·8 W004 45·6 TRN 017
GLASGOW GLG 350
GLASGOW GOW 115·4P
GLASGOW AC 325

| SID | RWY | ROUTEING (incl. Noise Preferential Routeing) | OBSTACLE CLEARANCE REQUIREMENTS | ALTITUDES | AIRWAY ROUTE |
|---|---|---|---|---|---|
| TLA 1H Jet A/C Only | 23 | Climb ahead via AC NDB onto GOW VOR R234. At GOW 014 turn left onto TRN VOR R009. At NORBO (TRN R009 017) turn left onto TLA VOR R280 to TLA VOR. | Maintain mnm 3·8% climb to 1200'. | Cross GOW 012 above 5000'. GOW 014 at 6000'. TLA VOR at 6000'. | Jet A/C leaving controlled airspace via TLA |
| TLA 1J Jet A/C Only | 05 | Straight ahead to GLG NDB. Turn left onto PTH VOR R240. At TRN VOR R013 turn left onto TRN VOR R009. At NORBO (TRN R009 017) turn left onto TLA VOR R280 to TLA VOR. | Maintain mnm 4·5% climb to 1500'. | Cross GLG NDB above 2000'. TRN VOR R020 at 6000'. TLA VOR at 6000'. | |

AVERAGE TRACK MILEAGE TO TLA: TLA 1H 71, TLA 1J 92

| CHANGE | LEVEL ACCELERATION INFO DELETED | 154A |

AERO INF DATE 29 Sep 94

© CIVIL AVIATION AUTHORITY 1994

## STARs via DAYNE — MANCHESTER

GENERAL INFORMATION
1 These procedures also apply to aircraft inbound to Woodford.
2 Standard routes may be varied at the discretion of ATC.
3 Cross SLPs or 3 min before holding facility at 250kts or less when at FL140 or below.
4 When TNT VOR is out of service DAYNE holding axis is aligned to the MCT VOR R135 between 11NM and 16NM.
5 When ROSUN hold is congested traffic from A2 (POL) and B1 (OTR) may, at ATC discretion, be routed to DAYNE via the DAY 1C/D STAR.
6 For radio communication failure procedures the clearance limit is DAYNE.

TRANSITION LEVEL - ATC
TRANSITION ALT 5000'

NOT TO SCALE

OTRINGHAM
OTR 113-9D
N53 41-9 W000 06-1
B1

OTR R265
DAY 1D

STOCK
N53 32-1 W001 49-1
WAL D48

SLP
POL D3

SLP STOCK

POLE HILL
POL 112-1D
N53 44-6 W002 06-1
A2

DAY 1C

POL R167
DAY 1C 1D

SLP
SLP

AMLET
N53 16-1 W001 50-2
POL D30 MCT D16
TNT D13

TNT 115-7D
N53 03-2 W001 40-1
R3 B4
UB4 UP6
A20
A2

SLP
TNT D5

TNT R315
DAY 1A

135°

315°

MCT R114
MCT R135

DAYNE
N53 14-4 W002 02-1
TNT D17
MCT D11

HOLDING
Min Alt 6000'

MANCHESTER
MCT 113-55D

GPWS NUISANCE WARNINGS
To minimise occurrences, aircraft en-route DAYNE Hold-RWY 24 Max IAS 210kts between TNT VOR R300 & R350 unless otherwise authorised by ATC.

DESCENT PLANNING - ATC REQUIREMENTS
When determining top of descent point, pilots should anticipate possible clearance to the lowest holding level (FL equivalent to 6000ft) by the SLP. Pilots unable to comply must notify ATC as soon as possible.
ACTUAL DESCENT CLEARANCE WILL BE AS DIRECTED BY ATC.

| STAR DESIGNATOR | VIA | ROUTE |
|---|---|---|
| | | TNT VOR-DAYNE |
| DAYNE 1A (DAY 1A) | R3/B4/UB4/UP6/A20/A2 | |
| | | POL VOR-AMLET-DAYNE |
| DAYNE 1C (DAY 1C) See Note 5 | A2 | |
| | | OTR VOR-STOCK-POL R167-AMLET-DAYNE |
| DAYNE 1D (DAY 1D) See Note 5 | B1 | |
| CHANGE | DAYNE 1A: VIA UB4/UP6 ADDED. | |

AERO INF DATE 11 Apr 96    701

---

## STARs via LPL NDB (POL VOR OP.) — LIVERPOOL

GENERAL INFORMATION
1 All inbound flights from other routes see MIRSI, ROSUN & DALEY STARs.
2 Under certain traffic conditions ATC may require aircraft to hold at MIRSI before proceeding to LPL NDB.
3 Aircraft inbound to Hawarden will route TNT VOR-WHI NDB-HAW NDB.
4 Standard Routes may be varied at the discretion of ATC.
5 Cross SLPs or 3 min before holding facility at 250kts at FL140 or below.
6 When POL VOR is out of service MIRSI holding axis is aligned to the WAL VOR R065 between 12NM and 17NM.
7 For radio communication failure procedures the clearance limit is LPL NDB.

TRANSITION LEVEL - ATC
TRANSITION ALT 5000'

DESCENT PLANNING - ATC REQUIREMENTS
When determining top of descent point, pilots should anticipate possible clearance to 3500ft by WHI NDB. Pilots unable to comply must notify ATC as soon as possible.
ACTUAL DESCENT CLEARANCE WILL BE AS DIRECTED BY ATC.

NOT TO SCALE

LIVERPOOL
LPL 349-5
N53 20-3 W002 43-4

SLP
WHI NDB

LPL QDM 345°
LPL 2A    10

272°

092°

HOLDING
Min Alt 2500'
Max FL100

WHITEGATE
WHI 368-5
N53 11-1 W002 37-3

TNT R289
LPL 2A    35

TNT 115-7D
N53 03-2 W001 40-1
R3 B4
UB4 UP6
A20
A2

| STAR DESIGNATOR | VIA | ROUTE |
|---|---|---|
| LIVERPOOL 2A (LPL 2A) | R3/B4/UB4 UP6/A20/A2 | TNT VOR-WHI NDB-LPL NDB |
| CHANGE | VIA UB4/UP6 ADDED. | |

AERO INF DATE 11 Apr 96    301

**Left** *Standard Terminal Arrival (STAR) Charts for Liverpool and Manchester* (CAA).

VOR radial back to the holding fix position.

In the event of a ground equipment failure at the VOR/DME installation, a stand-by procedure is published, based on an alternative VOR/DME or other radio beacon. In the case of DAYNE, the holding pattern is defined additionally by a radial and distance from the Manchester VOR/DME.

## Aircraft type and airfield designators

For flight planning and flight progress strip presentation, aircraft types have been allocated by ICAO a designator of not more than four characters. Where possible this conforms to the manufacturer's designation, or at least to part of it. For example, Boeing 707, 737, 747 are represented by B707, B737 and B747, an HS74 as an HS748, an SH36 a Shorts 360, and a BA41 a Jetstream 41.

The codes are often used on R/T, most being fairly obvious, but some are obscure. Controllers occasionally ask a pilot for his aircraft type and get an answer that is not very enlightening. Space does not permit a comprehensive listing, which would run into many hundreds of entries, but commonly heard designators are listed in Appendix 5.

Four-letter designators for airfields are often heard on HF R/T, but very rarely on VHF, and are allocated by ICAO on a worldwide basis for flight planning and telex purposes. British airfields are prefixed 'EG', hence EGLL for Heathrow, EGKK for Gatwick and EGCC for Manchester. A few European examples are EDDH (Hamburg), LFPO (Paris Orly), EBOS (Ostend), LSZH (Zurich) and LEMD (Madrid). American airports are prefixed 'K', as in KJFK (Kennedy) and KLAX (Los Angeles). A worldwide listing of the most important airfields can be found in the companion volume *International Air Band Radio Handbook*.

*An Airbus A320 cockpit with fully integrated displays, setting the standard for future aircraft* (Airbus Industrie).

*Chapter 14*

# Airline company messages

Included in the VHF air band and listed in Appendix 3 are blocks of frequencies, generally between 129.50 and 131.975, which are allocated for company operational communications and used for the exchange of information between commercial aircraft and their ground-based operations staff or handling agents. These behind-the-scenes messages are entirely separate from air traffic control, but are essential for the safe and efficient running of an airline or cargo service. Further down the scale, but no less important to their users, many flying schools have a company frequency to pass weather information to their offices and discuss flying bookings, etc.

In contrast to ATC exchanges, messages on company frequencies are very informal and often resemble a telephone conversation. An exception is where one frequency is shared by several operators or by one handling agent at a number of different airports. In this case the talking is kept to a minimum. Larger airlines have their own ops channels, for example British Midland's 'BD Ops' at East Midlands and British Airways' 'Speedbird Control' at Heathrow. Further sub-divisions include 'Speedbird Glasgow', 'Speedbird Manchester', 'Speedbird Tech' for advice on technical matters, and 'Speedbird Library' for charts and documentation. The BA Shuttle fleet has its own ops channel.

Other airlines, especially foreign ones, find it uneconomical to maintain their own ops office at each airport, and use the services of a handling agent instead. Best known is Servisair, a Stockport-based firm with offices at all the main and regional airports. A comprehensive service is provided, including passenger and cargo handling, organising refuelling, catering requirements, aircraft cleaning, the filing of flight plans, arranging slot times, crew meals and hotel bookings.

There is no standard phraseology for company messages, but the information is usually passed in a particular manner. In the initial call, the last two letters of the aircraft registration are often added as a suffix to the call-sign, for example 'Midland 85 Juliet Charlie'. Sometimes the flight number is deleted altogether, as in 'Britannia Alpha Kilo'. Time 'off blocks' or 'off chocks', ie the time taxying commenced, is passed first, followed by airborne time and ETA at destination. Fuelling requirements for the next sector (the next leg of a series of flights or the return trip) are given in the following manner: 'In tanks X tonnes or kilos. Burn off (or burn) X tonnes or kilos. Taxi X tonnes or kilos'. 'Burn off' is the amount of fuel estimated to be used. The term RTOW is sometimes heard; this stands for Regulated Take-Off Weight, the pre-computed weight for the aircraft plus passengers, fuel and cargo for a particular set of conditions, including runway length, whether its surface is wet or dry, temperature and certain other factors.

Passenger information is usually included in various forms. The total number of fare-paying passengers is passed, followed by the number of non-fare paying infants, for example '253 plus

2'. The infants are sometimes referred to as tenths ('2/10ths') or as decimals ('252.2 pax'). 'No specials' indicates that there are no special requirements. Disabled passengers may require a wheelchair for disembarkation: 'lift-off' if unable to walk, 'walk off' if able to get down the steps to the wheelchair. Other information passed via company messages is extremely varied, ranging from passengers' lost library books and special dietary requirements to requests for the police to meet rowdy passengers on arrival. Stand or gate numbers for parking at the terminal are relayed to the aircraft by ops, having been issued by the airport's Apron Control, an entirely separate function from ATC.

Such is the computerised complexity of modern transport aircraft that technical problems are frequently passed as so-called Fault Codes. These are a series of 6- to 8-digit numbers that can be interpreted by engineering ground staff. An ADD is an Allowable Deferred Defect, a minor fault that can be attended to at the end of the day's service. The Flight Data Recorder (FDR), familiarly known as the 'black box', records certain technical aspects of a flight that can be used to analyse accidents and incidents. Also heard are references to QARs, Quick Access Recorders. Unlike the FDR, a QAR is not a legal requirement, but it is now fitted to many of the world's airliners. The flight data fed into it is automatically monitored and subsequently analysed by ground staff. As an example, a Boeing 767's equipment may record up to 1,550 different parameters, covering a large number of operating aspects from engine health and Flight Director accuracy to fuel burn efficiency and Autoland precision. Any discrepancies can be rectified promptly, often with considerable cost savings to the operator, as well as increased safety. Unfortunately the QAR cassettes are soon filled up, hence the requests for new ones on reaching the destination. The solution to this disadvantage is the Optical QAR, an optical-disk-based device that offers up to eight times the memory capacity of the current QAR. It is now in the final stages of development and will also have datalink capability (see page 39).

# Aircraft Communications Addressing and Reporting System (ACARS)

ACARS was developed in the USA by ARINC to reduce voice communications. For example, an exchange of routine ops information taking up to 1 minute of congested VHF air-time can be compressed by ACARS into less than a second by means of a ground computer converting it into a print-out. As well as a flight deck unit for keyboard data entry, an aircraft equipped with ACARS is fitted with sensing devices that send data automatically to the ground station when the aircraft has performed certain manoeuvres such as a 'pushback' from the departure gate, take-off, landing and gate arrival. SITA, the European communications company, has a version known as AIRCOM, which is compatible with ACARS. Its use is increasing on this side of the Atlantic and it is possible for the amateur to decode the messages with the aid of a personal computer and equipment such as the Airmaster produced by Lowe Electronics (see addresses on page 126). ACARS has also got great potential for routine ATC messages, as proved by Canada and the UK, which have been passing oceanic clearances to selected airlines for several years via VHF datalinks and ACARS. Pilots must still, however, request the clearance and acknowledge receipt by voice, but in the next phase of the trial a single button push on the ACARS unit will confirm reception.

ACARS will one day make company voice communications obsolete, but for the moment listening to ops messages can be quite fascinating, and really give an insight into the intricacies of running an airline. Once again discretion is advised in discussing them, but the main impression gained is how well airlines look after their customers' individual needs.

## ACARS Frequencies (datalink)

136.90 136.925 136.95 136.975

# Chapter 15

# Air displays

Airshow frequencies are generally the same as those normally used by the airfield concerned; some may be allocated by the Civil Aviation Authority on a temporary basis for venues that are not airfields. If there is any doubt, the scanner search facility will soon locate the appropriate channels. Some receivers will search for active frequencies between preset upper and lower limits and automatically dump them into one of the memory banks. The receiver does all the work for you and at airshows the external aerial can be shortened or removed altogether so that only local frequencies will be found.

For those who prefer to plan ahead, airfield frequencies can be programmed in advance, and the search mode used to detect any non-standard ones that may be in use. If the location is a civil airfield, the number involved will be small. Military airfields normally have a much greater number of frequencies, some being secondary, back-up channels. On VHF, 122.1 is used as a standard frequency for Aerodrome Traffic Zone penetration by civil aircraft. This or another assigned VHF frequency is almost always used for the control of military airshows so as to cater for civil participants.

Many small airfields do not have a full ATC service. However, a simple air/ground radio channel or a rather more formal flight information service may be provided to pass basic data to pilots. When hosting an airshow, a few volunteer controllers will be on duty with a CAA temporary local validation of their ATC licences. The International Air Tattoo at Fairford in Gloucestershire, for example, relies on the same team of experienced controllers working in their spare time.

Radio calls are kept to a minimum during airshows to avoid breaking a pilot's concentration during a complex sequence of manoeuvres. As his 'slot' nears its end, he will be given a check of minutes to go. Some military display teams, such as the Red Arrows, have their own UHF frequency for interplane transmissions. The leader or his No 2 monitors the VHF channel and relays any ATC messages. Many other display teams simply use the airshow control frequency for their air-to-air messages, although they may be in a foreign language!

An expensive radio is no advantage at an airshow, as you are close to the transmitters and even the cheapest set can resolve broadcasts at that range. Your choice of antenna, usually so critical for quality reception, is also less restricted. Many listeners use a short length of flexible wire instead of the normal antenna, which means that the set can be stowed in a jacket pocket out of the way, with no loss of signal.

An important accessory is a pair of lightweight headphones or an earphone to overcome the noise of jet aircraft. Now on the market is a police-style earpiece costing around £9, which slips over the ear and provides many hours of comfortable listening with very little weight. Earphones offer another advantage: they increase your battery life and can make the difference between them lasting all day or dying in the middle of the show. The majority of modern receivers can use rechargeable cells, but these rarely last more than 4 to 6 hours of constant use, so a spare set of rechargeables is needed.

Batteries are an important consideration and many regular listeners use alkaline cells at an airshow. They are more expensive but will easily last 10 to 12 hours in all but the oldest of receivers. Some modern radios can run for 20 or more hours on a set and can thus last all weekend, which is useful if the show is a two-day event like the International Air Tattoo.

If your radio has memory banks, a good tip is to programme the basic ATC frequencies into one bank for rapid scanning and place display team channels into another for use during the individual routines. If you have a single-frequency set, your best plan is to locate the airshow controller (normally the tower frequency) and stick to this all day. It will provide almost everything you need and some teams will also use it for their air-to-air communications.

There are several less obvious benefits to be derived from using an air band radio. Airshow photography has always relied upon split-second timing to get the best shots. Tuning in to the voices of the pilots as they synchronise manoeuvres can assist in getting that special picture. Display items often catch the commentator unawares – the fast, low arrival of the Tornado, for example. The pilot has to inform ATC that he is running in and, if you are listening, you can be waiting, camera at the ready.

Perhaps your interest lies with video photography. The headphone socket provides a useful link to your radio if you use a camcorder. By joining a lead between the two, you will be able to add the radio broadcasts to your video soundtrack. Alternatively, you can just place your receiver near to the camcorder and the transmissions will still record well. It will also serve to cut out background chatter from people around you and result in a greatly enhanced video that really captures the spirit of the event.

Enthusiasts tend to deplore the extensive market areas seen at most displays, but they do have one advantage – the presence of numerous aviation suppliers. Their wares range from books and magazines to air band radios and navigation charts. The major outlets that make regular appearances include *FlyPast* magazine, Air Supply, Flightdeck (The Airband Shop), Javiation, Lowe Electronics, Midland Counties Publications, Stewart Aviation, Air-Britain and The Aviation Hobby Shop.

## Selected display team frequencies

Aquilla (Spain): 130.5 252.5
Blue Angels: 121.9 123.4 134.1 241.2 250.8
    251.6 275.35 307.7 360.4 384.4 391.9 395.9
Silver Eagles (Army Air Corps): 252.5
    372.625 312.0
Falcons: 255.1 (Air-to-Drop Zone Link)
Patrouille de France: 242.65 143.1
Patrouille de Suisse: 288.85
Red Arrows: 243.45 242.2
Royal Navy Helicopter Team: 135.975
    250.475
Russian Test Pilots: 125.35 (or airshow
    control frequency)
Thunderbirds: 120.45 123.4 124.935 235.25
    236.55 236.6 250.85 273.5 283.5 295.7 322.0
    322.6 382.9 394.0
Battle of Britain Memorial Flight: 120.8
Crunchie Flying Circus: 118.0

# Chapter 16

# Emergencies

Emergency situations with aircraft are fairly common, and although the word conjures up images of catastrophic failure or fire in the air, few are very dramatic, even if they do give the pilot some worrying moments. The most numerous are cockpit indications of undercarriage malfunctions, which may necessitate a low run past the tower for a visual check that the wheels are down. There is no guarantee that they are locked, however, but it gives the pilot some encouragement! Almost invariably the green lights come on when the jolt of the landing activates a stuck micro-switch.

Other frequent problems are doors coming open in flight, failed generators and lost fuel filler caps. On most light aircraft an open door is a noisy and draughty inconvenience rather than an actual hazard, but there some types on which the adverse effect on the airflow can reduce control. Hence, unlike in the USA where a pilot has formally to declare an emergency before the safety services are alerted, a British controller uses his or her judgment and almost always puts them on a Local Stand-by, working on the principle of 'better safe than sorry'. There is also the possibility that a minor problem with the aircraft may distract a pilot enough to make him misjudge the landing. For Royal Flights, a Stand-by is standard practice.

The scale of Rescue and Fire Fighting Services at a particular airport is determined by the overall length and maximum fuselage width of the largest aircraft handled on a regular basis. The lowest is the Special Category, licensed solely for flying instruction to take place. Then follow Categories 1 to 9, rising from an overall length of 9m progressively up to 76m. Bristol, a typical regional airport, is Cat 7, Heathrow Cat 9.

There are six standard categories of emergency beginning with the self-explanatory 'Aircraft Accident'. A 'Full Emergency' is arranged when it is known that an aircraft is, or is suspected to be, in such trouble that there is a danger of an accident. The problems include the thankfully rare fire in the air, fuel shortage and the not uncommon engine failure on multi-engined aircraft. In the latter case an experienced and properly trained commercial pilot should have no difficulty in making a safe landing as he is required to practice asymmetric flying at regular intervals and pass a check. The safety services are alerted, however, and at larger airports this usually means that outside services will be summoned automatically as a back-up.

Next comes the above-mentioned 'Local Stand-by', and the 'Aircraft Ground Incident', which covers occurrences other than accidents. These include fuel spillages and bomb scares on parked aircraft. A 'Weather Stand-by' is instituted when 'weather conditions are such as to render a landing difficult or difficult to observe'. Bad visibility is one obvious instance, a significant crosswind component another. The final category is 'Domestic Fire', which, as its title implies, covers such things as grass fires on and adjacent to the airfield and fire in its buildings. At major airports the rescue services have the use of a common frequency of 121.6 to talk directly with the aircraft crew when necessary.

A pilot requiring immediate assistance is expected to transmit a Distress Message with the prefix 'Mayday, Mayday, Mayday'. If the situation is less serious an Urgency Message with the prefix 'Pan, Pan, Pan' is used. Unfortunately pilots, particularly phlegmatic British ones, are loth to make too much of a fuss, so if you hear a 'Mayday' call, things have really reached the critical stage! The announcement of the loss of one engine, provided that there are more than one, is usually delivered in a matter-of-fact manner, together with a request for a diversion. This calm approach is sometimes self-defeating – a controller who would be sparked into instant action to clear a path for an aircraft that has abruptly turned into a glider in the circuit may think he has misheard if the magic word 'Mayday' is not used, and waste time asking for a repeat.

Aircraft in distress or lost, if they are not already in two-way contact with an ATC unit, may call on the International Distress Frequency of 121.5MHz. If they have a transponder the code 7700 can be selected to indicate an emergency. (This activates an alarm at every radar station able to receive the signal and also makes the radar blip pulsate to attract the controller's attention.) The Distress Frequency is monitored continuously by the RAF Distress & Diversion Cell (D&D) at West Drayton in Middlesex and at Prestwick in Scotland, which serve the areas south and north of 55°N respectively. They can provide a service to civil aircraft in emergency in addition to that for military aircraft on 243MHz UHF.

South of a line from Preston to the Humber there is a reasonable chance of establishing the position of an aircraft transmitting on 121.5 at quite low levels, except over the hilly areas of Wales and South West England. D/F bearings from 15 out-stations provide almost instant position-fixing by autotriangulation. The service is virtually guaranteed over most of the land mass to the east and south of Manchester above 3,000ft, and down to 2,000ft in the vicinity of London.

Pilots are encouraged to make practice Pan calls on 121.5, having first of all asked permission in case there is a real emergency in progress. It is extremely impressive to hear how quickly D&D can fix the aircraft's position even when it is not equipped with a transponder. Aircraft on transatlantic flights are required to monitor 121.5 continuously, and there have been many occasions when a high-flying airliner has relayed distress messages from some wave-hopping light aircraft on a delivery flight and alerted the rescue services.

Transmissions from an aircraft in distress have priority over all other messages. When a pilot is already in contact with an ATC unit, assistance should be sought on the frequency in use, otherwise a call should be made on 121.5. On hearing a distress call, all stations must maintain radio silence on that frequency, unless they themselves are required to render assistance, and should continue to listen on the frequency concerned until it is evident that assistance is being provided.

The recommended form of the distress message to be transmitted is somewhat long-winded, and it would have to be a very cool pilot who remembered to include everything (and in the right order!), even assuming that he had time to make the full call. All those that I have heard consisted of 'Mayday' three times, the call-sign and 'Engine failure'.

The information to be passed is as follows:

(a) Name of the station addressed (when appropriate)
(b) Call-sign and type of aircraft
(c) Nature of the emergency
(d) Intention of the person in command
(e) Present position, Flight Level/altitude and heading
(f) Pilot's qualifications as appropriate: (1) Student pilot; (2) No instrument qualification; (3) IMC rated; (4) Full instrument rating

Pilots are invited to use the call-sign prefix 'Tyro' when calling a military ATC unit or the D&D Cell, to indicate lack of experience. This code word will ensure that controllers do not issue instructions that the pilot may have difficulty in following.

The standard acknowledgment is 'GABCD [station] Roger Mayday', and further instructions follow without delay. It may be necessary to impose radio silence on all stations in the area or any particular station that interferes with emergency transmissions, usually unintentionally having just come on to the frequency. In either case the messages should take the form 'All stations Leeds Approach stop transmitting, Mayday' or 'GAMPT stop transmitting, Mayday'.

It may be a good idea to transfer aircraft from the frequency to avoid interfering with calls from or to the aircraft in distress: 'Mayday. All stations contact Leeds Tower on 120.3. Out.' When an emergency situation has been resolved, the station that has been controlling the traffic will broadcast a message that normal working will be resumed: 'Mayday. All stations Leeds Tower time 04 distress traffic GABCD ended. Out.'

When an aircraft is operating on a flight plan and fails to arrive within 30 minutes of its ETA, the controller at the destination is required to confirm the ATD from the departure airfield. Other set procedures known as Preliminary Overdue Action are also put into effect. After an hour, or sooner in certain cases, Full Overdue Action is taken by the parent ACC and a search launched for the missing aircraft.

Aircraft on a flight for which a plan has not been filed have no such protection, although they are required to 'book out' with the ATC unit at the departure aerodrome, assuming that one exists. The departure, together with time en route, fuel endurance and number of souls on board, are recorded, but no further action need be taken. If such an aircraft goes missing, it is often some time before people start asking questions, usually sparked off by anxious relatives.

Flight plans must be filed at least 30 minutes before requesting taxi clearance or start-up approval. A pilot may file one for any flight, but for certain categories they are mandatory. These include all IFR flights within controlled airspace, those that cross an international boundary, and for any flight where the destination is more than 40km from the aerodrome of departure and the aircraft's maximum total weight exceeds 5,700kg. In addition, a pilot is advised to file a plan if he intends to fly over the sea more than 10 miles from the coast, or over sparsely populated areas where Search and Rescue operations would be difficult.

For scheduled airline routes and other regularly recurring IFR flights with identical basic features, a repetitive flight plan saves operators and crews the chore of filing a separate plan each time. Often referred to as a 'stored plan', it is submitted by an operator for computer storage and repetitive use by ATC units for each individual flight.

## 'Airprox'

Until recently known as an 'Airmiss', an Airprox Report should be made whenever a pilot or controller considers that the distance between aircraft as well as their relative positions and speed have been such that the safety of the aircraft involved was or may have been compromised. A sense of proportion is required for this, however, as light aircraft in traffic circuits occasionally get horrendously close to one another, usually through inexperience and/or not keeping a good look-out.

Pilots flying under IFR in controlled airspace may well file if they see another aircraft that they believe is closer to them than required by the separation rules. In a radar-controlled environment this may be 4 instead of 5 miles, which a pilot flying under VFR would consider ludicrous.

All Airprox Reports are investigated, not so much as to allot blame but to try to prevent a recurrence by examining the circumstances. The degree of actual risk of collision is assessed and regular summaries of the most serious cases are published for all to read. In the past, when circulation was restricted, the press had to rely on leaked reports. Unfortunately one that they never heard about was the large pink pig, which an Army helicopter nearly rammed one hazy day over the River Thames. It was an advertising balloon that had broken its moorings and drifted away! Most make very dull reading, an exception being the celebrated Boeing 737/UFO encounter near Manchester in 1994!

## Radio failures

If an aircraft suffers a radio failure there are published procedures to which the pilot is expected to adhere. A 'squawk' of 7600 set on the transponder will alert an ATC unit to his problem, provided that it has SSR capability. If essential navigation equipment has also failed, pilots are advised as a last resort to carry out a special procedure to alert the radar controller to the fact that they need assistance. The aircraft is to fly at least two triangular patterns before resuming its course, as follows:

| Aircraft speed | Length of leg |
|---|---|
| 300kt or less | 2 minutes |
| More than 300kt | 1 minute |

*Transmitter failure only*
Right-hand turns

*Complete failure*
Left-hand turns

If the controller should notice such a manoeuvre (and RAF experiments show that they often do not!), he is to advise the Distress & Diversion Cell of the position and track, and continue to plot the aircraft while it is in radar cover. A 'shepherd' aircraft will then be sent out to lead it, hopefully, to a safe landing.

Quite often the failure is of the transmitter only and the controller can instruct the aircraft to make one or more turns and check if the pilot is complying. If it becomes obvious that the receiver is working, normal radar service is resumed. There are some subtle ways by which the aircraft's altitude and other information can be ascertained, such as 'After passing FL50 turn left heading 270'.

There are occasions when an aircraft receiver is working correctly but the reply transmitted is unintelligible at the ground station because the speech is badly distorted or non-existent, perhaps because the microphone is unserviceable. Military pilots are briefed to use a special code that makes use of the carrier wave only. The pilot presses his transmitter button a certain number of times according to the following code:

**One short transmission** – Yes (or an acknowledgment)
**Two short transmissions** – No
**Three short transmissions** – Say again
**Four short transmissions** – Request homing
**One long transmission (2 seconds)** – Manoeuvre complete (eg, steady on heading)
**One long, two short, one long** – The aircraft has developed another emergency

A controller will be alerted to the presence of an aircraft with this kind of failure if he hears, or sees on the VDF, four short carrier wave transmissions. The controller should then interrogate the pilot, using the call-sign 'Speechless Aircraft' if the identity of the aircraft cannot be discovered, to find out what assistance is required. He must be careful to ask questions that can be answered with a direct 'yes' or 'no'. The code is now recommended for use by civilian pilots as it can be explained easily by the controller during the first few transmissions.

# Chapter 17

# Military air band

Military ATC employs a block of frequencies between 225 and 400MHz, audio modulated (AM) as in the civil VHF air band. Although technically the Ultra High Frequency (UHF) band does not start until 300MHz, they are usually referred to as UHF and are normally spaced 25kHZ apart. Theoretically this produces 7,000 separate channels, and although many are in use for airfield and area ATC, it leaves a very large number available for a variety of uses. These include in-flight refuelling, bombing and gunnery range operations, air-to-air frequencies for formation flying, satellite links, and, in the case of the USAF in Britain, numerous ops and Command Post channels.

Blocks of frequencies, known as TADs (Tactical Air Designators), are allocated for air defence interception purposes by RAF radar units. Each channel has a code number, such as TAD 122. An anomaly is the use by the RAF and USAF of a few frequencies around 142MHz. To save time-consuming manual tuning, many military aircraft have pre-set radio frequencies, referred to as 'Studs' ('Button' or 'Push' to the Americans) and used in the same way as the push buttons on a car radio. For example, the current allocation for a Hawk based at RAF Valley is as follows:

Stud 1: Ground Movements Control; Stud 2: Tower; Stud 3: Departures; Stud 4: Mona; Stud 5: Quiet frequency; Stud 6: Approach; Stud 7: Radar; Stud 8: Radar; Stud 9: NATO common; Stud 10: Low level; Stud 11: Air-to-air; Stud 12: Air-to-air; Stud 13: Air-to-air; Stud 14: London Mil; Stud 15: London Mil; Stud 16: Scottish Mil; Stud 17:

Llanbedr Approach; Stud 18: Llanbedr Tower; Stud 19: Duty Instructor/Ops; Stud 20: Not allocated.

Military aviation in Britain is organised much the same as its civil counterpart, although the ultimate purpose of a considerable amount of military ATC is to bring aircraft together (formation join-ups, air-to-air refuelling, interceptions, etc) rather than to keep them apart. Most airfields have a Ground Movements Controller as well as a Tower Controller, who is known also as the 'local' controller. The controller who sequences traffic on to final approach is the Director, the next stage being the Talkdown Controller, who uses Precision Approach Radar (PAR) to bring the aircraft down to visual contact with the runway. PAR, discontinued in UK civil ATC about 20 years ago in favour of ILS, uses two radar displays. One shows the aircraft and final approach in plan view, the other the picture from the side, which monitors deviations above and below the glide path. The pilot can thus be given height as well as heading corrections.

The RAF makes considerable use of ILS installations, but few are rated more accurate than the minimum civil Category 1 (minimum of 200ft cloud base and 600 metres RVR). Efforts are being made to improve this situation to counter the planned demise of PAR, MLS (Microwave Landing System) being seen as the eventual replacement for both systems.

RAF rules governing runway occupancy, separation and other procedures are similar to those in civil ATC. R/T phraseology is, however, somewhat different, although it is planned to bring it into line with civilian practice as an ongoing process. Military jet circuits tend to be relatively tight and are more oval-shaped than civil practice (see page 57). Military controllers use 'two in', 'three in', etc, for the number of aircraft present in the circuit. The 'finals' call is made just before turning base leg. 'Roll' is used instead of the civil 'touch and go', and an 'overshoot' is a low approach rather than a go around. A 'run and break' is a useful method of killing excess speed by approaching the runway, pulling up and turning downwind for a close-in final. USAF bases in Britain use some of the American phraseology as described in *International Air Band Radio Handbook*.

R/T exchanges are often clipped and difficult for the layman to understand; for example, two clicks on the mike button often serves as an acknowledgment. Also, the use of oxygen mask microphones tends to depersonalise voices, but it does make many RAF transmissions instantly identifiable as such! Ground operations frequencies at RAF and USAF bases can be found in the 30–39, 68–69, 72–80 and 406–414MHz ranges, all NFM mode.

Military aviation thrives on initials and code words. Among the many to be heard on UHF are 'PD' (Practice Diversion), 'RTB' (Return To Base), 'Homeplate' (base), 'Chicks' (friendly fighter aircraft), 'Playmate' (aircraft being worked with), and 'Pogo' (switch to channel . . . ). The Americans have their own jargon, such as 'Code One' (a fully serviceable aircraft), 'RON' (Remain Overnight), 'TOT' (time on target), 'Lima Charlie' (loud and clear), 'Victor freek' (VHF frequency), and 'Uniform' (UHF frequency).

London Air Traffic Control Centre (Military) is co-located with the civil LATCC at West Drayton near Heathrow Airport to form the London Joint Area Organisation (LJAO). To meet the requirements of all airspace users, the civil controllers provide air traffic services to en route GAT (General Air Traffic) flights, usually within the airways system and within fixed geographical sectors, and the military controllers give a service in a more flexible fashion to OAT (Operational Air Traffic) flights. OAT flights are generally those that cannot conform to the requirements of flights within airways and other regulated airspace.

Within the airways system GAT, including military traffic operating as GAT, is normally given priority over OAT. Exceptions are made, however, for such operations as military aircraft engaged in the calibration of a radar system. Conversely, outside the airways and upper route structures OAT generally gets priority over off-route GAT. The Initial Contact Frequencies (ICFs) for each sector at what is known from its call-sign as 'London Mil' are monitored permanently. LJAO is not equipped with dedicated VHF frequencies, so when a VHF service is required use has to be made of the civil sector spare VHF frequency, subject to availability and the approval of the Chief Sector Controller. The Central (Mil) Sector, formerly known as Daventry, is the busiest of the six sectors, the others being Northwest, Clacton, Dover/Lydd, Seaford/Hurn and London Upper.

Flight Plans are vitally important for the efficient operation of the system. GAT Plans are processed in the normal way by the civil computer, while those for OAT are fed into the military Myriad computer by the RAF Air Movements Section. If any of the flight plans affect LJAO airspace the relevant flight progress strips are printed and distributed to the appropriate sectors.

As one military controller working in LJAO remarked, it soon becomes obvious that most of the aircraft based in the east of England want to exercise in the west, and those from the west want to exercise in the east! The problem is that to get to those areas the aircraft need to cross one of the busiest air route complexes in the world, colloquially known as 'the Ambers' after their now obsolete designation. In most cases the crossing is achieved with very little fuss due to constant co-ordination with the civil controllers on the spot.

Virtually all crossings of the airways are

accomplished by means of a 'cleared level', which means that no aircraft under civil control will be allowed to occupy the negotiated level for the period that the military aircraft is crossing. When this is not possible owing to busy traffic situations, the military controller is permitted to use radar separation to achieve a safe crossing, a procedure known as 'taking five'. The name comes from the prescribed separation of at least 5 nautical miles or 5,000ft vertically from any GAT aircraft in the airway. Obviously it is easier to 'take five' with a fighter aircraft than a transport owing to the higher speed and manoeuvrability.

When this method is being employed and there is a possibility of a conflict with one particular aircraft, the controller can co-ordinate with his civil opposite number. When a course of action is agreed, the military controller is able to reduce separation against that one aircraft to the standard radar separation required, depending on its flight level, ie 5 miles horizontally or 1,000ft vertically (2,000ft above FL245). In an emergency, when neither a radar nor procedural crossing can be obtained, an airway may be crossed at an intermediate 500ft level, ie a level of 1,000ft plus 500ft. If already at a 1,000ft level, the aircraft must climb 500ft before entering the airway.

A further method of crossing airways is via the Radar Video Corridors that have been established at the points most frequently required to be crossed by military flights. The Lichfield RVC in the north-west Midlands facilitates crossings at either FL110 or FL180, while the Scunthorpe RVC runs through airway Bravo 1 at FL110, being controlled by London Mil. The Daventry RVC allows crossings at FL100 or FL110, and the Westcott RVC takes military traffic across the airways system just north of London at FL230 or FL240. Over Mid-Wales, the Niton RVC is available for transits at FL110 or FL120. Brize Radar at Brize Norton in Oxfordshire provides a service for the Swindon RVC at FL230 or FL240, while

Yeovilton Radar does the same for Alpha 25. These 'blocks' of airspace simplify crossing procedures, but the pilot must still request a prior clearance from the controlling authority.

Every other sector in the LJAO is similar in operation to the Central Sector, if not quite so busy. On the Northwest Sector a slight difference exists in that the Manchester Sub-Centre controls all the airspace up to and including FL195, so requests for clearances through these levels have to be made direct to Manchester by the military controller. On the Clacton, Dover and Seaford Sectors handovers are made between LJAO and foreign military agencies, chiefly Mazout Radar in France and Belga Radar in Belgium, the aircraft being transferred to the appropriate frequency when it reaches the FIR boundary. North of 55°N, roughly an east-west line through Newcastle, Scottish Mil at Prestwick operates on the same lines as London Mil.

Most of the UK airspace at and above FL245 up to FL660 is designated as a Mandatory Radar Service Area (MRSA) with an ATC radar unit responsible for each sector. It is compulsory for pilots intending to fly in the MRSA to call the appropriate radar unit and fly under its instructions except when operating as civil air traffic or under air defence radars. The North Wales Military Training Area (MTA) and the Lincolnshire Military Reserved Airspace (MRA) are established within the MRSA to afford freedom of operation for aircraft engaged in exercises incompatible with radar control. The Lincolnshire MRA is co-ordinated by RAF Waddington and stretches upwards from FL245 to FL350. The North Wales MTA, under RAF Valley, has limits of FL245 and FL450. Outside the published hours of training activity MTAs revert to normal MRSA status.

Aerial Tactics Areas (ATAs) reach from FL50 up to FL245 and enable high-energy combat manoeuvres to be carried out by formations of up to six aircraft. Current examples are The Wash ATA, the primary users of which are Coningsby, Cottesmore and Wittering, and the Lakenheath ATA, mainly used by Lakenheath itself. Within The Wash ATA is the ACMI Range (see page 33).

Military units also offer a Lower Airspace Radar Advisory Service (LARS) outside controlled airspace up to FL100 for both military and civil aircraft, and a similar service up to FL245 within what is termed 'Middle Airspace'. Its availability is subject to the range and cover of the particular radar in use as well as controller workload. The procedure when within approximately 30 miles of the radar unit is to establish R/T contact on the appropriate frequency using the phraseology '[ATC unit] this is [aircraft call-sign] request Lower Airspace Radar Service'. Pilots may be asked to 'stand by for controller'. When asked, they are to pass aircraft type, position and heading, Flight Level or altitude, intentions and type of service required. The latter may be a radar advisory or information service (see page 82 for details).

Military Aerodrome Traffic Zones (MATZs) normally consist of a circle of a radius of 5 nautical miles from the aerodrome up to 3,000ft above aerodrome level, together with one or more 'stubs' out to 5 miles protecting the approach paths of the instrument runways. A MATZ Penetration Service is provided to civil aircraft, the common frequency being 122.1. Traffic information will be given together with any instructions necessary to achieve separation from known or observed traffic in the zone. In some areas MATZs may overlap to form a combined zone; in this case the altimeter pressure setting will be passed to aircraft as a 'Clutch QNH'.

The RAF Distress & Diversion Cells at West Drayton and Prestwick have already been described in Chapter 16. 'London Centre', as it is known by its call-sign, now has a computer-based facility that can calculate and display the position of any aircraft transmitting on the military distress frequency of 243MHz. If a crash or ditching occurs, Search and Rescue (SAR) is co-ordinated either by Plymouth Rescue Co-ordination Centre (RCC) or Kinloss

Aeronautical RCC in North East Scotland, depending on the location; their call-signs are 'Plymouth Rescue' and 'Kinloss Rescue', and HF frequencies are employed because of their long range. The primary day frequency is 5.680kHZ; 3.023 is used at night. They are shared by the two RCCs, and since both are worldwide common frequencies, other units such as Stavanger can be heard on them at times, as well as ground units such as Mountain Rescue Teams (RAF call-sign 'Alpine') and civilian equivalents (for example Kendal MRT, 'Mintcake')!

Of course the emergencies do not just involve aircraft; they may be ships in distress, climbing accidents, floods and a variety of other incidents. A Temporary Danger Area is established around the site so that SAR ops can be continued without interference from press aircraft and other non-essential intruders. When an aircraft is fitted with an ELT (Emergency Locator Transmitter) or a downed pilot activates an SARBE (SAR Beacon), the signals will be picked up by SARSAT (Search and Rescue Satellite Aided Tracking). The system is highly sensitive in detecting transmissions on 121.5, 243 and 406MHz and alerting the rescue services – so sensitive in fact that a stolen beacon was traced to a bedroom wardrobe. The satellite picked up the transmissions, an RAF helicopter went to the general area and homed in further with its own direction-finding equipment. A landing was made in a playing field behind the house and the culprit later said in court that he had found the beacon on a bus! He was not believed.

Operational control of No 32 (The Royal) Squadron, which has taken over the duties of The Queen's Flight, is vested in the RAF. Royal Flight status is often extended to other reigning sovereigns, Prime Ministers and other Heads of State as a courtesy. Contrary to popular opinion, there are no special increased separations for Royal Flights; they are treated exactly the same as

**Right** *Military Aerodrome Traffic Zones (MATZs) (CAA).*

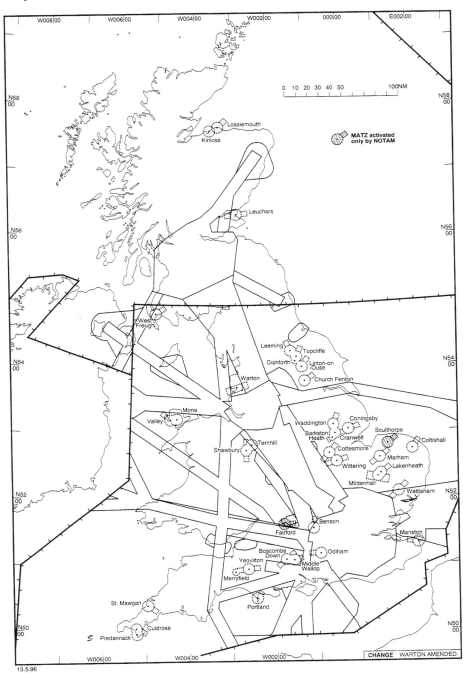

CHANGE   WARTON AMENDED.

13.5.96

any other aircraft in controlled airspace, although a higher priority is given where necessary as the Royal personage usually has to meet a tight schedule.

Royal Flights in fixed-wing aircraft are always provided with controlled airspace to cover the entire flight path when it is within UK airspace. This coverage is obtained by the establishment of Purple airways for the entire route and special Control Zones at the departure and destination airfields if these are not already in existence. Purple airways normally extend for 5 miles on either side of the route and may coincide with existing airways of the national system. The vertical dimensions, relevant radio frequencies, times and any other pertinent information will be detailed in the NOTAM concerning the flight.

The NOTAM is prepared by the Airspace Utilisation Section whenever a Royal flight is arranged. It is distributed by post to the ACCs and airfields concerned, normally providing at least 48 hours' warning. All Purple airspace is notified as Class A, ie any aircraft within it must fly by IFR at all times. In the case of temporary Control Zones, ATC may issue Special VFR clearances to pilots unable to comply with the IFR requirements and thus ensure positive separation at all times.

Purple airspace is not normally established for Royal helicopter flights, but a Royal Low Level Corridor, marked by a series of check-points, is promulgated. These check-points will be approximately 20 miles apart and will usually coincide with turning points on the route. Pilots flying near the Corridor are expected to keep a good look-out and maintain adequate separation from the Royal helicopter. The NOTAM will incorporate a list of nominated aerodromes from which pilots may obtain information on the progress of the flight.

The person on board a Royal Flight used to be readily identifiable by the call-sign, for example 'Kittyhawk' when HM The Queen was on board, 'Rainbow' for the Duke of Edinburgh, 'Unicorn' for the Prince of Wales, and 'Leopard' for Prince Andrew. However, for various reasons only 'Kittyhawk' and 'Rainbow' now remain in use. 'Kittyhawk', followed by the two-figure number allocated to the individual pilot of No 32 (The Royal) Squadron with the suffix 'R', is now used for all Royal Flights except when the Duke of Edinburgh is at the controls, when it becomes 'Rainbow'. For VIP flights the 'R' is deleted. Training and positioning flights are identified by 'Kitty' and the pilot's number. For security reasons, a plain 'Ascot' call-sign is used for flights to and from Northern Ireland.

US Air Force operations from British bases are handled in a similar way to those of their RAF opposite numbers. They have their own controllers in the airfield towers, but approach control may be centralised and co-ordinated as at Lakenheath and nearby Mildenhall. Similar arrangements can be found at various RAF stations where London Mil operates a Centralised Approach Control service.

American bases make extensive use of Standard Instrument Departures (SIDs), an example being Lakenheath's Thetford Two Departure to the east, associated waypoints being designated Mike Charlie One and Mike Charlie Six, the latter being on the London/Amsterdam UIR boundary. They connect with a network of upper airspace TACAN (Tactical Air Navigation) Routes across Britain and mainland Europe linking TACANs, the military equivalent of the civil VOR/DME. There are a number of other US military reporting points not shown on normal charts, including Gate Alpha, an East Coast range exit point, and Liberty, north-east of Norwich, for aircraft inbound to Lakenheath.

To preserve security, some military transmissions may employ DVP (Digital Voice Protection) techniques. The speech is electronically digitised, mixed at random, then transmitted. A compatible receiver unscrambles the sequence and restores its

**Right** *The Military TACAN Route System* (CAA).

# UPPER AIRSPACE MILITARY TACAN ROUTE SYSTEM

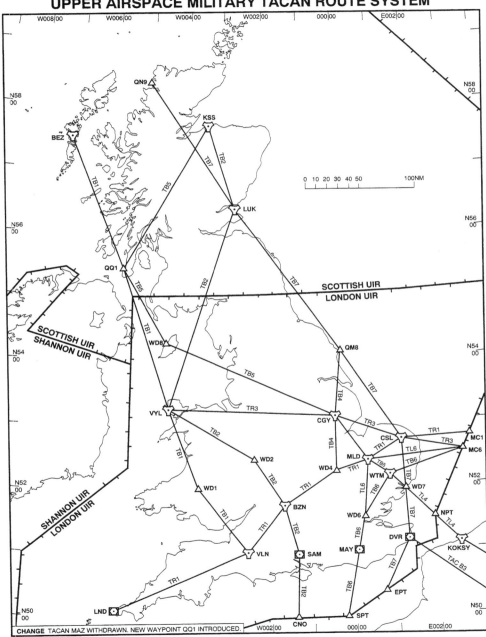

CHANGE TACAN MAZ WITHDRAWN. NEW WAYPOINT QQ1 INTRODUCED.

29.1.96

intelligibility. There are several code words for this secure mode; USAF AWACS aircraft, for example, refer to it as 'in the green'. Other terms are 'going tactical' and 'going crypto'. Some NATO strike aircraft are able to engage a frequency-hopping communications system 'Have Quick', which uses eight channels in sequence to foil the eavesdropper. However, a receiver with a very fast scan rate can still monitor the messages, although a developed version is highly secure because of its ability to race through many more frequencies right across the UHF band.

Military aviation makes considerable use of the HF bands, both the RAF and the USAF having their own networks, as does the Royal Canadian Air Force. Other foreign air forces are also represented, but since the transmissions are made in the native language they are of little interest. The RAF's Flight Watch HF network is known as the Strike Command Integrated Communications System (STCICS). It is operated from RAF Upavon in Wiltshire with the call-sign 'Architect'. Its task is to handle the military equivalent of company messages, arrange telephone patches to home stations and operations centres, and provide met and other information on request.

The UK Air Defence System runs a separate net providing communications between Sector Operations Centres and interceptor aircraft patrolling the UK Air Defence Regions. 'Friendly', 'Unknown' and 'Zombie' (Russian) aircraft are investigated, although the latter category is now virtually non-existent. Positions are given by the Georef system, a worldwide RAF system of grid squares, each designated by a four-letter code. They can be found on the En Route Charts published by the RAF and available to the public from the address on page 130. Positions in latitude and longitude are converted into a code of four letters and four numbers. In the example shown, aircraft Friendly 1234 is at 58N 02W (MKPP0000). It is thus possible to listen to interceptions and plot their progress!

The USAF equivalent to STCICS is GHFS, the Global HF System, which divides the world into 14 Zones. It was known until recently as GCCS, the Global Command and Control System, but the command and control function has been downgraded with the relaxation in superpower relations. The English base is at Croughton (first syllable pronounced as in 'crowd') in Northamptonshire, call-sign 'Croughton Radio'. Its primary frequency is 11176kHZ, sometimes referred to as 'Triple One Upper'. This is a common GHFS frequency used also by Incirlik in Turkey and Ascension Island, among others, and they too can be monitored under good reception conditions. The most frequent users are the transports of Air Mobility Command, giving details of loads and unserviceabilities to their destinations or ops centres. The latter are sometimes designated by a code name such as 'Phantom Ops', the European Airlift Control Centre at Ramstein, Germany, or 'Falcon Ops' at Torrejon, Spain.

When an aircraft crew wish to call an Airlift Command Centre they often use the blanket call-sign 'Mainsail' to alert GHFS stations that a phone patch is required. The ground station will respond only if the aircraft signal is reasonably strong and clear. It is not uncommon for Croughton to have several aircraft 'queuing' for phone patches, so there are a number of back-up frequencies available. Many of the calls involve met information known as 'Metro' (pronounced 'Mee-tro'). Aircrew may offer PIREPS, pilot reports of weather conditions encountered en route. This can be useful because the aircraft's serial number and type are usually quoted as well as its tactical call-sign if one is in use. Capsule messages can also be heard, periodically updating operation instructions to transport aircraft.

GHFS channels are interrupted frequently by Air Combat Command

**Right** *An example of aircraft positioning using the Georef system. Aircraft Friendly 1234 is at 58N 02W (MKPP0000).*

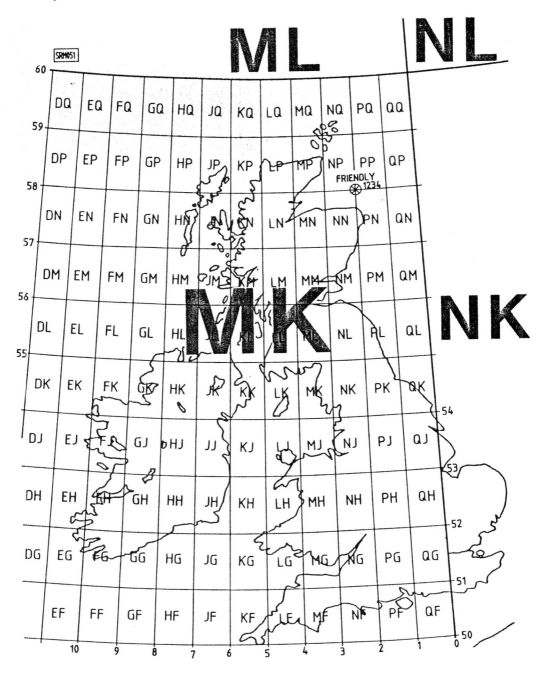

'Foxtrot' routine mission status broadcasts, known as 'Skybird' after the blanket call-sign for ACC ground stations. Part of the former Strategic Air Command (SAC) fail-safe system, now incorporated in ACC, they test communications between aircraft, ground stations and missile silos. Should the US ever have been involved in a nuclear exchange the 'go code' would have been transmitted via this network. Consisting of a string of alpha-numerics, these coded messages have been going out on HF since at least the early 1960s. The ground stations' initial call to all SAC aircraft, 'Skyking, Skyking, do not answer, do not answer', will be familiar to regular HF listeners.

The broadcasts on GHFS are repeats of those going out on the former SAC's own group of frequencies, known as 'Giant Talk'. A basic form of security is the use of a channel designator such as 'Sierra 391', rather than the actual frequency. As with many military HF frequencies, they can be 'dead' for long periods. Ground stations employ imaginative call-signs that are changed daily, examples being 'Acidman', 'Chipmouse', 'Big Daddy' and 'Red Cedar'. Another system is used by the US Air Force in Europe (USAFE, pronounced 'You-safe-ee'), which enables tactical aircraft to remain in contact with base while on practice missions as far afield as the North of Scotland.

The other major HF network is the Canadian Military Aeronautical Communication System (MACS). Once easy to monitor in the UK, Lahr Military has now closed down since the RCAF withdrawal from Germany, but Trenton in Ontario and St John's in Newfoundland can be heard at times. Not specifically aeronautical is the 'Mystic Star' network, controlled from Andrews Air Force Base, which enables the US President, other VIPs and high-ranking officers to maintain contact with Washington DC. Over 600 separate HF frequencies are available and many of the conversations are scrambled or consist of encoded messages. The US Navy has its own HF net, which often involves

aircraft as well as ships. US Coast Guard aircraft can sometimes be heard over the Eastern Seaboard of the USA talking to their bases. Other miscellaneous users of the HF band include anti-drug-running aircraft and the so-called Hurricane Hunters tracking storms.

The call-signs employed by military aircraft take many forms. Most common for RAF aircraft until recently was the tri-graph, eg ABC12. However, most first-line aircraft have adopted an alpha-numeric system, usually changed every 24 hours, examples being 8JL06, a Tornado, and F5G20, a Puma. The first two characters are always a letter/number or number/letter sequence, while the third character is always a letter, and the three together are known as the call-sign root. The last two characters are the mission identifier and are always numbers allocated at random. If a flight of aircraft is operating the same mission, ie in formation, an additional suffix letter is used.

Another style resembles the USAF tactical call-sign ( for example Carbon Two, a Tornado). One of the reasons for the change was a clash with the ICAO three-letter code allocations. On one confusing occasion in which I was involved, an RAF Tristar, SAU14, was identified by the London computer as a Saudi Airways Tristar. The RAF decided to fall in line with the ICAO system and registered a number of three-letter prefixes for training units, examples being VYT and CWL (Valley and Cranwell respectively). More are listed in Appendix 6.

RAF Air Support Command use 'Ascot' as a prefix, the aircraft type and unit or base being identified as in the following examples, individual call-signs being numbered sequentially from the round figure quoted: 4000 – Hercules, RAF Lyneham; 5000 – Hercules, RAF Lyneham; 7500–7749 BAe 125 of 32 Squadron, Northolt; 9200–9399 – VC10, Lyneham. Individual call-signs, eg 'Ascot 1609', are known as Task numbers.

'Rafair' is another prefix of long standing, used for transit purposes or overseas operations. Some RAF units have special call-signs reserved for formation flights; these include 'Isis' Formation (Oxford University Air Squadron) and 'Haggis' Formation for East Lothian UAS. RAF Valley Hawks sometimes use 'Cobra' or 'Python' Formation as well as 'Jester' and 'Viper', instructors' call-signs inspired by the film *Top Gun*! References to a 'four-ship' mean that there are four aircraft in the formation. Two Wessex helicopters were recently heard using 'Goat' Formation, a reference to the squadron's official badge, which incorporates a goat in the design. The USAF and US Army make considerable use of so-called tactical call-signs such as 'Foster' 15, the number being the pilot's personal designation, but there are frequent anomalies, an example being 'Tail Pipe Delta', an SR-71. These prefixes are changed periodically, although having said that there are many that have been retained for years, and some are included in Appendix 6.

When a formation is involved, the leader will handle all voice communications with the ground. To find out how many aircraft are in the flight, listen for a frequency change and count each aircraft checking in on the new channel. 'Shark 21 Flight, check', '2!', '3!', '4!', etc. The same procedure is used for all formations, whether they be military or civil. Air Mobility Command transports generally use the aircraft serial, referred to as the 'tail number', prefixed by 'Reach'. However, since Operation 'Desert Shield' alpha-numeric codes have been employed as well, eg 'Reach' 7M8RH. On occasion the suffix has represented a particular exercise, eg 'FL' for Flintlock and 'RF' for Reforger. The US Navy is another alpha-numeric user, Navy 6 Golf 086 for example, the first two characters often referring to the code painted on the aircraft.

Other foreign air forces use self-evident prefixes such as Danish, Saudi, etc. 'Aussie' identifies the Royal Australian Air Force

*The tower at RAF Leeming, a wartime building topped with a modern Visual Control Room (S. G. Jones).*

and 'Kiwi' the Royal New Zealand Air Force; the Greeks use 'Hellenic Air Force', but the Norwegians hide behind 'Juliet Whiskey'. French Air Force transport aircraft often use 'Cotam', the initials of this arm of the Air Force, while the French Navy uses 'FMN' or sometimes 'France Marine'. 'Mission' and up to four figures is a NATO prefix frequently used by German military aircraft as well as those of other air forces, including the RAF.

# Chapter 18

# Air band radios

In the early days of air band radios back in the 1960s, there were only two or three types available. The variety then grew steadily, prices came down and some were miniaturised to true pocket size. Manufacturers came and went, some to obscurity, others to the more lucrative field of two-way communications equipment. Today the potential purchaser is faced with a bewildering selection of sets from around £15 up to well over £900. It is also a fact that performance is not always proportional to price.

I do not intend to give a *Which?* magazine type of survey on the best to buy as I have not had the opportunity to test all those listed. Nor have I included all the cheap models stocked by various High Street outlets; some of these are excellent, but beware of those that claim to cover the air band but stop at 135 or even 130MHz, thus depriving you of the upper section of the band, which extends up to 137MHz.

The major drawback with all the cheaper receivers is the absence of an accurate tuning facility, so you are never quite sure to which frequency you are tuned until you have listened for a while. Some radios cover the entire air band with a 1-inch scale and if, say, 124.2 is tuned, transmissions on the adjacent frequencies of 124.0, 124.05, 124.10 and 124.15, and 124.25, 124.30, 124.35 and so on, may be picked up as well. They are not usually as loud as the primary frequency being monitored, but are annoying and confusing, particularly when a powerful transmission from a nearer source swamps the aircraft in which you are interested. A longer scale makes tuning easier but has no effect on the lack of discrimination.

We now move on to the realm of synthesised receivers controlled by microprocessors. The required frequency is keyed in and displayed digitally on an LCD display (similar to a pocket calculator), overlaps with adjacent frequencies being virtually eliminated. These sets are known colloquially as 'scanners' and specific frequencies can be stored in a memory maintained by a separate battery or an EEPROM (Electronically Erasable Programmable Read-Only Memory) when the radio is switched off. Some scanners are able to store up to 1,000 channels, divided into 10 memory banks for easier management. In scanning mode the radio scans through them continuously, only stopping when a transmission is received and resuming the scan when it ceases. Use of the 'Delay' button will enable the reply to be heard as well, assuming that this comes almost immediately. If 'Hold' is selected the scan will stop at the first active frequency and stay there until 'Scan' is pressed again. You can also 'lock out' certain frequencies that transmit continuously, such as Volmet and ATIS.

Many scanners are designed as base stations (desk-top models) and are not easily portable, while others are hand-held portables that tend to 'eat' batteries. Investment in rechargeable batteries and a transformer for home use is obviously desirable. The former are now usually supplied with the set as standard, along with a mains charger. It is a good idea to obtain a second rechargeable battery pack so that the two can be alternated; life between charges is only a few hours. The more expensive sets are advertised as communications receivers because they are able to monitor far more than merely aviation messages. It all depends on whether you wish to listen to bus and taxi drivers, the gas board and the many other users of the public service bands, as well as marine and other bands.

The ideal set for the aviation enthusiast receives 108 to 137MHz and 225 to 400MHz in 25kHz steps. However, 12.5kHz steps are useful for some offset carriers (see below) and some consideration should be given to the 8.33kHz spacing described below when buying a new set, in order to cover possible developments. These frequency ranges take in both the civil and military air bands. Some receivers claim to do this but leave gaps, so it is essential to make a careful study of the set's capabilities before deciding which one to purchase. Advice from existing owners is also an advantage, as all sets have their own little peculiarities.

There are theoretically 760 channels in the communications (COM) section of the civil air band, comprising 118.0 to 136.975 inclusive. In the UK most of the spacings are 50kHz, ie 118.10, 118.15, etc. Many of the intervening 25kHz frequencies, eg 118.125, 118.175 and 118.225, remain as yet unallocated, often because they are already in use over Europe and their range has to be protected from interference by other stations. A crisis is looming in civil VHF frequency allocations because of increasing traffic and the new ATC sectors required to control it.

In September 1994 an ICAO regional air navigation meeting in Vienna concluded that the 8.33kHz AM voice system is the only practicable solution that can be implemented within a short time scale. Not all European countries are experiencing frequency congestion at present, but it is likely to spread gradually to most of the region over the next five years. The strategy is to implement the 8.33 mode in a progressive way. Initially, 8.33 channel spacing will be introduced in the core area of Europe – southern United Kingdom, Benelux, Germany, France, Switzerland, Austria and northern Italy – where the problem is most noticeable. The initial phase is scheduled to begin in 1998 and implementation will be extended to other areas in the 2000–2003 period.

The implications of the change are considerable, bearing in mind the confusion caused by recent allocations of new frequencies when the upper limit of the air band was increased from 136 to 137MHz. Some eastern European airliners were unable to contact British ATC centres and had to revert to back-up channels below 136. From the air band enthusiast's point of view, most older scanners are not capable of tuning at 8.33 intervals, but such steps are standard in new-model receivers coming on to the market. Perhaps it will not be necessary in Britain's skies as there are several other proposals under discussion to relieve the shortage of frequencies. They include persuading the Ministry of Defence to release the 225–230MHz portion of the military air band for civil use and doing the same thing with NATO to take over the 380–399.975MHz military sub-band. A further possibility is the reallocation of the 410–430MHz sub-band currently in use for military airfield ground operations. Whatever happens, any 8.33 allocations are likely to be restricted to stations controlling high-level civil traffic.

Most of the en route control frequencies are transmitted from up to four remote locations to render the coverage as wide as possible. To eliminate the characteristic screech, known as a heterodyne, when more than one station transmits simultaneously, an offset carrier system is used. The offsets are ±5kHz for a two-carrier system, ±7.5kHz and 0kHz for a three-carrier, and ±7.5kHz and ±2.5kHz for a four-carrier system. Therefore, where the sensitivity of the receiver allows, reception may be improved by tuning the set slightly higher or lower than the published frequency.

There are a great number of features on

**Left** *AOR AR 8000, the current top-of-the-range scanner* (AOR UK Ltd).

**Above** *Yupiteru VT-125, a dedicated air band scanner* (James Newell, via Air Supply).

today's radios and it is important to find out exactly what is or is not included in the purchase price. Some require separate aerials, others power supplies and battery chargers. All the specialised dealers hold stocks of accessories, such as aerials, headphones, earpieces, spare crystals and assorted plugs, leads and adaptors.

As has been stated before, VHF reception is 'quasi-line of sight', so the higher the

**Above** *Left to right – Yupiteru MVT 7100, WIN 108, VT-125, MVT 7000, Nevada MS 100 desk-top scanner and VT-225 in foreground* (Air Supply).

**Left** *Steepletone dial-tuned air band receivers* (Air Supply).

aerial the better the result. If the usual telescopic aerial or rubber antenna supplied with the set proves inadequate, a remote antenna can be purchased, or an aerial can be made very cheaply at home.

Ron Bishop of the Ulster Aviation Society has kindly supplied me with details of how to do this. He writes: 'A simple radio aerial can be made from a piece of rod or wire whose length is a simple fraction (one-quarter or one-half) of the wavelength you want and orientated the same way that the signal is polarised. For VHF air band, quarter-wave is 50–60cm (20–24in) and the orientation is vertical. If you have a place at home where you do a lot of listening it is worth rigging up a more permanent half-wave dipole costing about 50p, which will substantially improve reception, particularly with the cheaper sets.

'Get two pieces of metal rod or stiff wire, each a quarter-wave long. Fix them end to end on a small block of wood or other insulator, with a gap of about 4cm between the two ends. Attach the central core of a piece of coaxial cable to the upper element and the screening (braiding) wire to the lower element. TV aerial coaxial cable will do, but UR43 cable from an electronics shop matches the impedance of the set much better. At the set end, fit the appropriate connector (BNC or mini-jack) and plug it into the aerial socket of the set. Experience shows that more sophisticated aerials are not necessarily more effective.'

A wide variety of commercial aerials are available. Richard McLachlan of Lowe Electronics at Matlock covers the basic types as follows: 'The man who needs to do some head-scratching is the man who can hear the aircraft OK but can only just hear the ground station in the background noise. In this case an improvement somewhere could make all the difference. If the whip aerial supplied with the receiver is all that is being used, an outside aerial on the chimney is definitely a good thing! If you already have an outside aerial – which must, of course, be a proper air band aerial rather than a TV or FM aerial – raising it another 10 feet helps. Improvements can also be made in the coaxial cable used to connect aerial to receiver. If by re-routing it you can shorten it, great, but if you can't get it any shorter than about 40ft, consider using UR67 coaxial cable – expensive, but offering much lower losses than cheaper cable.

'For VHF air band it would be hard to beat the ground plane type of aerial, and Lowe's own LAB can be recommended. The LAB is a vertical folded dipole aerial with four radial elements, each around 18in long, protruding from the base at right angles. Because it is designed for air band use, it will give better performance on air band than almost any other aerial available, including wideband types designed for general use with scanners. Ideally it should be mounted as high as possible in the clear, but is still capable of good results if left swinging from a rafter in your loft!

'However, if you wish to listen to military UHF as well as civil VHF, an aerial is needed that will cover the whole range from 100 to 500MHz. The professionals use a discone aerial for this purpose, and Lowe stocks a good range of them. Although looking like a demented hedgehog, they are the only simple aerial to work over a wide frequency range and the performance is first class.

'As all signals in the VHF air band are vertically polarised, mobile operation is quite straightforward since a vertical whip aerial is easy to fix and use. For quick fitting to a vehicle a magnetic mount is useful. Lowe's most popular whip aerial for the air band listener is the MG125B. Reasonably priced, it consists of a complete whip, magnetic mounting base, cable and fitted plug.'

Newcomers to air band listening are recommended to buy one of the inexpensive sets first to familiarise themselves with what is being said and its meaning. When hooked on air band (and it doesn't take very long!), one can move on to a more ambitious receiver. Second-hand models are often advertised in the aviation and radio magazines, and many dealers offer a good selection of trade-ins. It can be argued, however, that right from the start an investment in a proper air band scanner is desirable. This avoids the shortcomings of cheap sets already described. As ever, it all depends on money!

A further method of improving reception is a pre-amplifier (usually abbreviated to pre-amp), which fits between the antenna and the receiver on a hand-held model or inside the case of a base station. The device boosts the received signals and feeds them into the receiver. Results can vary but it may be possible to receive, say, the ground transmissions from a distant airport that were previously audible only as 'noise'.

The performance of some scanners can be boosted by computer control. An example is the AR3000A, which, with the aid of ACEPAC-3 software obtainable from AOR (UK) Ltd, can be run from an IBM-compatible computer and a standard serial lead. By exploiting the memory capabilities of the computer, more memory banks can be programmed and, if required, they can be uploaded to the AR3000A's internal memory for subsequent use without the computer. An 'activity count' mode is available where you can set the scanner searching a given bank of memory channels with the programme performing a percentage count of the activity on each. This can be for virtually any period you like and a printed report is supplied at the end! This is very useful for assessing the listening possibilities of particular air band frequencies. These are just a couple of useful functions – external computer control gives virtually unlimited flexibility.

Those with access to the Internet will find an almost infinite range of aviation information, including new frequencies and procedures discovered by enthusiasts and unusual visiting aircraft, often with advance warning of their arrival. Questions can be addressed to the professionals; for example, Houston Airport, Texas, has its own air traffic control web site!

## ATC computer simulations

Air band enthusiasts may want to go a stage further and learn some of the techniques of ATC themselves via a computer simulation. Probably the earliest available was designed for the Spectrum 128K about eight years ago. Known as Heathrow Air Traffic Control (it also featured a simulation for Amsterdam/ Schiphol), the tape was useful in its day, but by the standards of modern personal computers is very primitive. One of the best was TRACON II by the US company Wesson International, but regrettably Wesson have moved upwards into professional ATC simulation and no longer market the program. A second-hand copy is

certainly worth seeking out. TRACON is an acronym for Terminal Radar Control, a system on which the London CCF is modelled. The areas on the disk are Los Angeles, San Francisco, Chicago, Miami and Boston. A supplementary disk by the Edinburgh firm Gemini International includes a number of UK TMAs, including Scottish, London, Manchester, Belfast, Birmingham and Jersey. Unfortunately the procedures and traffic are still basically North American, which somewhat detracts from its value.

One can choose the scenario, from rate of traffic to be handled and weather conditions to pilot competency ('perfect' to 'lousy'!) as well as several other factors, and a mark is awarded at the end of each exercise. R/T is done by a synthesised voice in conjunction with commands via mouse or keyboard. My main criticism with these simulations is that one is expected to handle far more airspace and traffic than a real-life TRACON controller. Having said that, I recommend that anyone seriously contemplating a career in ATC through the CAA selection process, etc, should try to master these simulations. The training in basic radar vectoring, separation and level allocation is invaluable in laying the foundation for proper training with professional simulators, then real aircraft. Apart from this, your aptitude or lack of it will soon become obvious! BAO's Tower features airport control at several US locations and is said to be very realistic.

For the flying side of the operation there are many excellent flight simulators available, including Airbus A320. One of the best is SubLogic's Flight Assignment ATP. It is basically a Boeing 737-200 (747, 767, Airbus and even Shorts 360 as well, but the differences are cosmetic rather than real). Navigation is by VOR rather than INS, but you certainly learn how to do it, complete with all the ATC communications. Some programmes can be run in conjunction with ATC simulations. There are several good fast jet simulations, the best perhaps being Tornado. However, some of the products on offer are little more than 'shoot 'em up' games rather than serious simulations. The software is not cheap and one needs time and dedication to digest the comprehensive manuals and achieve reasonable competency. R. C. Simulations and Transair Pilot Shop have a wide range of ATC and flight simulators; their addresses are on page 126.

## A selection of air band radios currently available

NB Prices may vary as currencies fluctuate.

**Price range: £15–£35**
*Pye TRO170; Realistic Jetstream; Steepletone SAB9; Steepletone SAB11; Stewart 2087* – All have VHF air band and AM/FM broadcast bands.

**Price range: £75–£100**
*Commtel 202S* – Hand-held scanner. VHF air band, partial UHF air band.
*Steepletone MRB8* – VHF air band/AM and FM broadcast/Marine band.

**Price range: £105–£150**
*Bearcat UBC120XLT* – Hand-held scanner. VHF air band, etc.
*Bearcat UBC860XLT* – Desk-top scanner. VHF air band, etc.
*Netset PRO-44* – Hand-held scanner. VHF air band, etc.
*Realistic PRO-63* – Hand-held scanner. VHF air band, etc.
*WIN 108* – Hand-held scanner. VHF air band only.

**Price range: £150–£200**
*Bearcat UBC220XLT* – Hand-held scanner. VHF air band, etc.
*Netset PRO-46* – Hand-held scanner. VHF air band, etc.
*Realistic PRO-29* – Hand-held scanner. VHF air band, etc.
*VT-125* – Hand-held scanner. VHF air band, etc.

**Price range: £200–£250**
*Commtel 204* – Hand-held scanner. VHF and UHF air band, etc.

*Netset PRO-2032* – Desk-top scanner. VHF air band, etc.
*Realistic PRO-26* – Hand-held scanner. VHF and UHF air band, etc.
*Trident TR-980* – Hand-held scanner. VHF and UHF air band, etc.
*Yupiteru VT-225* – Hand-held scanner. VHF and UHF air band, etc.

**Price range: £250–£300**
*Alinco DJ-X1D* – Hand-held scanner. VHF and UHF air band, etc.
*AR 2700* – Hand-held scanner. VHF and UHF air band, etc.
*Trident TR-2400* – Hand-held scanner. VHF and UHF air band, etc.
*Yupiteru MVT-7100* – Hand-held scanner. VHF and UHF air band, etc.

**Price range: £300–£350**
*AR 1500EX* – Hand-held scanner. VHF and UHF air band, HF SSB, etc.
*Bearcat UBC9000XLT* – Desk-top scanner. VHF and UHF air band, etc.
*Welz WS-1000* – Hand-held scanner. VHF and UHF air band, etc.
*Yupiteru MVT-7100EX* – Hand-held scanner. VHF and UHF air band, etc.
*Yupiteru MVT-8000* – Desk-top scanner. VHF and UHF air band, etc.

**Price range: £350–£400**
*AOR AR-8000* – Hand-held scanner. VHF and UHF air band plus HF SSB, etc.

**Price range: Around £950**
*AR 3000A* – Desk-top scanner. VHF and UHF air band, HF SSB and much more, including computer control.

For some details of shortwave/HF sets, see Chapter 9.

## Principal air band and hobby suppliers

Air Supply, 97 High Street, Yeadon, Leeds LS19 7TA. Tel 0113 250 9581.
Alan Hooker Radio Communications, 42 Nether Hall Road, Doncaster DN1 2PZ. Tel 01302 325690.

ASK Electronics Ltd, 248/250 Tottenham Court Road, London W1P 9AD. Tel 0171 637 0353/0590.

The Aviation Hobby Centre, 1st Floor, Main Terminal Building, Birmingham Airport, Birmingham B26 3QJ. Tel 0121 782 2112.

The Aviation Hobby Shop, 4 Horton Parade, Horton Road, West Drayton, Middlesex UB7 8EA. Tel 01895 442123.

The Aviation Shop, Spectator Terraces, Manchester Airport M22 5SZ. Tel 0161 499 0303.

BUCHair Shop, Spectators Terrace, Gatwick Airport.

Flightdeck, The Airband Shop, 192 Wilmslow Road, Heald Green, Cheadle, Cheshire SK8 3BH. Tel 0161 499 9350.

Haydon Communications, 132 High Street, Edgware, Middlesex HA8 7EL. Tel 0181 951 5781/2.

Javiation, Carlton Works, Carlton Street, Bradford, West Yorkshire BD7 1DA. Tel 01274 732146.

Lowe Electronics Ltd, Chesterfield Road, Matlock, Derbyshire DE4 5LE. Tel 01629 580800.

152 High Street, Chesterton, Cambridge CB4 1NL. Tel 01223 311230.

117 Beaumont Road, St Judes, Plymouth PL1 4PQ. Tel 01752 257224.

79/81 Gloucester Road, Patchway, Bristol BS12 5QJ. Tel 0117 931 5263

High Street, Handcross, West Sussex. Tel 01444 400786

12 Station Road, Crossgates, Leeds. Tel 0113 232 8400

Unit 18B, Airport Industrial Estate, Newcastle NE3 2EF. Tel 0191 214 5424.

Martin Lynch, 140–2 Northfield Avenue, Ealing, London W13 9SB. Tel 0181 566 1120.

Multicom 2000, Radio House, 37 Cunningham Way, Eaton Socon, St Neots, Huntingdon, Cambs PE19 3NJ. Tel 01480 406770.

Nevada Communications, Mail Order: 189 London Road, North End, Portsmouth, Hants PO2 9AE. Tel 01705 662145. Showrooms: 1A Munster Road, Portsmouth PO2 9BS.

Northern Shortwave Centre, Blackdyke Road, Kingstown Industrial Estate, Carlisle, Cumbria CA3 0PJ. Tel 01228 590011.

Raycom Communications Systems Ltd, International House, 963 Wolverhampton Road, Oldbury, Warley, West Midlands B69 4RJ. Tel 021 552 0073.

R. C. Simulations, The Hangars, Bristol Airport, Lulsgate, Bristol BS19 3EP. Tel 01275 474550.

The Short Wave Centre, 95 Colindeep Lane, Sprowston, Norwich NR7 8EQ. Tel 0603 788281.

The Short Wave Shop, 18 Fairmile Road, Christchurch, Dorset BH23 2LJ. Tel 01202 490099.

SRP Trading, Mail Order: Unit 20, Nash Works, Forge Lane, Belbroughton, Nr Stourbridge, Worcs. Tel 01562 730672. Shop: 1686 Bristol Road South, Rednall, Birmingham B45 9TZ. Tel 0121 460 1581.

Stewart Aviation, PO Box 7, Market Harborough, Leics LE16 8AW. Tel 01536 770962.

Touchdown Aviation Shops, 4 Tavistock Road, West Drayton, Middlesex UB7 7QT. Tel 01895 434510

5A Mill Street, Mildenhall, Suffolk IP28 7DN. Tel 01638 515971/718811.

Transair Pilot Shop, West Entrance, Fairoaks Airport, Chobham, Nr Woking, Surrey GU24 8HU. Tel 01276 858533

50a Cambridge Street, London SW1V 4QQ. Tel 0171 976 6787.

Waters & Stanton Electronics, Warren House, 22 Main Road, Hockley, Essex SS5 4QS. Tel 01702 206835/204965

12 North Street, Hornchurch, Essex RM11 1QX. Tel 01708 444765.

World Radio Centre, Adam Bede High Tech Centre, Derby Road, Wirksworth, Derbyshire DE4 4BG. Tel 01629 825926.

# Chapter 19

# Charts and related documents

Almost as important as an air band radio itself is the acquisition of a set of radio navigation charts. These are essential to build up an overall picture of the UK airways system and the positions of its beacons and reporting points.

En route charts are published by three organisations for the United Kingdom: the Royal Air Force, British Airways Aerad and Jeppesen. The USAF produces its own charts, but these are more difficult to obtain. Obviously the information on the different charts is fundamentally the same, but the presentation differs quite considerably. There is also some variation in the areas covered and only the RAF charts for the UK show the whole of the British Isles on one sheet. This is separated into two charts, 411H for high altitudes and 412S/412N for low altitudes. The low-level charts are drawn to an approximate scale of 14 nautical miles to the inch, while the high-level ones are about 28 miles to the inch.

British Airways Aerad charts for the UK cover high altitude (H109/108) at a scale of 30 miles to the inch. They feature most of Western Europe except Spain and the North of Scotland. Low altitude is covered by EUR 1/2 to a scale of about 17 miles to the inch, as far north as Edinburgh and including parts of France and Germany. Chart EUR 3 shows the rest of Scotland.

Aerad also produce a wide range of other related documentation, including Standard Instrument Departure charts, Standard Arrival charts and airport and apron layouts. Aerad's other important publication, much prized by enthusiasts, is the *Europe and Middle East Supplement*, one of a set of four that cover the entire world. It is a soft-backed book packed with information on airports, including their aids, runway lengths and radio frequencies.

The other chart publisher is Jeppesen Sanderson Inc, an American firm whose main distributor in the UK is CSE Aviation at Oxford Airport. Two sheets cover the UK, one for high level (Ref E(HI)3 and 4) and one for low altitudes (Ref E(LO)1 and 2). The company also produces a wide variety of associated data, the most important of which are airport approach charts.

The CAA distributes a wide range of charts, including topographical maps, which are of only limited use to air band listeners, SIDs and STARs. The CAA is of course responsible for the UK Aeronautical Information Publication, known as the *Air Pilot*. This is really the bible for aviators in Britain's airspace but it is an extremely bulky document, divided into several volumes. Of particular interest are the AGA, COM and RAC sections, detailing aerodromes and ground aids, communications and ATC rules and procedures. It is, needless to say, very expensive and incorporates a regular updating and amendments service. All airport briefing offices have copies and you may be able to get permission to 'browse', especially if you have some bona fide aviation connection, such as being a flying club member.

At first sight, radio navigation charts are a perplexing welter of intersecting lines, symbols and figures, but, like any other

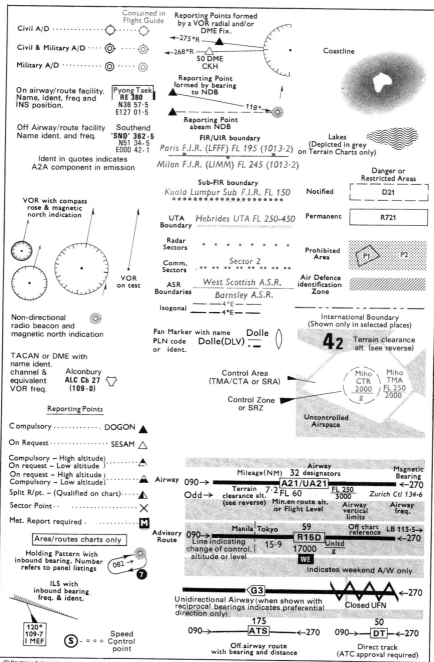

**Left** *Radio navigation chart legend* (British Airways Aerad).

**Below** *Section of an Aerad chart for Southern England* (British Airways Aerad).

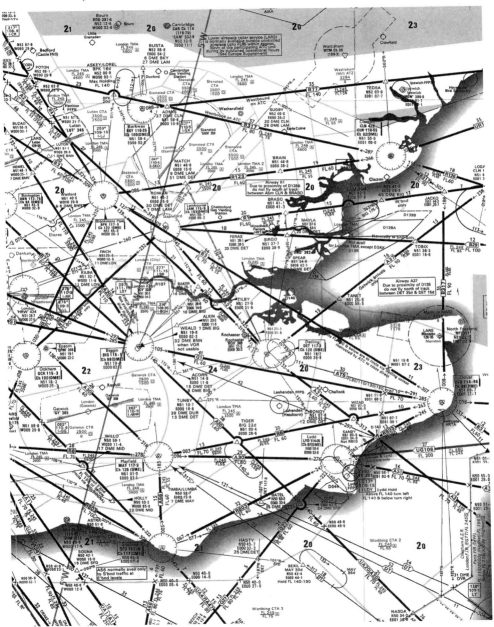

maps, there is a key and with a few minutes' study they become logical. The radio beacons are identified by name and a three- or two-letter abbreviation. Wallasey, for example, may be referred to by ATC and aircraft as Wallasey or Whiskey Alpha Lima. The frequency of 114.1MHz on which the beacon radiates will be adjacent to its name on the chart. Also shown on the chart are the names of airways, their bearings in both directions, the distances in nautical miles between reporting points, the heights of their bases and upper limits, and the lowest available cruising levels.

Many of the charts are stocked by air band radio suppliers, but they can also be purchased direct from the publishers or their agents at the addresses listed below. Out-of-date charts are often available from airshow stalls and air band dealers. Provided that they are not too old, say more than 12 months, they can still be very useful.

# Suppliers of airways charts, flight guides and related material

*British Airways*, Aerad Customer Services, Aerad House, PO Box 10, Heathrow Airport, Hounslow, Middlesex TW6 2JA.

*CSE Aviation Ltd* (Jeppesen Agents), Oxford Airport, Kidlington, Oxford OX5 1RA.

*Royal Air Force*, No 1 Aeronautical Documents Unit, RAF Northolt, West End Road, Ruislip, Middlesex HA4 6NG.

*Civil Aviation Authority*, Printing and Publishing, Greville House, 37 Gratton Road, Cheltenham, Gloucestershire GL50 2BN.

*Air Supply*, 97 High Street, Yeadon, Leeds LS19 7TA.

*Interproducts*, 8 Abbot Street, Perth PH2 0EB.

*Pooleys*, Elstree Aerodrome, Elstree, Hertfordshire WD6 3AW.
Wycombe Airpark (Booker), Marlow, Buckinghamshire SL7 3DR.
16 New Quebec Street, London W1.

*Transair Pilot Shop*, West Entrance, Fairoaks Airport, Chobham, Nr Woking, Surrey GU24 8HX.
50a Cambridge Street, London SW1V 4QQ.

# Appendix 1

# Beacons and reporting points

The centrelines of airways are marked by navigational beacons positioned at strategic intervals, such as where the airway changes direction or where one or more of them intersect. Airway beacons are mostly VORs with a co-located DME to indicate range, but some, Lichfield being a major example, are NDBs. With the aid of a radio navigation chart it is easy to find those nearest to your home.

Many of the reporting points are not beacons at all, but hypothetical positions formed where certain radials from two VORs intersect, and are given a standard five-letter name. This may be related to a geographical feature such as the name of a nearby town, and is often a distortion of the real name to arrive at five letters. Examples are LAMMA south of Edinburgh (Lammermuir Hills), SAPCO near Sapcote in Leicestershire and REXAM near Wrexham. Others are purely artificial but often imaginative, derived from sources such as children's comics (BEENO, DANDI, TOPPA) and naval heroes (BENBO, HARDY, DRAKE). ROBIN in the East Midlands commemorates Robin Hood, and GRICE in Scotland a retired Supervisor at Scottish ACC!

As described in Chapter 6, each major airport has one or more terminal beacons. Well known are the LBA at Leeds, the NEW at Newcastle and the GOW at Glasgow. Even if the destination is not mentioned in transmissions while on airways, such routeings as Pole Hill-LBA will immediately give a clue. 'A standard WILLO Arrival Runway 26 Right' will identify the destination as Gatwick.

Similarly, knowledge of the runway designators at various airports will be useful. Since the trend is to a single main runway with an instrument approach at both ends, with perhaps one subsidiary for light aircraft, one can soon become familiar with those in one's home area. Examples are Birmingham 15/33, Heathrow 09L & 09R/27L & 27R, Glasgow 05/23 and Manchester 06/24.

A, B, G, and R signify regional air routes, prefixed by U when in the upper airspace (ie above FL245). Regional area navigation routes are designated UH (Link Route to Polar Tracks), UL (Link Route to oceanic airspace), UN and UP. SL is a Supersonic Link Route and UT a non-regional area nav route. Suffixes N, S, E and W indicate compass points; for example, R1N and R1S are parallel one-way routes. Advisory Routes are suffixed D.

# Beacons and reporting points

VOR frequencies are in MHz and NDBs in kHz.

| Name | Frequency | Code | Type | Approximate location |
|------|-----------|------|------|----------------------|
| Aberdeen | 114.3 | ADN | VOR | Scottish East Coast |
| Abdal | | | RP | Bristol CTA-Bristol, Cardiff and Filton arrivals |
| Absil | | | RP | UA37 |
| Acorn | | | RP | London TMA-Gatwick SIDs |
| Admis | | | RP | B317-R77, etc |
| Adson | | | RP | R37 |
| Agano | | | RP | Channel Islands CTZ |
| Akelo | | | RP | Supersonic Link Routes |
| Alcon | | | RP | UL613-UP6 |
| Alice | | | RP | Aberdeen HMRs |
| Alkin | | | RP | Holding pattern for London/City |
| Alloy | | | RP | East Shetland Basin |
| Alvin | | | RP | G1 E of Brecon |
| Alwyn | | | RP | East Shetland Basin |
| Amlet | | | RP | Manchester TMA |
| Amman | | | RP | On G1 in South Wales |
| Angel | | | RP | UL74, North Sea |
| Angla | | | RP | Channel Islands CTZ |
| Angus | | | RP | B2/B226 intersection |
| Annet | | | RP | UL722, London/France boundary |
| Apple | | | RP | UN590 |
| Artha | | | RP | Manchester TMA |
| Arvok | | | RP | Eire, junction of UB2/UA38 |
| Askey | | | RP | London TMA-Stansted/Luton STARs |
| Askil | | | RP | UT7 |
| Aspen | | | RP | UR24, S of Bournemouth |
| Aspit | | | RP | UN582 |
| Astra | | | RP | Holding pattern for Gatwick |
| Avant | | | RP | Gatwick STARs |
| Bagin | | | RP | Gatwick STARs |
| Bakat | | | RP | SL4 SOTA |
| Baker | | | RP | B4, SE England |
| Bakur | | | RP | UA38, London/Dublin boundary |
| Balis | | | RP | Aberdeen HMRs |
| Banba | | | RP | UB10, London/Dublin boundary |
| Bandu | | | RP | SOTA |
| Banlo | | | RP | SL2 SOTA |
| Barix | | | RP | SL3-SL5-SOTA |
| Barkway | 116.25 | BKY | VOR | Nuthampstead, Herts |
| Bartn | | | RP | Manchester TMA |
| Basav | | | RP | R77-UA37-UR77 |
| Baset | | | RP | UG1, Wiltshire |
| Batel | | | RP | London TMA |
| Batsu | | | RP | UN611 |

| Name | Frequency | Code | Type | Approximate location |
|------|-----------|------|------|----------------------|
| Bedfo | | | RP | Near Bedford on UB4 |
| Beech | | | RP | SE England on G27 |
| Beeno | | | RP | North Sea, junction of UB1/UB7 |
| Begas | | | RP | SOTA |
| Begda | | | RP | UB39-UW502 |
| Begto | | | RP | Heathrow STARs |
| Beket | | | RP | W5D S of Sumburgh |
| Belfast | 117.2 | BEL | VOR | East of Belfast City |
| Benbecula | 114.4 | BEN | VOR | Outer Hebrides |
| Benbo | | | RP | On A1 south of Worthing |
| Bendy | | | RP | Solent CTA |
| Benix | | | RP | Channel Islands CTZ |
| Benty | | | RP | Sumburgh Heli Routes |
| Berek | | | RP | Gatwick STARs |
| Berry Head | 112.7 | BHD | VOR | On A25 near Torquay |
| Besop | | | RP | UB2-UP6 |
| Bevav | | | RP | Channel Islands CTZ |
| Bewli | | | RP | Heathrow and Gatwick STARs |
| Bexil | | | RP | Gatwick STARs |
| BIA | 339 | | NDB | Bournemouth Airport |
| Biggin | 115.1 | BIG | VOR | SE holding pattern for Heathrow |
| BIR | 406 | | NDB | Birmingham Locator Beacon |
| Birch | | | RP | Birmingham STARs |
| Biski | | | RP | SL1-SL7-SOTA |
| Blaca | | | RP | Edinburgh/Glasgow STARs |
| Blufa | | | RP | UB1 Amsterdam/London boundary |
| Blusy | | | RP | UB29 Amsterdam/London boundary |
| Bodam | | | RP | Sumburgh Helicopter Routes |
| Bogna | | | RP | Heathrow/Gatwick SIDs |
| Bonby | | | RP | W3D-Inverness |
| Bondy | | | RP | SE of London TMA |
| Borma | | | RP | UN582-UN611 |
| Borve | | | RP | Aberdeen HMRs |
| Bovingdon | 113.75 | BNN | VOR | NW holding pattern for Heathrow |
| Bovva | | | RP | Heathrow hold when Bovingdon out of service |
| Bowes | | | RP | North Yorkshire |
| Boyne | | | RP | W911D, Irish Sea |
| BPL | 420 | | NDB | Blackpool Airport |
| Brain | | | RP | R123 Essex |
| Braso | | | RP | R1 E of Lambourne |
| Brecon | 117.45 | BCN | VOR | A25/G1, South Wales |
| BRI | 380 | | NDB | Bristol Airport |
| Brill | | | RP | Channel Islands CTZ |
| Bripo | | | RP | R8 Bridport, Dorset |
| Brookmans Park | 117.5 | BPK | VOR | North of London |
| Bruce | | | RP | W910D SE of Tiree |
| Bryna | | | RP | UW502 |
| Buken | | | RP | North Yorkshire |

| Name | Frequency | Code | Type | Approximate location |
|------|-----------|------|------|----------------------|
| Burnham | 421 | BUR | NDB | Berkshire |
| Burni | | | RP | Manchester/Liverpool STARs |
| Busta | | | RP | London TMA |
| Buzad | | | RP | A20/B3, SE Midlands |
| Calda | | | RP | NW of Manchester |
| Cambo | | | RP | UR72, London/France boundary |
| Carnane | 366.5 | CAR | NDB | Isle of Man on DG27 |
| Casel | | | RP | Isle of Man Arrivals |
| Caval | | | RP | UR168, London/France boundary |
| CDF | 388.5 | | NDB | Cardiff Airport |
| Cedar | | | RP | Birmingham SIDs/STARs |
| Chanl | | | RP | En route hold inbound Gatwick |
| Chase | | | RP | Holding pattern for Birmingham |
| Chelt | | | RP | B39-UA251-UB39 |
| Chiltern | 277 | CHT | NDB | North of Heathrow |
| Chinn | | | RP | NE Scotland on W3D |
| Chubb | | | RP | Channel Islands CTZ |
| CL | 328 | | NDB | Carlisle Airport |
| Clacton | 114.55 | CLN | VOR | Essex coast |
| Cliff | | | RP | English Channel off SE coast |
| Clonmel | 387 | CML | NDB | Eire, junction of UB2/UG1 |
| Clyde | | | RP | Scottish TMA |
| Codey | | | RP | Farnborough |
| Colre | | | RP | Londonderry holding pattern |
| Compton | 114.35 | CPT | VOR | Berkshire |
| Conga | | | RP | Manchester SIDs |
| Cork | 114.6 | CRK | VOR | Eire |
| Costa | 111.8 | COA | VOR | Belgian coast on B29 |
| Cowly | | | RP | South Midlands |
| Crewe | | | RP | Birmingham STARs |
| Croft | | | RP | North of Manchester TMA |
| CT | 363.5 | | NDB | Coventry Airport |
| Cumbo | | | RP | Edinburgh SIDs |
| Cumri | | | RP | UN863 |
| Daley | | | RP | Manchester/Liverpool STARs |
| Dalky | | | RP | B2, Shannon/Scottish boundary |
| Dandi | | | RP | UA37, Scottish/Copenhagen boundary |
| Daventry | 116.4 | DTY | VOR | South Midlands |
| Davot | | | RP | W3D, S of Inverness |
| Dawly | | | RP | UA25/UR8 off Devon coast |
| Dayne | | | RP | Holding pattern for Manchester |
| Dean Cross | 115.2 | DCS | VOR | West of Carlisle |
| Degos | | | RP | UN517 |
| Denby | | | RP | S of Pole Hill VOR |
| Depso | | | RP | East Shetland Basin |
| Detling | 117.3 | DET | VOR | Kent |
| Dieppe | 115.8 | DPE | VOR | French coast on A1E |
| Didel | | | RP | UA29-UL3 |
| Dikas | | | RP | UA25-UB40-UG1 |

| Name | Frequency | Code | Type | Approximate location |
|------|-----------|------|------|----------------------|
| DND | 394 | | NDB | Dundee Airport |
| Dogga | | | RP | UB1/UB13, North Sea |
| Donna | | | RP | Heathrow STARs |
| Dover | 114.95 | DVR | VOR | Near town |
| Downi | | | RP | Aberdeen |
| Drake | | | RP | English Channel on UA34 |
| Dublin | 114.9 | DUB | VOR | North of city |
| Duffy | | | RP | N Ireland |
| Dumba | | | RP | Scottish TMA |
| Dundrum | | | RP | South of Belfast VOR on B2 |
| Dunlo | | | RP | UN570-UP6 |
| Eagle | | | RP | Biggin Hill instrument approach |
| Easin | | | RP | Southern North Sea HMRs |
| Eastwood | | | RP | Holding pattern for Gatwick |
| Ebony | | | RP | Birmingham STARs |
| EDN | 341 | | NDB | Edinburgh Airport |
| Eider | | | RP | East Shetland Basin |
| Elder | | | RP | UR1W/UA34W, Isle of Wight |
| Eldin | | | RP | B5-UB5 |
| Elgar | | | RP | N863-UN863 |
| Emjee | | | RP | UW534 |
| EMW | 393 | | NDB | East Midlands Airport |
| Epsom | 316 | EPM | NDB | Holding pattern for Heathrow when Ockham out of service |
| Ering | | | RP | B29-UB29 |
| Ermin | | | RP | Plymouth Instrument Approaches |
| Ernan | | | RP | UN550-UN560 |
| Evrin | | | RP | UG1, Dublin/London boundary |
| Eskdo | | | RP | Edinburgh STARs |
| Evrin | | | RP | UL1-UP4 |
| EX | 337 | | NDB | Exeter Airport |
| Exmor | | | RP | North Devon |
| Fambo | | | RP | North Sea on UB13 |
| Fawbo | | | RP | UA34W, London/France boundary of London TMA |
| Ferit | | | RP | UB29-UM14 |
| Finch | | | RP | A20 |
| Findo | | | RP | SW of Perth |
| Finma | | | RP | A47/B71 |
| Fiwud | | | RP | W2D |
| Flame | | | RP | East Shetland Basin |
| Forty | | | RP | NE of Aberdeen |
| Foyle | | | RP | Scottish TMA |
| Frank | | | RP | London TMA-Northolt SIDs |
| Fulma | | | RP | W958D NW of Turnberry |
| Fyner | | | RP | En route hold W910D |
| Gabad | | | RP | North Sea E of Clacton |
| Gapli | | | RP | UR8-SOTA |
| Gater | | | RP | NE England |

| Name | Frequency | Code | Type | Approximate location |
|------|-----------|------|------|---------------------|
| Gavel | | | RP | W5D S of Sumburgh |
| Gelki | | | RP | Belfast TMA |
| Gerpa | | | RP | Northern Radar Advisory Area |
| Gibso | | | RP | R8, south coast |
| Gilda | | | RP | UG39-UM14-UR12 |
| Giper | | | RP | SOTA |
| Girva | | | RP | Glasgow STARs |
| Glasgow | 115.4 | GOW | VOR | Airport holding pattern |
| Glesk | | | RP | S of Aberdeen on B22 |
| Goles | | | RP | UB1-UB105 |
| Gonut | | | RP | UH70 |
| Goodwood | 114.75 | GWC | VOR | South coast on UR25 |
| Gordo | | | RP | UR23, Scottish/Copenhagen boundary |
| Gorse | | | RP | Aberdeen Heli Routes |
| Grice | | | RP | North boundary of Scottish TMA |
| GST | 331 | | NDB | Gloucestershire Airport |
| Guernsey | 109.4 | GUR | VOR | On UR1 |
| Gulda | | | RP | Channel Islands CTZ |
| Gunpa | | | RP | UP19, UP610 |
| Gunso | | | RP | SOTA |
| Halif | | | RP | UL613-UN590-UR4 |
| Hanky | | | RP | LTMA entry fix to PEPIS Hold |
| Hardy | | | RP | S of Seaford on A1 |
| Hasty | | | RP | SE England on W8 |
| Hawke | | | RP | A1-G27-UA1-UG27 |
| Haydo | | | RP | SE England |
| Hazel | | | RP | UR8/UR1W, southern England |
| HB | 420 | | NDB | Belfast/City Airport |
| HBR | 350.5 | | NDB | Humberside Airport |
| Heidi | | | RP | A2/W1 intersection |
| Hemel | | | RP | Herts |
| Henton | 433.5 | HEN | NDB | Bucks |
| Heron | | | RP | Off Ayrshire coast |
| Hilly | | | RP | Heathrow STARs |
| Holly | | | RP | Gatwick STARs |
| Honiley | 113.65 | HON | VOR | S of Birmingham airport |
| HRW | 424 | | NDB | London Heathrow |
| Inlak | | | RP | UB29-UB39 |
| Inverness | 109.2 | INS | VOR | Inverness Airport |
| Isle of Man | 112.2 | IOM | VOR | Southern tip of island |
| Izack | | | RP | Sumburgh Heli Routes |
| Jacko | | | RP | W1/R1, North Sea |
| Jersey | 112.2 | JSY | VOR | Near airport |
| Karil | | | RP | Channel Islands CTZ |
| Karno | | | RP | On N862 |
| Kathy | | | RP | UR1/UA34W, English Channel |
| Kelly | | | RP | Isle of Man Arrivals |
| Kenet | | | RP | In Wiltshire, on G1 |
| Kenuk | | | RP | SOTA |

| Name | Frequency | Code | Type | Approximate location |
|------|-----------|------|------|----------------------|
| Kidli | | | RP | Oxford area A34-B321, etc |
| Killiney | 378 | KLY | NDB | UB2/UR14, near Dublin |
| Kindr | | | RP | Woodford |
| Kippa | | | RP | UB105 |
| Kirby | | | RP | Manchester TMA |
| Kista | | | RP | W3D, SW of Sumburgh |
| Klonn | | | RP | B2D, Scottish/Stavanger boundary |
| Kokal | | | RP | W3D |
| Koksy | 114.5 | KOK | VOR | Belgian coast on G1 |
| Koley | | | RP | UL7, North Sea |
| Komik | | | RP | UA37-UB105 |
| Konan | | | RP | UG1, Amsterdam/London boundary |
| Lager | | | RP | Southern North Sea |
| Lakey | | | RP | Manchester/Liverpool STARs |
| Lambourne | 115.6 | LAM | VOR | NE holding pattern for Heathrow |
| Lamma | | | RP | S of Edinburgh on UR38 |
| Lanak | | | RP | Glasgow STARs |
| Lands End | 114.2 | LND | VOR | Lands End |
| Larck | | | RP | Gatwick STARs |
| Lasno | | | RP | SOTA |
| LBA | 402.5 | | NDB | Leeds/Bradford Airport |
| LCY | 322 | | NDB | London/City Airport |
| Lerak | | | RP | Channel Islands CTR |
| Lesta | | | RP | B4-UB4-UP6 |
| Libba | | | RP | Scottish TMA |
| Lichfield | 545 | LIC | NDB | Midlands junction of A1E/W37 |
| Liffy | | LFY | RP | B1, London/Dublin boundary |
| Lindy | | | RP | UG1, W of Woodley VOR |
| Lirki | | | RP | UH71 |
| Lisbo | | | RP | Lisburn, NI |
| Lizad | | | RP | UG4, France/London boundary |
| Logan | | | RP | North Sea off Essex |
| Lomon | | | RP | Scottish TMA boundary |
| Lonam | | | RP | North Sea London/Amsterdam boundary |
| Lorel | | | RP | London TMA |
| Lovel | | | RP | Manchester TMA |
| LPL | 349.5 | | NDB | Liverpool Airport |
| Lucco | | | RP | Gatwick STARs |
| Lumba | | | RP | Gatwick STARs |
| Lusit | | | RP | Channel Islands CTZ |
| Luton | 345 | LUT | NDB | Holding pattern for airport |
| Lynas | | | RP | Anglesey on B1 |
| Lyneham | 282 | LA | NDB | Wiltshire |
| Machrihanish | 116.0 | MAC | VOR | Kintyre, Scotland |
| Madli | | | RP | UN863 |
| Magee | | | RP | Holding pattern for Belfast/City |
| Malby | | | RP | G1 between BCN and Kenet |
| Manchester | 113.55 | MCT | VOR | On the airport |
| Mango | | | RP | UR12, Essex |

| *Name* | *Frequency* | *Code* | *Type* | *Approximate location* |
|--------|-------------|--------|--------|------------------------|
| Manta | | | RP | Channel Islands CTZ |
| Maple | | | RP | Birmingham SIDs/STARs |
| Margo | | | RP | South Scotland |
| Match | | | RP | R123, Essex |
| Matik | | | RP | UN615 |
| Matim | | | RP | Supersonic Link Routes |
| Mayfield | 117.9 | MAY | VOR | W17/A34E/A30, Sussex |
| Mayla | | | RP | London TMA |
| Merly | | | RP | UB40/UB37, Bristol Channel |
| Midhurst | 114.0 | MID | VOR | Sussex |
| Milde | | | RP | Southern North Sea |
| Mimbi | | | RP | G1 Brize inbounds |
| Minqi | | | RP | Channel Islands CTZ |
| Mirsa | | | RP | Hold for Manchester/Liverpool |
| Mocha | | | RP | W5D, S of Sumburgh |
| Molak | | | RP | UN545 |
| Monty | | | RP | Mid Wales on A25 |
| Moody | | | RP | Plymouth |
| Moray | | | RP | W4D, SE of Wick |
| Morby | | | RP | Morecambe Bay |
| Morka | | | RP | UA1 |
| Moris | | | RP | UW501 |
| Mulit | | | RP | UL74, North Sea |
| Mulla | | | RP | Irish Sea on B2 |
| Mynda | | | RP | N863-UN863 |
| Nadir | | | RP | B2D, North Sea |
| Nakid | | | RP | UG4-UR116 |
| Nanti | | | RP | Liverpool SIDs |
| Nasda | | | RP | London/City, Stansted and Luton STARs |
| Nedul | | | RP | Solent CTA arrivals |
| Nelsa | | | RP | B4-Leeds Bradford SIDs |
| Nevil | | | RP | London/Brest boundary on W8 |
| Nevis | | | RP | UN585-UN601 |
| Newcastle | 114.25 | NEW | VOR | Newcastle Airport and en route aid |
| New Galloway | 399 | NGY | NDB | South Scotland |
| Nicky | 117.4 | NIK | VOR | Belgian coast |
| Nigit | | | RP | UB39-UP2 |
| Nipit | | | RP | UN537 |
| Niton | | | RP | Mid-Wales on A25 |
| Nobal | | | RP | Aberdeen area |
| Nokin | | | RP | Manchester/Liverpool STARs |
| Norbo | | | RP | Glasgow SIDs |
| Norda | | | RP | Channel Islands CTZ |
| Norla | | | RP | UR37, Dublin/London boundary |
| Norry | | | RP | Berkshire |
| Norse | | | RP | E Shetland Basin Route Structure |
| Northlight | | | RP | Irish Sea on W927D |
| Numpo | | | RP | UA25-UP2 |
| Ockham | 115.3 | OCK | VOR | SW holding pattern for Heathrow |

| Name | Frequency | Code | Type | Approximate location |
|------|-----------|------|------|----------------------|
| Olgud | | | RP | Gatwick/Heathrow STARs |
| Olive | | | RP | Birmingham STARs |
| Olker | | | RP | UN614 Hebrides UCA |
| Olney | | | RP | A20/W1 intersection |
| Omimi | | | RP | UN510-UN520-SOTA |
| Omoko | | | RP | SL1-SL5-SOTA |
| Orist | | | RP | UR24, London/France boundary |
| Ormer | | | RP | Channel Islands CTZ |
| Ortac | | | RP | UR1/UR14, France/London boundary |
| Orvik | | | RP | UG11, SE of Sumburgh |
| Oskal | | | RP | UN611 |
| Ospol | | | RP | G27 |
| Ottringham | 113.9 | OTR | VOR | Humberside on B1/UB1 |
| Oysta | | | RP | Channel Islands CTZ |
| Pampus | 117.8 | PAM | VOR | Holland |
| Pavlo | | | RP | UL3-UR72 |
| Pepis | | | RP | R41-W5-UR41 |
| Perch | | | RP | Channel Islands CTZ |
| Perth | 110.4 | PTH | VOR | Central Scotland |
| Phili | | | RP | UN502 |
| Pikey | | | RP | Channel Islands CTR |
| Pikod | | | RP | UN502 |
| Plymo | | | RP | En route hold (UR8) |
| Pole Hill | 112.1 | POL | VOR | N of Manchester on A1 |
| Pompi | | | RP | Gatwick STARs |
| Porla | | | RP | UW501-UW502 |
| Poton | | | RP | B4/W1, S Midlands |
| Radno | | | RP | South Wales on W39 |
| Ranok | | | RP | W3D, N of Glasgow |
| Ratka | | | RP | UN510-UN520-SOTA |
| Rebka | | | RP | Channel Islands CTR |
| Redfa | | | RP | R1N, London/Amsterdam boundary |
| Remsi | | | RP | UP6-UR4 |
| Replo | | | RP | UA37-UG39 |
| Rexam | | | RP | Wrexham on A25 |
| Ribel | | | RP | N of Pole Hill VOR |
| Rilka | | | RP | Supersonic Link Routes |
| Ringa | | | RP | Irish Sea on B2 |
| Robbo | | | RP | Scottish TMA |
| Robin | | | RP | North Midlands B4-R3 |
| Ronak | | | RP | UN602-UN611 |
| Ronar | | | RP | A1D, NW Scotland |
| Rosun | | | RP | Manchester/Liverpool STARs |
| Rowan | | | RP | London TMA |
| Royce | | | RP | UW534-UW550 |
| Rupas | | | RP | Channel Islands CTZ |
| Rusel | | | RP | Aberdeen Heli Routes |
| Saber | | | RP | Heathrow/Stansted/Luton STARs |
| Sadal | | | RP | London/City STARs |

| Name | Frequency | Code | Type | Approximate location |
|---|---|---|---|---|
| St Abbs | 112.5 | SAB | VOR | Scottish East coast on UR23 |
| St Inglevert | 387 | ING | NDB | French coast |
| Salco | | | RP | UR1, France/London boundary |
| Samon | | | RP | UL7, North Sea |
| Sandy | | | RP | South coast on A2 |
| Sapco | | | RP | A2/W37, Midlands |
| Sapot | | | RP | W3D |
| Seaford | 117.0 | SFD | VOR | South coast on A2 |
| Setel | | | RP | North-west of Pole Hill VOR |
| Shannon | 113.3 | SHA | VOR | SW Eire |
| Shapp | | | RP | Cumbria on B4 |
| Shark | | | RP | Holding pattern Jersey Airport |
| Shrub | | | RP | Aberdeen |
| Sider | | | RP | UG11, Reykjavik/Scottish |
| Silok | | | RP | Sumburgh Heli Routes |
| Silva | | | RP | UR4, North Sea |
| Singa | | | RP | UW538 |
| Sirgo | | | RP | UB29-UR12 |
| Sitet | | | RP | UA34, France/London boundary |
| Sitko | | | RP | B1-UA37-UB1 |
| Skate | | | RP | UL74, North Sea |
| Skery | | | RP | On A25 S of BHD |
| Skeso | | | RP | UA25, France/London boundary |
| Slany | | | RP | G1 Dublin/London boundary |
| Slyda | | | RP | Irish Sea on B3 |
| Smoki | | | RP | NE Scotland on W4D |
| SND | 362.5 | | NDB | Southend Airport |
| Sotol | | | RP | UR4 |
| Southampton | 113.35 | SAM | VOR | On airport |
| Spear | | | RP | Kent |
| Spike | | | RP | Aberdeen area |
| Spijkerboor | 113.3 | SPY | VOR | Holland |
| Sprat | | | RP | UA37 |
| Stafa | | | RP | Eccleshall, Staffs |
| Stira | | | RP | Edinburgh/Glasgow STARs |
| Stoat | | | RP | UL613-UM14 |
| Stock | | | RP | Manchester/Liverpool SIDs |
| Stornoway | 115.1 | STN | VOR | Outer Hebrides |
| Strumble | 113.1 | STU | VOR | Coast of SW Wales |
| Sudby | | | RP | London TMA |
| Supap | | | RP | UN502-UR72 |
| Swany | | | RP | Bristol Channel on UB40 |
| Tabit | | | RP | N553D-W958D |
| Tadex | | | RP | UN551-UN560 |
| Takas | | | RP | UN490-SOTA |
| Talla | 113.8 | TLA | VOR | South Scotland |
| Tanet | | | RP | Kent on A37 |
| Taran | | | RP | Heathrow/Gatwick STARs |
| Tartn | | | RP | Edinburgh STARs |

| Name | Frequency | Code | Type | Approximate location |
|------|-----------|------|------|----------------------|
| Tawny | | | RP | Heathrow hold when Lambourne out of service |
| TD | 347.5 | | NDB | Teesside Airport |
| Tebra | | | RP | UG39 |
| Tedsa | | | RP | R77-UR77 |
| Telba | | | RP | UA25E/UA34, S of Crewe |
| Tesgo | | | RP | SL4-SL7 |
| Thred | | | RP | R41-Solent CTA arrivals |
| Tiger | | | RP | En route hold, Heathrow STARs |
| Tilby | | | RP | London TMA |
| Timba | | | RP | Gatwick STARs |
| Tirik | | | RP | Aberdeen area |
| Tiver | | | RP | UA25-UL3 |
| Tivli | | | RP | UG4, Dublin/London boundary |
| Tobix | | | RP | Gatwick STARs |
| Tolka | | | RP | UW39, Dublin/London boundary |
| Tomin | | | RP | Aberdeen Heli Routes |
| Tompo | | | RP | Exeter IAPs |
| Toppa | | | RP | UL74, London/Amsterdam boundary |
| Tovri | | | RP | UN491 (SOTA) |
| Trent | 115.7 | TNT | VOR | North Midlands |
| Tripo | | | RP | R1, Essex coast |
| Trout | | | RP | B2D NE of Aberdeen |
| Tubot | | | RP | UR23, North Sea |
| Tunby | | | RP | London TMA |
| Tunel | | | RP | London TMA |
| Tunit | | | RP | Channel Islands CTZ |
| Turnberry | 117.5 | TRN | VOR | S of Prestwick |
| Tuton | | | RP | UN863 |
| Tweed | | | RP | Edinburgh STARs |
| Tysti | | | RP | Aberdeen area |
| Ullap | | | RP | W6D-Inverness |
| Unrok | | | RP | UN502-UT7 |
| Upton | | | RP | On B1, Yorkshire |
| Vanin | | | RP | Isle of Man Arrivals (W2D) |
| Vatry | | | RP | R14-UR14 |
| Vesta | 116.6 | VES | VOR | Denmark |
| Veule | | | RP | A1, French coast |
| Waffu | | | RP | A47-G27-UA47-UG27 |
| Wallasey | 114.1 | WAL | VOR | Wirral Peninsula |
| Weald | | | RP | Heathrow hold when Biggin out of service |
| Welin | | | RP | Herts |
| Westcott | 335 | WCO | NDB | South Midlands |
| Wesul | | | RP | UM14-UR1 |
| Whitegate | 368.5 | WHI | NDB | Manchester TMA, SW corner |
| Wick | 113.6 | WIK | VOR | Northern Scotland |
| Willo | | | RP | Holding pattern for Gatwick |
| Wizad | | | RP | West of Dover on W17 |
| Wobun | | | RP | South Midlands |

| *Name* | *Frequency* | *Code* | *Type* | *Approximate location* |
|--------|-------------|--------|--------|------------------------|
| Woodley | 352 | WOD | NDB | G1/A1E, Berkshire |
| Worthing | | WOR | RP | South coast |
| Wotan | | | RP | G1 |

## The Morse Code

| | | | | | |
|---|---|---|---|---|---|
| A | • — | J | • — — — | S | • • • |
| B | — • • • | K | — • — | T | — |
| C | — • — • | L | • — • • | U | • • — |
| D | — • • | M | — — | V | • • • — |
| E | • | N | — • | W | • — — |
| F | • • — • | O | — — — | X | — • • — |
| G | — — • | P | • — — • | Y | — • — — |
| H | • • • • | Q | — — • — | Z | — — • • |
| I | • • | R | • — • | | |

# Appendix 2

# Airways frequency allocation

| Airways | Area | Call-sign | Freq | Remarks (Freq as directed) |
|---|---|---|---|---|
| A1 | Turnberry–N54°30' | Scottish Control | { 126.25<br>123.375 | **0700–2145**<br>**2145–0700** |
| | N54°30'–Abm Stafford | | | |
| | *above FL195* | London Control | { 131.05 | 129.1, 134.425, 136.2 |
| | *at or below FL195* | Manchester Control | 126.65 | 124.2, 130.925 |
| | Abm Stafford–Birmingham | | | |
| | *above FL195* | London Control | 131.125 | 129.2 |
| | *at or below FL195* | Manchester Control | 124.2 | 130.925, 128.475 |
| | Birmingham–Abm Westcott | London Control | 130.925 | 127.875, 130.075, 133.975 |
| | S of COWLY–FIR Boundary | London Control | 131.125 | 129.2, 135.325, 136.6, 132.45 |
| A2 | Between TALLA and N54°30' | Scottish Control | 123.375 | |
| | Between N54°30' and Abm Lichfield | | | |
| | *above FL195* | London Control | 131.05 | 134.425, 136.2 |
| | *at or below FL195* | Manchester Control | 124.2 | 130.925 |
| | Between Abm Lichfield and Abm Birmingham | | | |
| | *above FL195* | London Control | 127.1 | 127.875, 131.25, 134.425 |
| | *at or below FL195* | Manchester Control | 124.2 | |
| | Between Abm Birmingham and Brookmans Park | London Control | 130.925 | 127.875, 133.975, 134.425 |
| | S of Brookmans Park to FIR Boundary | London Control | 128.425 | 132.45, 132.6, 134.45 |
| A20 | FIR Boundary–Biggin | London Control | 128.425 | 134.45 |
| | Biggin–Abm Birmingham | London Control | 127.1 | 127.875, 131.125, 132.45 |
| | Abm Birmingham–Pole Hill | | | |
| | *above FL195* | London Control | 131.05 | 129.1, 136.2 |
| | *at or below FL195* | Manchester Control | 124.2 | 126.65 |
| A25 | Dean Cross–N54°30' | Scottish Control | { 123.375<br>126.25 | **0700–2145**<br>**2145–0700** |
| | N54°30'–MONTY | | | |
| | *above FL195* | London Control | 135.575 | 129.1, 134.425, 126.875 |
| | *at or below FL195* | Manchester Control | 125.1 | 136.4 |
| | MONTY–Cardiff | London Control | 133.6 | |
| | Cardiff–N50°00' | London Control | 126.075 | 127.7, 135.25 |
| | N50°00'–Southern Boundary of Channel Islands Zone | Ch Isles Control | 125.2 | |

| Airways | Area | Call-sign | Freq | Remarks (Freq as directed) |
|---|---|---|---|---|
| **A30** | Within London FIR | *London Control* | 128.425 | |
| **A34** | Within London FIR | *London Control* | 135.325 | 124.275, 131.125 |
| **A37** | Entire Route | *London Control* | 129.6 | 136.55, 118.475, 133.45, 133.525 |
| **A47** | Pole Hill–Lichfield | | | |
| | *above FL195* | *London Control* | 131.05 | 129.1, 136.2 |
| | *at or below FL195* | *Manchester Control* | 126.65 | 124.2 |
| | Lichfield–Abm Birmingham | | | |
| | *above FL195* | *London Control* | 131.125 | |
| | *at or below FL195* | *Manchester Control* | 124.2 | 128.475 |
| | Abm Birmingham–Abm Westcott | *London Control* | 131.125 | 129.2 |
| | COWLY–FIR Boundary | *London Control* | 130.925 | 132.45, 132.325, 127.875, 136.6, 133.075, 133.975 |
| **A56** | Within London FIR | *London Control* | 135.325 | 136.6 |
| **B1** | W of Wallasey | | | |
| | *above FL195* | *London Control* | 135.575 | 128.05, 134.425 |
| | *at or below FL195* | *Manchester Control* | 125.1 | |
| | Wallasey–BARTN | | | |
| | *above FL195* | *London Control* | 135.575 | 134.425 |
| | *at or below FL195* | *Manchester Control* | 125.1 | |
| | BARTN–Ottringham | | | |
| | *above FL195* | *London Control* | 131.05 | 136.2, 126.875 |
| | *at or below FL195* | *Manchester Control* | 126.65 | 124.2 |
| | E of Ottringham | *London Control* | 126.775 | 128.125, 121.325, 136.275, 133.525 |
| **B2** | N of TMA | *Scottish Control* | 124.5 | |
| | S of TMA | *Scottish Control* | 123.775 | |
| **B3** | Belfast–W005°00′ | *Scottish Control* | 123.775 | |
| | W005°00′–Wallasey | | | |
| | *above FL195* | *London Control* | 135.575 | 129.1 |
| | *at or below FL195* | *Manchester Control* | 125.1 | |
| | Wallasey–STAFA | | | |
| | *above FL195* | *London Control* | 135.575 | 129.1 |
| | *at or below FL195* | *Manchester Control* | 125.1 | 124.2 |
| | STAFA–Abm Birmingham | | | |
| | *above FL195* | *London Control* | 131.125 | 121.025, 129.2 |
| | *at or below FL195* | *Manchester Control* | 125.1 | 124.2, 130.925 |
| | Abm Birmingham–Brookmans Park | | | |
| | *above FL195* | *London Control* | 127.1 | 127.875, 131.125 |
| | *at or below FL195* | *London Control* | 124.925 | 133.975 |
| | S of Brookmans Park–FIR Boundary | *London Control* | 128.425 | 134.9, 132.6, 132.45 |
| **B4** | Detling–Brookmans Park | *London Control* | 128.425 | 134.45, 132.6, 132.45 |
| | Brookmans Park–Abm Birmingham | *London Control* | 127.1 | 131.125, 127.875 |
| | Abm Birmingham–ROBIN | | | |
| | *above FL195* | *London Control* | 127.1 | 124.925 |
| | *at or below FL195* | *Manchester Control* | 124.2 | 126.65 |
| | ROBIN–Pole Hill | | | |
| | *above FL195* | *London Control* | 131.05 | 136.2, 126.875 |

| Airways | Area | Call-sign | Freq | Remarks (Freq as directed) |
|---|---|---|---|---|
| | *at or below FL195*<br>Pole Hill–N54°30′ | *Manchester Control* | 124.2 | 126.65 |
| | *above FL195* | *London Control* | 131.05 | 126.875, 136.2 |
| | *at or below FL195* | *Manchester Control* | 126.65 | 124.2 |
| | N54°30′–GRICE | *Scottish Control* | 123.375 | |
| B5 | ELDIN–DOGGA | *London Control* | 126.775 | 121.325, 128.125, 133.525, 134.25 |
| | NEW–TALLA | *Scottish Control* | 124.5 | |
| B11 | Within London FIR | *London Control* | 135.05 | 129.425, 136.6 |
| B29 | Within London FIR | *London Control* | 129.6 | 136.55, 118.475, 127.95 |
| B39 | MALBY–RADNO | *London Control* | 133.6 | 136.4 |
| | RADNO–TOLKA | *London Control* | 135.575 | 136.875 |
| B53 | Entire Route | | | |
| | *above FL195* | *London Control* | 135.575 | 129.1, 126.875 |
| | *at or below FL195* | *Manchester Control* | 125.1 | 124.2 |
| B226 | Entire Route | *Scottish Control* | 124.5 | |
| B317 | Daventry–Abm Barkway | *London Control* | 127.1<br>130.925 | 127.875, 131.125 |
| | Abm Barkway–20N of Dover | *London Control* | 129.6 | 136.55, 127.95, 118.475, 133.45, 133.525, 136.275 |
| | 20N of Dover–Dover | *London Control* | 134.9 | 128.425, 134.45 |
| B321 | Honiley–Abm Westcott | *London Control* | 131.125 | 129.2 |
| | Abm Westcott–5N of Compton | *London Control* | 132.45<br>130.925 | 133.6 |
| | 5N of Compton–PEPIS | *London Control* | 132.45 | 135.05, 127.7 |
| G1 | W of Brecon | *London Control* | 133.6 | 129.375, 136.4 |
| | Brecon–Abm Compton | *London Control* | 133.6 | 134.75, 136.4 |
| | E of Abm Compton–FIR Boundary | *London Control* | 132.45<br>134.9 | 132.6, 128.425 |
| G27 | N of N50°00′ | *London Control* | 128.425 | 136.6, 134.9, 135.05 |
| R1 | ORTAC–Midhurst | *London Control* | 135.05 | 132.3, 124.275, 129.425 |
| | Midhurst–FIR Boundary | *London Control* | 129.6<br>132.45 | 118.475, 136.55, 133.45, 133.525 |
| R3 | Wallasey–ROBIN | | | |
| | *above FL195* | *London Control* | 135.575 | 126.875, 134.425 |
| | *at or below FL195* | *Manchester Control* | 125.1 | 124.2 |
| R8 | BRIPO–Southampton | *London Control* | 126.075 | 124.425, 135.05 |
| | Southampton–Midhurst | *London Control* | 135.325 | 129.425, 136.6 |
| | Midhurst–Dover | *London Control* | 134.9 | 128.425, 134.45 |
| R12 | Entire Route | *London Control* | 132.45<br>129.6 | 136.55, 133.45, 133.525, 118.475 |
| R14 | Within London FIR | *London Control* | 133.6 | |
| R25 | Entire Route | *London Control* | 135.325 | 132.45 |
| R37 | Entire Route | *London Control* | 135.05 | 129.425, 136.6 |
| R41 | ORTAC–Southampton | *London Control* | 135.05 | 132.3, 129.425, 136.6 |
| | Southampton–Abm Compton | *London Control* | 132.45 | 132.6, 131.125, 129.2 |
| | Abm Compton–Westcott | *London Control* | 130.925 | 127.875, 133.075 |
| R84 | Entire Route | *London Control* | 135.05 | 132.3, 136.6, 129.425 |

| Airways<br>Area | | Call-sign | Freq | Remarks (Freq as directed) |
|---|---|---|---|---|
| **R126** | Entire Route | *London Control* | 135.325 | 118.475, 136.55 |
| **R803** | Entire Route | *London Control* | 135.325 | 136.6 |

## Upper ATS routes

| Airways | Area | Call-sign | Freq | Remarks (Freq as directed) |
|---|---|---|---|---|
| **UA1** | N of N54°30' | *Scottish Control* | 129.225 | |
| | N54°30'–Abm Lichfield | *London Control* | 131.05 | 129.1, 136.2, 126.875 |
| | Abm Lichfield–Abm COWLY | *London Control* | 131.125 | 133.7, 129.2 |
| | Abm COLWY–UIR Boundary | *London Control* | 135.325 | 135.425, 136.6, 127.425, 132.45 |
| **UA2** | Machrihanish–N54°30' | *Scottish Control* | 129.225 | |
| | N54°30'–TRENT | *London Control* | 131.05 | 129.1, 136.2, 126.875 |
| | TRENT–Brookmans Park | *London Control* | 127.1 | 131.125, 127.875 |
| | Brookmans Park–UIR Boundary | *London Control* | 128.425 | 132.45, 132.6, 134.45, 127.425 |
| **UA20** | Entire Route | *London Control* | 128.425 | 127.425, 134.45 |
| **UA25** | N of N54°30' | *Scottish Control* | 129.225 | |
| | N54°30'–S of Wallasey | *London Control* | 135.575 | 129.1, 134.425, 126.875 |
| | S of Wallasey–S of Brecon | *London Control* | 133.6 | 136.4 |
| | S of Brecon–UIR Boundary | *London Control* | 126.075 | 127.7, 135.25 |
| **UA29** | BAKUR–MERLY | *London Control* | 133.6 | 129.375, 136.4 |
| | MERLY–SALCO | *London Control* | 126.075 | 132.95 |
| **UA30** | Entire Route | *London Control* | 128.425 | 127.425, 135.425, 132.6 |
| **UA34** | Wallasey–TELBA | *London Control* | 135.575 | 129.1, 126.875 |
| | TELBA–Abm Woodley | *London Control* | 131.125 | 120.025, 129.2 |
| | Abm Woodley–UIR Boundary | *London Control* | 135.325 | 124.275, 127.425, 132.45, 136.6 |
| **UA37** | DANDI–Gabbard | *London Control* | 126.775 | 127.1, 128.125, 133.525 |
| | Gabbard–Detling | *London Control* | 129.6 | 133.525, 118.475, 136.6 127.425 |
| **UA47** | Daventry–Woodley | *London Control* | 131.125 | 120.025, 129.2 |
| | S of Woodley–UIR Boundary | *London Control* | 135.325 | 127.425, 135.425 |
| **UA251** | Pole Hill–TELBA | *London Control* | 131.05 | 129.1, 136.2 |
| | TELBA–EXMOR | *London Control* | 133.6 | 134.75, 136.4 |
| **UB1** | Liffey–Wallasey | *London Control* | 135.575 | 134.425, 126.875 |
| | Wallasey–Ottringham | *London Control* | 131.05 | 126.875, 129.1, 136.2 |
| | E of Ottringham | *London Control* | 126.775 | 128.125, 121.325, 133.525, 136.275 |
| **UB2** | GELKI–Perth | *Scottish Control* | 129.225 | 125.675 |
| | Perth–KLONN | *Scottish Control* | 134.775 | 133.675 |
| **UB3** | Belfast–W005°00' | *Scottish Control* | 129.225 | 125.675 |
| | W005°00'–N53°00' | *London Control* | 135.575 | 129.1 |
| | N53°00'–Brookmans Park | *London Control* | 133.7 | 120.025, 127.1, 129.2 |
| | Brookmans Park–Dover | *London Control* | 128.425 | 134.9, 127.425, 132.6 |
| **UB4** | FINDO–N54°30' | *Scottish Control* | 129.225 | |
| | N54°30'–LESTA | *London Control* | 131.05 | 134.425, 126.875, 129.1, 136.2 |

| Airways | Area | Call-sign | Freq | Remarks (Freq as directed) |
|---|---|---|---|---|
| | LESTA–Brookmans Park | *London Control* | 127.1 | 129.2, 131.125, 127.875 |
| | S of Brookmans Park–UIR Boundary | *London Control* | 128.425 | 132.45, 127.425, 134.45, 132.6 |
| **UB5** | N of FAMBO | *Scottish Control* | 134.775 | 129.225 |
| | S of FAMBO | *London Control* | 126.775 | 128.125, 133.525, 121.325, 136.275 |
| **UB10** | Within London UIR | *London Control* | 133.6 | 129.375, 136.4 |
| **UB11** | Within London UIR | *London Control* | 135.05 | 124.275, 129.425, 135.425, 136.6 |
| **UB29** | Compton–Abm Brookmans Park | *London Control* | 127.425 | 132.45, 132.6 |
| | E of Abm Brookmans Park–UIR Boundary | *London Control* | 129.6 | 133.525, 118.475, 136.275, 127.425 |
| **UB39** | Midhurst–RADNO | *London Control* | 133.6 | 127.425, 132.45 |
| | RADNO–TOLKA | *London Control* | 135.575 | 127.425 |
| **UB40** | DIKAS–SWANY | *London Control* | 133.6 | 136.4 |
| | SWANY–BANLO | *London Control* | 126.075 | 132.95 |
| **UB71** | Entire route | *London Control* | 127.425 | 134.9, 131.125, 129.2 |
| **UB105** | Within London UIR | *London Control* | 126.775 | 128.125, 133.525, 136.275, 121.325 |
| **UG1** | UIR Boundary–Abm Woodley | *London Control* | 133.6 | 129.375, 134.75 |
| | Abm Woodley–UIR Boundary | *London Control* | 134.9 | 127.425, 134.75, 128.425, 135.425 |
| **UG4** | Within London UIR | *London Control* | 126.075 | 132.95 |
| **UG11** | Within Scottish UIR | *Scottish Control* | 133.675 | 134.775 |
| **UG106** | Within London UIR | *London Control* | 134.9 | 127.425, 128.425 |
| **UH70** | Aberdeen–Wick–GONUT | *Scottish Control* | 133.675 | 134.775 |
| **UH71** | Sumburgh–LIRKI | *Scottish Control* | 133.675 | 134.775 |
| **UH73** | GRICE–Machrihanish | *Scottish Control* | 129.225 | 125.675 |
| **UL1** | W of Abm Woodley–UIR Boundary | *London Control* | 133.6 | 134.75, 136.4 |
| | E of Abm Woodley–UIR Boundary | *London Control* | 134.9 | 127.425, 135.425, 128.425 |
| **UL7** | N of SKATE | *Scottish Control* | 133.675 | 134.775 |
| | S of SKATE | *London Control* | 126.775 | 128.125 |
| **UL74** | Entire Route | *London Control* | 126.775 | 128.125, 121.325 |
| **UL722** | Entire Route | *London Control* | 126.075 | 132.95 |
| **UN862/ 863/865** | Berry Head–SKELSO/SALCO | *London Control* | 126.075 | 135.25 |
| **UR1** | ORTAC/MID to Lambourne | *London Control* | 135.05 | 124.275, 135.325, 136.6, 129.425 |
| **UR123** | Lambourne–UIR Boundary | *London Control* | 136.55 | 133.45, 118.475, 133.525, 127.425 |
| **UR4** | IOM–Pole Hill | *London Control* | 128.05 | 135.575 |
| | Pole Hill–DANDI | *London Control* | 126.775 | 128.125, 133.525 |
| **UR8** | GALPI–Southampton | *London Control* | 126.075 | 132.95, 132.6 |
| | Southampton–Midhurst | *London Control* | 135.325 | 124.275, 127.425, 135.425 |
| **UR14** | YATRY–SWANY | *London Control* | 133.6 | 131.2, 129.375, 136.4 |
| | SWANY–EXMOR | *London Control* | 126.075 | 132.6 |
| **UR23** | Glasgow–SAB | *Scottish Control* | 129.225 | 120.675 |
| | SAB–GORDO | *Scottish Control* | 133.675 | 134.775 |

| *Airways* *Area* | *Call-sign* | *Freq* | *Remarks (Freq as directed)* |
|---|---|---|---|
| UR24 ORIST–ASPEN | *London Control* | 135.325 | 129.425 |
| UR25 Entire Route | *London Control* | 135.325 | 124.275, 136.6, 135.425 |
| UR37 Southampton–Abm Midhurst | *London Control* | 135.05 | 124.725, 136.6 |
| Abm Midhurst–Dover | *London Control* | 134.9 | 124.275, 128.425, 124.725 |
| UR38 Newcastle–N57°15′ | *Scottish Control* | 134.775 | 129.225 |
| N57°15′–Stornoway | *Scottish Control* | 133.675 | 134.775 |
| UR40 GAPLI–LIZAD | *London Control* | 126.075 | 132.95 |
| UR41 ORTAC–Southampton | *London Control* | 135.05 | 129.425, 136.6 |
| Southampton–Westcott | *London Control* | 131.125 | 127.425, 120.025, 135.425 |
| UR84 ORTAC–Midhurst | *London Control* | 135.05 | 127.425, 129.425, 136.6 |
| UR126 Entire Route | *London Control* | 136.55 | 133.525, 118.475, 129.6 |
| UR168 Lands End–CAVAL | *London Control* | 126.075 | 132.95 |
| UT7 Lands End–NOTRO | *London Control* | 126.075 | 132.95 |
| NOTRO–ASKIL | Brest Control | 129.5 | |

## Lower ATS advisory routes

| | | | |
|---|---|---|---|
| A1D FIR Boundary–Stornoway | *Scottish Control* | 127.275 | |
| Stornoway–Glasgow | *Scottish Control* | 127.275 | |
| B2D Within Scottish FIR | *Scottish Control* | 131.3 | |
| G4D Within London FIR | *London Control* | 126.075 | 127.7 |
| N552D Entire Route | *Scottish Control* | 127.275 | |
| N562D Entire Route | *Scottish Control* | 127.275 | |
| N573D Entire Route | *Scottish Control* | 127.275 | |
| R8D Within London FIR | *London Control* | 132.6 | |
| W2D W of FLWUD | | | |
| *above FL195* | *London Control* | 135.575 | 129.1, 134.425 |
| *at or below FL195* | *Manchester Control* | 125.1 | |
| E of FLWUD | | | |
| *above FL195* | *London Control* | 131.05 | 134.425, 126.875, 136.2 |
| *at or below FL195* | *Manchester Control* | 126.65 | 124.2 |
| W3D S of Inverness | *Scottish Control* | 124.5 | |
| Inverness–Sumburgh | *Scottish Control* | 131.3 | |
| W4D Within Scottish FIR | *Scottish Control* | 131.3 | |
| W5D Within Scottish FIR | *Scottish Control* | 131.3 | |
| W6D Stornoway–W005°00′ | *Scottish Control* | 127.275 | |
| W005°00′–Inverness | *Scottish Control* | 131.3 | |
| W911D N of N54°30′ | *Scottish Control* | 124.5(a) | |
| S of N54°30′ | | | |
| *above FL105* | *Scottish Control* | 123.775 | |
| *at or below FL105* | *Manchester Control* | 125.1 | |
| W928D Entire Route | *Scottish Control* | 123.775 | |
| W958D Entire Route | *Scottish Control* | 127.275 | |

(a) Communications will be with *Scottish Control* on 128.5 outside the hours of operation of NRASA.

| Airways<br>Area | Call-sign | Freq | Remarks (Freq as directed) |
|---|---|---|---|

## Northern radar advisory service area

| | | | |
|---|---|---|---|
| N of W911D | *Scottish Radar* | 124.5 | |
| S of W911D | *Pennine Radar* | 128.675 | |

## Hebrides upper control area

| | | | |
|---|---|---|---|
| S of line N57 | | | |
| 30°W010°00′–TIR–N56°36′ W004°10′ | *Scottish Control* | 129.225 | 125.675 |
| N of line N57 | | | |
| 30°W010°00′–TIR–N56°36′ W004°10′ | *Scottish Control* | 133.675 | |

# Appendix 3

# VHF air band frequencies

## Frequencies of airports and airfields

*Aberdeen:* Tower: 118.1 GMC: 121.7 Approach: 120.4 Radar: 121.25/128.3 ATIS: 121.85/114.30
  Info: 135.175
*Aberporth:* AFIS: 122.15
*Alderney:* Tower: 125.35 Approach (Guernsey): 128.65
*Andrews Field:* A/G: 130.55
*Anglia Radar:* 125.275/128.925
*Ashcroft Farm:* A/G: 122.525 (by arrangement)
*Audley End:* A/G: 122.35 (by arrangement)
*Badminton:* A/G: 123.175
*Bagby:* A/G: 123.25
*Barra:* A/G: 118.075
*Barrow (Walney):* Tower: 123.2
*Barton:* A/G: 122.7
*Beccles:* A/G: 134.6
*Belfast (Aldergrove):* Tower: 118.3 GMC: 121.75 Approach/Radar: 120.0/120.9 ATIS: 128.2
*Belfast City:* Tower: 130.75 Approach: 130.85 Radar: 134.8
*Bembridge, Isle of Wight:* AFIS: 123.25
*Benbecula:* Tower/Approach: 119.2
*Benson:* Tower: 130.25 Zone: 120.9
*Beverley/Linley Hill:* A/G: 123.05
*Biggin Hill:* Tower: 134.8 Approach: 129.4 ATIS: 121.875
*Birmingham:* Tower: 118.3 GMC: 121.8 Approach: 118.05 Radar: 131.325 ATIS: 120.725
*Blackbushe:* AFIS: 122.3
*Blackpool:* Tower: 118.4 Approach/Radar: 119.95 ATIS: 121.75
*Bodmin:* A/G: 122.7
*Booker (Wycombe Air Park):* AFIS: 126.55 GMC: 121.775
*Boscombe Down:* Tower: 130.75 Radar: 126.7
*Bourn:* A/G: 129.8
*Bournemouth:* Tower: 125.6 Approach: 119.625 Radar: 118.65 ATIS: 121.95 GMC: 121.7
*Breighton:* A/G: 129.8
*Bristol (Filton):* Tower: 132.35 Approach/Radar: 122.725/127.975
*Bristol (Lulsgate):* Tower: 133.85 Approach: 128.55 Radar: 124.35 ATIS: 126.025
*Brize Norton:* Tower: 126.5 Radar: 134.3/119.0/133.75 Ops: 130.075
*Brough:* A/G: 130.55
*Bruntingthorpe:* A/G: 122.825
*Caernarfon:* A/G: 122.25
*Cambridge:* Tower: 122.2 Approach: 123.6 Radar: 130.75

*Campbeltown:* AFIS: 125.9
*Cardiff:* Tower: 125.0 Approach: 125.85 Radar: 124.1 ATIS: 119.475
*Carlisle:* Tower/Approach: 123.6
*Chivenor:* A/G: 130.2
*Chichester (Goodwood):* Tower: 120.65 Approach: 122.45
*Church Fenton:* Tower: 122.1 Approach: 126.5
*Clacton:* A/G: 135.4
*Colerne:* Tower/Approach: 122.1
*Coltishall:* Tower: 122.1 MATZ: 125.9
*Compton Abbas:* A/G: 122.7
*Coningsby:* Tower: 122.1 Approach: 120.8
*Cosford:* Tower: 118.925 GMC: 121.95
*Cottesmore:* Tower: 122.1 Approach: 130.2
*Coventry:* Tower/Approach: 119.25/124.8 Radar: 122.0 GMC: 121.7 ATIS : 126.05
*Cranfield:* Tower: 134.925 Approach/Radar: 122.85 ATIS: 121.875
*Cranwell:* Tower: 122.1 Approach: 119.375
*Cromer Micro:* A/G: 129.825
*Crowfield:* A/G: 122.775
*Crowland:* A/G: 130.1
*Culdrose:* Tower: 122.1 Approach: 134.05
*Cumbernauld:* AFIS: 120.6
*Deanland:* A/G: 129.725
*Deenethorpe:* A/G: 120.275
*Denham:* A/G: 130.725
*Derby:* A/G: 118.35
*Dublin:* Tower: 118.6 GMC: 121.8 Approach: 121.1/119.55/118.5 ATIS: 124.525
*Dundee:* Tower/Approach: 122.9
*Dunkeswell:* A/G: 123.475
*Dunsfold:* Tower: 124.325 Approach: 135.175 Radar: 122.55
*Duxford:* AFIS: 122.075 Ops: 122.675
*Eaglescott:* A/G: 123.0
*Earls Colne:* A/G: 122.425
*East Midlands:* Tower: 124.0 GMC: 121.9 Approach: 119.65 Radar: 120.125 ATIS: 128.225
*Edinburgh:* Tower: 118.7 GMC: 121.75 Approach: 121.2 Radar: 128.975 ATIS: 132.075
*Elstree:* A/G: 122.4
*Enniskillen:* (St Angelo) A/G: 123.2
*Enstone:* A/G: 129.875
*Exeter:* Tower: 119.8 Approach: 128.15 Radar: 119.05
*Fadmoor:* A/G: 123.225
*Fairoaks:* A/G: 123.425
*Falmouth Radar:* 122.1
*Farnborough:* Tower: 122.5 Approach: 134.35 PAR: 130.05 Zone: 125.25 Ops: 130.375
*Fenland:* AFIS/A/G: 122.925
*Flotta:* A/G: 122.15
*Ford:* A/G: 122.0
*Fowlmere:* A/G: 120.925
*Full Sutton:* A/G: 132.325
*Gamston:* A/G: 130.475
*Gigha Island:* A/G: 123.05
*Glasgow:* Tower: 118.8 GMC: 121.7 Approach: 119.1 Radar: 119.3/121.3 ATIS: 132.175
*Glenrothes:* A/G: 130.45

*Gloucestershire:* Tower: 122.9 Approach: 125.65 Radar: 120.975 ATIS: 127.475
*Great Yarmouth (North Denes):* Tower: 123.4
*Guernsey:* Tower: 119.95 Approach: 128.65 Radar: 118.9/124.5 GMC: 121.8 ATIS: 109.4
*Halfpenny Green:* AFIS: 123.0
*Halton:* A/G: 130.425
*Haverfordwest:* A/G: 122.2
*Hawarden:* Tower: 124.95 Approach: 123.35 Radar: 130.25
*Henstridge:* A/G: 130.25
*Hethel:* A/G: 122.35
*Highland Radar:* 134.1/126.1
*Hucknall:* A/G: 130.8
*Huddersfield (Crosland Moor):* A/G: 122.2
*Humberside:* Tower: 118.55 Approach: 124.675 Radar: 123.15 ATIS: 124.125
*Insch:* A/G: 129.825
*Inverness (Dalcross):* Tower/Approach: 122.6
*Ipswich:* A/G: 118.325
*Islay (Port Ellen):* AFIS: 123.15
*Isle of Man (Ronaldsway):* Tower: 118.9 Approach/Radar: 120.85/118.2/125.3
*Isle of Wight (Sandown):* A/G: 123.5
*Jersey:* Tower: 119.45 GMC: 121.9 Approach: 120.3 Radar: 118.55/120.3 Zone: 125.2/120.45 ATIS: 112.2
*Kinloss:* Tower: 122.1 Approach: 119.35 PAR: 123.3
*Kirkwall:* Tower/Approach: 118.3
*Lakenheath:* Tower: 122.1 Approach: 128.9 Depcon: 123.3
*Lands End (St Just):* Tower: 130.7
*Lasham:* A/G: 129.9 FLS Aerospace: 122.875
*Lashenden (Headcorn):* A/G: 122.0
*Leeds-Bradford:* Tower: 120.3 Approach: 123.75 Radar: 121.05 ATIS: 118.025
*Leeming:* Tower: 120.5/122.1 MATZ: 127.75
*Lee-on-Solent:* A/G: 135.7
*Leicester:* AFIS/A/G: 122.125
*Lerwick (Tingwall):* A/G: 122.6
*Leuchars:* Tower: 122.1 Approach: 129.15 Radar: 123.3
*Linton-on-Ouse:* MATZ: 129.15 PAR: 123.3
*Little Gransden:* A/G: 130.85
*Little Snoring:* A/G: 122.4
*Liverpool:* Tower: 118.1 Approach/Radar: 119.85 Radar: 118.45
*Llanbedr:* Tower/Radar: 122.5
*London/City:* Tower: 118.075/127.95 Approach: 132.7 Radar: 128.025 ATIS: 127.95
*London Control:* See Appendix 2
*London/Gatwick:* Tower: 124.225/134.225 GMC: 121.8 Director: 126.825/118.95/129.025 Delivery: 121.95
    ATIS: 128.475
*London/Heathrow:* Tower: 118.7/118.5/124.475 GMC: 121.9 Director: 119.725/120.4/134.975/
    Radar: 119.9/125.625 ATIS: 133.075 ATIS: 113.75/115.1/123.9 Delivery: 121.975
*London Mil:* West: 135.15 East: 135.275 Northwest: 127.45
*London Stansted:* Tower: 123.8 Approach: 125.55 Radar: 126.95/123.8 ATIS: 127.175 GMC: 121.725
*London (Westland Heliport):* Battersea Tower: 122.9
*Londonderry (Eglinton):* Tower: 122.85 Approach: 123.625
*Lossiemouth:* Tower: 118.9 Approach: 119.35 Radar: 123.3
*Luton:* Tower: 132.55 GMC: 121.75 Approach: 129.55/128.75/126.725 Radar: 127.3 ATIS: 120.575
*Lydd:* Tower/Approach: 120.7/131.3
*Lyneham:* Tower: 118.425 Approach: 118.425 Radar: 123.3

*Manchester:* Tower: 118.625 Radar: 119.4/121.35 Arrivals: 118.575 GMC: 121.7/121.85 ATIS: 128.175
*Manchester Control:* See Appendix 2
*Manston:* Tower: 119.275/122.1 Approach: 126.35/129.45 Radar: 123.3
*Marham:* Tower: 122.1 Approach: 124.15 Radar: 123.3
*Marston Moor:* A/G: 122.975
*Merryfield:* Tower: 122.1
*Middle Wallop:* Tower: 122.1 Approach: 126.7
*Mildenhall:* Tower: 122.55
*Mona:* AFIS: 122.0
*Netherthorpe:* A/G: 123.275
*Newcastle:* Tower: 119.7 Approach: 124.375 Radar: 118.5 ATIS: 114.25
*Newton:* Tower/Approach: 119.125/122.1
*Newtownards:* A/G: 123.5
*Northampton (Sywell):* AFIS/A/G: 122.7
*Northolt:* Tower: 124.975 Radar: 130.35 Departures: 120.325
*North Weald:* A/G: 123.525
*Norwich:* Tower: 124.25 Approach: 119.35 Radar: 128.325
*Nottingham:* A/G: 122.8
*Oaksey Park:* A/G: 122.775
*Oban:* A/G: 130.1 Micro: 129.825
*Odiham:* Tower: 122.1 MATZ: 125.25
*Old Sarum:* A/G: 123.2
*Old Warden (display days only):* 123.05 120.6
*Oxford:* Tower: 118.875 Approach: 125.325 GMC: 121.95 ATIS: 121.75
*Panshanger:* A/G: 120.25
*Pennine Radar:* 128.675
*Penzance Heliport:* A/G: 118.1
*Perranporth:* A/G: 119.75 Gliders: 130.1
*Peterborough (Conington):* A/G: 129.725
*Peterborough (Sibson):* A/G: 122.3
*Plockton:* Bond Helicopters: 122.375
*Plymouth (Roborough):* Tower: 122.6 Approach: 133.55
*Plymouth Radar:* 121.25
*Pocklington:* A/G: 130.1
*Popham:* A/G: 129.8
*Portland:* Tower: 122.1 Radar: 124.15
*Prestwick:* Tower: 118.15 GMC: 121.8 Approach: 120.55 Radar: 119.45 ATIS: 127.125
*Redhill:* Tower: 120.275
*Rochester:* AFIS: 122.25
*St Mawgan:* Tower: 123.4 Approach: 122.1/126.5 Radar: 125.55/123.3
*Sandtoft:* A/G: 130.425
*Scarborough (Willy Howe):* A/G: 130.125
*Scatsta:* Tower/Approach: 123.6 Radar: 122.4
*Scilly Isles:* Tower: 123.15
*Scottish Control:* See Appendix 2
*Seething:* A/G: 122.6
*Shanwick Radio:* 127.9/123.95/127.65/135.525/133.8
*Shawbury:* Tower: 122.1 Approach/MATZ: 120.775
*Sherburn-in-Elmet:* A/G: 122.6
*Shetland Radar:* 118.15
*Shipdham:* A/G: 119.55

*Shobdon:* A/G: 123.5
*Shoreham:* Tower: 123.15 Approach: 125.4 ATIS: 132.4
*Silverstone:* A/G: 121.075
*Sleap:* A/G: 122.45
*Southampton:* Tower: 118.2 Approach: 128.85 Solent Zone: 120.225/131.0 ATIS: 113.35
*Southend:* Tower: 127.725 Approach: 128.95 ATIS: 121.8
*Stapleford Tawney:* A/G: 122.8
*Stornoway:* Tower/Approach: 123.5
*Strathallan:* A/G: 129.9
*Strubby Heliport:* A/G: 122.375
*Sturgate:* A/G: 130.3
*Sumburgh:* Tower: 118.25 Approach: 123.15 Radar: 118.15/119.25/130.05 ATIS: 125.85
*Swansea:* Tower/Approach: 119.7
*Swanton Morley:* A/G: 123.5
*Syerston:* A/G: 125.425
*Tatenhill:* A/G: 124.075
*Teesside:* Tower: 119.8 Approach: 118.85 Radar: 128.85
*Thames Radar:* 132.7
*Thruxton:* A/G: 130.45
*Tilstock:* A/G: 122.075
*Tiree:* AFIS: 122.7
*Tresco:* A/G: 130.25
*Truro:* A/G: 129.8
*Turweston:* A/G: 122.175
*Unst:* A/G: 130.35 Ops: 123.45/123.1
*Valley:* Tower: 122.1 Approach: 134.35
*Waddington:* Approach: 127.35 Radar: 123.3
*Walton Wood Heliport:* A/G: 123.625
*Warton:* Tower: 130.8 Approach: 124.45
*Wattisham:* Tower: 122.1 Approach: 124.925 Radar: 123.3/124.925 A/G (Anglia Base): 129.975
*Wellesbourne Mountford:* A/G: 124.025
*Welshpool:* A/G: 123.25
*West Freugh:* Tower: 122.55 Approach/Radar: 130.05/130.725
*Weston Super Mare:* Tower: 122.5 Approach: 129.25
*White Waltham:* A/G: 122.6
*Wick:* Tower/Approach: 119.7 Ops: 130.375
*Wickenby:* A/G: 122.45
*Wigtown:* A/G: 123.05
*Winfield:* A/G: 123.5
*Wittering:* Tower: 122.1 MATZ: 130.2 (Cottesmore)
*Woodford:* Tower: 126.925 Approach: 130.75 Radar: 130.05
*Woodvale:* Tower: 119.75 Approach: 121.0
*Wroughton:* A/G: 123.225
*Wycombe Air Park (Booker):* A/G: 126.55 GMC: 121.775
*Yeovil (Judwin):* Tower: 125.4 Approach: 130.8
*Yeovilton:* Tower: 122.1 MATZ: 127.35
*York/Rufforth:* A/G: 129.975

# Air band frequencies in numerical order

Note: Many of the offshore oil and gas field frequencies are shared between one or more installations; all current frequencies are listed below.

*MHz*

| | |
|---|---|
| 118.025 | Leeds ATIS |
| 118.05 | Birmingham Radar |
| 118.075 | London (City) Tower/Barra AFIS |
| 118.10 | Liverpool Tower/Aberdeen Tower/ Penzance Heliport/Scilly Isles |
| 118.15 | Prestwick Tower |
| 118.20 | Ronaldsway Radar/Southampton Tower |
| 118.25 | Sumburgh Tower |
| 118.30 | Birmingham Tower/Belfast (Aldergrove) Tower/Kirkwall Tower/Approach |
| 118.325 | Ipswich Tower & Approach |
| 118.35 | Derby A/G |
| 118.40 | Blackpool Tower |
| 118.425 | Lyneham Tower |
| 118.45 | Liverpool Radar |
| 118.475 | London Control |
| 118.50 | Heathrow Tower/Newcastle Radar/Dublin Radar |
| 118.55 | Jersey Tower/Humberside Tower |
| 118.575 | Manchester Arrivals (Stack Control) |
| 118.60 | Dublin Tower |
| 118.625 | Manchester Tower |
| 118.65 | Bournemouth Radar |
| 118.70 | Edinburgh Tower/Heathrow Tower/Shannon Tower |
| 118.80 | Glasgow Tower/Cork Radar |
| 118.825 | London Control Departures via Brookmans Park |
| 118.85 | Teesside Approach |
| 118.875 | Oxford Tower |
| 118.90 | Guernsey Radar/Isle of Man Tower |
| 118.925 | Cosford Tower |
| 118.95 | Gatwick Director |
| 119.00 | Brize Zone |
| 119.05 | Exeter Radar |
| 119.10 | Glasgow Approach |
| 119.125 | Newton Tower/Approach |
| 119.20 | Benbecula Tower |
| 119.25 | Coventry Tower/Sumburgh Radar |
| 119.275 | Manston Tower |
| 119.30 | Glasgow Radar/Cork Tower |
| 119.35 | Lossiemouth Approach/Norwich Approach |
| 119.375 | Cranwell Approach |
| 119.40 | Manchester Approach |
| 119.425 | London (City) Tower |
| 119.45 | Jersey Tower/Prestwick Radar |
| 119.475 | Cardiff ATIS |
| 119.55 | Shipdham A/G/Dublin Radar |
| 119.60 | Prestwick Approach |
| 119.625 | Bournemouth Approach |
| 119.65 | East Midlands Approach |
| 119.70 | Swansea Tower/Approach/Wick Tower/Newcastle Tower |
| 119.725 | Heathrow Director |
| 119.75 | Perranporth A/G/Woodvale Tower |
| 119.775 | London Control Departures via Bovingdon |
| 119.80 | Exeter Tower/Teesside Tower |
| 119.85 | Liverpool Approach/Radar |
| 119.875 | Scottish FIS |
| 119.90 | Heathrow Radar/Cork Approach |
| 119.95 | Blackpool Radar/Guernsey Tower |
| 119.975 | Coningsby Tower |
| 120.00 | Belfast (Aldergrove) Radar |
| 120.025 | London Control |
| 120.075 | Tyne Oil Platform |
| 120.10 | Brussels Radar |
| 120.125 | East Midlands Radar |
| 120.175 | London Control Inbounds via LUMBA/TIMBA |
| 120.20 | Shannon Approach |
| 120.225 | Solent Approach |
| 120.25 | Panshanger A/G |
| 120.275 | Deenethorpe A/G |
| 120.30 | Jersey Approach/Leeds Tower |
| 120.325 | Northolt Departures |
| 120.40 | Aberdeen Approach |
| 120.425 | Barkston Tower |
| 120.45 | Jersey Zone |
| 120.475 | London SIDs via Midhurst |
| 120.50 | Leeming Tower |
| 120.525 | London Control Departures via Detling |
| 120.55 | Prestwick Approach |
| 120.575 | Luton ATIS |
| 120.60 | Cumbernauld Tower |
| 120.625 | Stansted Approach |
| 120.65 | Goodwood Tower |
| 120.70 | Lydd Tower |

| | |
|---|---|
| 120.775 | Shawbury Radar |
| 120.80 | Coningsby Radar |
| 120.85 | Ronaldsway Approach/Radar |
| 120.90 | Belfast (Aldergrove) Radar/Benson Zone |
| 120.925 | Fowlmere A/G/Cork ATIS |
| 120.975 | Gloster Radar |
| 121.00 | Woodvale Approach |
| 121.05 | Leeds Radar |
| 121.075 | Silverstone A/G |
| 121.10 | Dublin Approach |
| 121.20 | Edinburgh Approach |
| 121.225 | London Control |
| 121.25 | Aberdeen Radar/Manston Tower/Plymouth Radar |
| 121.275 | London Control |
| 121.30 | Glasgow Radar |
| 121.325 | London Control |
| 121.35 | Manchester Radar |
| 121.40 | Shannon Radar |
| 121.50 | DISTRESS |
| 121.60 | Fire and Rescue Services |
| 121.70 | Manchester GMC/Aberdeen GMC/Glasgow GMC/Bournemouth GMC/Cork Tower |
| 121.75 | Luton GMC/Aldergrove GMC/Edinburgh GMC/Blackpool ATIS/Oxford ATIS |
| 121.775 | Wycombe GMC |
| 121.80 | Birmingham GMC/Dublin GMC |
| 121.85 | Aberdeen ATIS/Manchester GMC |
| 121.875 | Biggin Hill ATIS/Cranfield ATIS |
| 121.90 | Jersey GMC/Heathrow GMC/East Midlands GMC |
| 121.975 | Heathrow Delivery |
| 121.95 | Gatwick GMP/Oxford GMC/Cosford GMC/Bournemouth ATIS |
| 122.00 | Coventry Radar/Ford Tower/Lashenden Tower/Wattisham Tower/Baldonnel Approach/Mona AFIS/Forties Oil Field |
| 122.025 | Argyll Oil Platform |
| 122.05 | BA Ops |
| | Newcastle/Brymon/Heavylift/Keenair/East Shetland Basin |
| 122.075 | Tilstock A/G /Duxford AFIS |
| 122.10 | Brize Norton Radar/Church Fenton Tower/Culdrose Tower/Leuchars Tower/Lyneham Radar/Shawbury Tower/Newton Tower |

| | |
|---|---|
| 122.125 | Leicester A/G |
| 122.15 | Flotta/Approach/Aberporth AFIS |
| 122.175 | Beryl Oil Field/Turweston A/G |
| 122.20 | Huddersfield (Crosland Moor)/Cambridge Tower/Haverfordwest |
| 122.225 | UK East Coast Offshore |
| 122.25 | Leicester/Rochester/Caernarfon/Brent Oilfield, North Sea |
| 122.30 | Blackbushe/Sibson |
| 122.325 | Esmond Oil Field |
| 122.35 | Hethel/Lexair Ops Luton/Gulf Air Ops/Aurigny Ops/East Shetland Basin |
| 122.375 | Strubby Heliport/Plockton/East Shetland Basin/UK West Coast Offshore |
| 122.40 | Little Snoring/Elstree/Scatsta Radar |
| 122.425 | Earls Colne A/G |
| 122.45 | Belfast (City) Radar/Goodwood Approach/Sleap/Wickenby/Piper Oil Field |
| 122.475 | Balloons |
| 122.50 | Farnborough Tower/Llanbedr Tower & Approach/Weston Super Mare Tower |
| 122.525 | Ashcroft Farm/Clyde Oil Field |
| 122.55 | Mildenhall Tower/West Freugh Tower |
| 122.60 | Inverness Tower/Plymouth (Roborough) Tower/Seething/Sherburn-in-Elmet A/G/Swansea Tower/White Waltham |
| 122.625 | Viking Oil Field |
| 122.65 | Brae Oil Field |
| 122.675 | Duxford Ops |
| 122.70 | Barton/Compton Abbas/Sywell/Silverstone/Bodmin/Tiree |
| 122.725 | Bristol Filton Approach |
| 122.75 | Common Range Info freq |
| 122.775 | Oaksey A/G/Scott Oil Platform |
| 122.80 | Nottingham/Stapleford/East Shetland Basin/Cranfield Approach/Eglinton Tower/Approach |
| 122.825 | Bruntingthorpe A/G |
| 122.875 | FLS Aerospace Lasham/Hewett Oil Field |
| 122.90 | Battersea Heliport/Dundee Tower/St Mawgan Tower/Gloster Tower |
| 122.925 | Fenland |
| 122.95 | Helicopter Depcom/Ekofisk Oilfield North Sea/BIH Aberdeen/Lasham |

| | |
|---|---|
| 123.00 | Halfpenny Green AFIS/Piper Bravo |
| 123.05 | Beverley A/G/Peterhead Heliport (Brittair)/Stevenage/Old Warden/Gigha Island/Brent Log (East Shetland Basin)/Wigtown A/G |
| 123.025 | Ravenspurn Oil Field |
| 123.10 | Search and Rescue (Scene of Search) |
| 123.15 | Humberside Approach/Shoreham Tower/Sumburgh Approach/Port Ellen |
| 123.175 | Badminton A/G |
| 123.20 | Barrow A/G/Old Sarum A/G |
| 123.225 | Wroughton A/G/Fadmoor A/G/Thames Oil Field |
| 123.25 | Isle of Wight (Bembridge)/Bagby/Welshpool/UK West Coast Offshore |
| 123.30 | Common Military Radar Frequency |
| 123.35 | Hawarden Approach |
| 123.375 | Scottish Control TMA |
| 123.40 | Lyneham Approach/St Mawgan Tower |
| 123.425 | Fairoaks A/G |
| 123.45 | Great Yarmouth (North Denes)/Redhill/Bristow Helicopters/Leman Platform |
| 123.475 | Dunkeswell A/G |
| 123.50 | Isle of Wight Sandown/Netherthorpe/Newtownards/Shobdon/Stornoway/Strathallan/Swanton Morley/Winfield |
| 123.525 | North Weald |
| 123.55 | East Scotland Offshore |
| 123.575 | Viking Oil Field |
| 123.60 | Cambridge Approach/Carlisle Tower & Approach/Alderney Tower |
| 123.625 | Leman Field/Walton Wood Heliport |
| 123.65 | Gamston/Coal Aston (Sheffield)/Heathrow Executive Handling/Brymon Ops/Beatrice Oil Platforms |
| 123.70 | Amsterdam Radar |
| 123.75 | Leeds Approach/Benson Approach |
| 123.80 | Stansted Tower |
| 123.85 | Amsterdam Control |
| 123.90 | Heathrow ATIS |
| 123.95 | Oceanic Clearance for Aircraft registered west of 30°W |
| 124.00 | East Midlands Tower |
| 124.025 | Wellesbourne A/G |
| 124.05 | Scottish Control |
| 124.075 | Tatenhill A/G |
| 124.10 | Cardiff Radar |
| 124.125 | Humberside ATIS |
| 124.15 | Marham Radar/Portland Radar |
| 124.20 | Manchester Control South-East/Trent |
| 124.225 | Gatwick Tower |
| 124.25 | Norwich Radar |
| 124.30 | Amsterdam FIS |
| 124.325 | Dunsfold Tower |
| 124.35 | Bristol (Lulsgate) Radar |
| 124.375 | Newcastle Approach |
| 124.40 | Topcliffe Radar |
| 124.45 | Warton Radar |
| 124.475 | Heathrow Tower |
| 124.50 | Guernsey Radar/Scottish Control |
| 124.525 | Dublin ATIS |
| 124.55 | Copenhagen Control |
| 124.60 | London Flight Information (East of Alpha One) |
| 124.65 | Dublin Control |
| 124.675 | Humberside Approach |
| 124.70 | Shannon Control |
| 124.75 | London Flight Information (West of Alpha One) |
| 124.80 | Coventry GMC |
| 124.90 | Manston Tower/Campbeltown AFIS |
| 124.925 | Wattisham Approach |
| 124.95 | Hawarden Tower |
| 124.975 | Northolt Tower |
| 125.00 | Cardiff Tower/Topcliffe Approach |
| 125.10 | Manchester Control West |
| 125.15 | Paris Volmet (in French) |
| 125.175 | Placid Oilfield |
| 125.20 | Jersey Zone |
| 125.25 | Farnborough Zone/Odiham Radar |
| 125.275 | Anglia Radar |
| 125.30 | Ronaldsway Radar |
| 125.325 | Oxford Approach |
| 125.35 | Boscombe Approach/Waddington Zone/Middle Wallop MATZ |
| 125.40 | Shoreham Approach/Yeovil (Judwin) Tower |
| 125.425 | Syerston A/G |
| 125.45 | Paris Control |
| 125.475 | London FIS (North of Bravo 1) |
| 125.50 | Brest Control |
| 125.55 | St Mawgan Radar/Stansted Zone |
| 125.60 | Bournemouth Tower |
| 125.65 | Gloster Approach |

| | |
|---|---|
| 125.675 | Scottish Control |
| 125.70 | Paris Information (North) |
| 125.725 | Scottish Volmet |
| 125.75 | Amsterdam Radar |
| 125.80 | London Control Radar Departures via Brookmans Park and Clacton |
| 125.85 | Cardiff Approach |
| 125.875 | Northolt PAR |
| 125.90 | Coltishall Radar/Campbeltown AFIS |
| 125.95 | Manchester Control North |
| 126.00 | Paris Volmet (in English) |
| 126.025 | Bristol ATIS |
| 126.075 | London Control |
| 126.10 | Highland Radar/Paris Info (South) |
| 126.15 | Dusseldorf Control |
| 126.20 | Amsterdam Met/Madrid Met |
| 126.25 | Scottish Control TMA |
| 126.275 | Birmingham ATIS |
| 126.30 | London Control Inbounds via Bovingdon |
| 126.35 | Manston Radar |
| 126.40 | Bordeaux Volmet (in English) |
| 126.50 | Church Fenton Approach/Coningsby MATZ/Leuchars Approach/St Mawgan Approach/Brize Tower |
| 126.55 | Wycombe Air Park (Booker) |
| 126.60 | London Volmet North |
| 126.65 | Manchester Control North-East |
| 126.70 | Boscombe Approach/Middle Wallop Approach |
| 126.725 | Luton Approach |
| 126.75 | Brussels (West Sector) |
| 126.775 | London Control |
| 126.80 | Geneva Met |
| 126.825 | Gatwick Director |
| 126.85 | Scottish Control |
| 126.875 | London Control Inbounds via LOREL |
| 126.90 | Brussels Information |
| 126.925 | Woodford Tower |
| 126.95 | Stansted Approach |
| 127.00 | Dublin Volmet/Copenhagen Met |
| 127.05 | Frankfurt Control |
| 127.10 | London Control Lydd Sector West |
| 127.15 | Benson PAR |
| 127.175 | Stansted ATIS |
| 127.20 | Zurich Volmet |
| 127.25 | Cotswold Radar |
| 127.275 | Scottish FIS |
| 127.30 | Luton Radar |
| 127.35 | Waddington Radar/Yeovilton Radar |
| 127.40 | Bremen Met/Marseille Met |
| 127.425 | London Upper Sector East |
| 127.45 | London Mil Northwest |
| 127.475 | Gloucestershire ATIS |
| 127.50 | Shannon Control (Cork Sector) |
| 127.60 | Barcelona Met/Frankfurt Met |
| 127.65 | Oceanic Clearance for Aircraft registered east of 30°W (including Australia) |
| 127.70 | London Control |
| 127.725 | Southend Tower |
| 127.75 | Leeming MATZ/Air UK Ops |
| 127.80 | Brussels Met |
| 127.85 | Reims Control |
| 127.875 | London Control |
| 127.90 | Shanwick Radio |
| 127.95 | London (City) Tower |
| 127.975 | Filton Approach |
| 128.025 | London (City) Radar |
| 128.10 | Paris Control |
| 128.125 | London Control North Sea |
| 128.15 | Exeter Approach |
| 128.175 | Manchester ATIS |
| 128.20 | Aldergrove ATIS/Brussels East |
| 128.225 | East Midlands ATIS |
| 128.25 | London Military |
| 128.30 | Aberdeen Radar/Netheravon Tower |
| 128.325 | Norwich Radar |
| 128.35 | Dutch Military |
| 128.40 | Pisa Volmet |
| 128.425 | London Control |
| 128.45 | Manston Approach |
| 128.475 | Gatwick ATIS |
| 128.50 | Scottish Control (TMA) |
| 128.55 | Bristol Approach |
| 128.60 | London Volmet South/Oslo Met |
| 128.65 | Guernsey Approach |
| 128.70 | London Military Radar |
| 128.75 | Luton Approach |
| 128.80 | Brussels Control |
| 128.85 | Southampton Tower/Approach/Teesside Radar |
| 128.90 | Lakenheath MATZ |
| 128.925 | Anglia Radar |
| 128.95 | Southend Approach |
| 128.975 | Edinburgh Radar |
| 129.00 | Brest Control |
| 129.025 | Gatwick Director |
| 129.075 | London Control |
| 129.10 | London Control Pole Hill/Irish Sea |

| | |
|---|---|
| 129.15 | Linton-on-Ouse MATZ/Leuchars Approach |
| 129.175 | Dublin North |
| 129.20 | London Control Daventry |
| 129.275 | London Control Inbounds via LOREL |
| 129.30 | Amsterdam Control |
| 129.375 | London Control |
| 129.40 | Biggin Hill Tower |
| 129.425 | London Control |
| 129.45 | Manston Approach |
| 129.50 | Brest Control |
| 129.55 | Luton Approach |
| 129.60 | London Control Clacton Sector |
| 129.65 | Brussels Control East Sector |
| 129.70 | Fort William Heliport/Gannet Oil Field |
| 129.725 | Peterborough/Conington A/G/Deanland A/G |
| 129.75 | BMA Ops/UK Gatwick/Air Express/Filton Ops/Frigg Oil Platform |
| 129.775 | Liverpool Bay Gas Field/Forties Alpha |
| 129.80 | Popham/Breighton/Truro/Bourn |
| 129.825 | Insch A/G/Cromer Micro/Oban Micro |
| 129.85 | Waterford Tower |
| 129.875 | Enstone/Rough Oil Field |
| 129.90 | Hang Gliders/Lasham |
| 129.95 | East Shetland Basin |
| 129.975 | Gliders/Rufforth A/G |
| 130.00 | Boscombe PAR |
| 130.05 | Farnborough Radar/Sumburgh Director/Woodford Approach/West Freugh Approach |
| 130.075 | Brize Ops/Servisair Gatwick |
| 130.10 | Gliders |
| 130.125 | Scarborough (Willy Howe) |
| 130.15 | Deptford Down (Salisbury Plain) Ops/UK West Coast Offshore |
| 130.175 | Ryanair Manchester/Reed Aviation |
| 130.20 | Cottesmore Radar/Chivenor A/G/East Shetland Basin |
| 130.25 | Benson Tower/Hawarden Radar/Henstridge A/G/Tresco |
| 130.275 | Henstridge/UK East Coast Offshore |
| 130.30 | Sturgate A/G |
| 130.35 | Northolt Radar (On request)/Unst A/G |
| 130.375 | Air Hanson Ops/Farnborough Exec/Heathrow/Wick Ops/Forties Alpha |
| 130.40 | Gliders |
| 130.425 | Sandtoft/Halton/Unicom for Emergency Controlling Authorities |
| 130.45 | Thruxton/Skegness/Glenrothes |
| 130.475 | Retford/Gamston |
| 130.50 | Cowes Week Heliport/Henley Regatta/etc |
| 130.55 | Brough A/G/Andrews Field/Brands Hatch (Shawline Ops) |
| 130.575 | Shell Ops |
| 130.60 | British Caledonian Ops/Servisair Ops |
| 130.625 | BAF Ops West/Norwich Handling |
| 130.65 | Dan-Air Ops/Air 2000 Ops |
| 130.70 | Land's End Tower |
| 130.725 | Denham/Freugh Radar/MCPO 1 Oil Platform |
| 130.75 | Belfast (City) Tower/Boscombe Down Tower/Cambridge Radar/Woodford Radar |
| 130.80 | Hucknall/Samlesbury Tower/Warton Tower/Yeovil (Judwin) Approach/East Shetland Basin |
| 130.85 | Belfast City Approach/Little Gransden A/G |
| 130.875 | Alba Oil Platforms |
| 130.90 | Rome Radar |
| 130.925 | London Control |
| 130.95 | Shannon ATIS |
| 131.00 | Southampton Radar |
| 131.05 | London Control North East UIR (Pole Hill) |
| 131.10 | Brussels Control (West Sector) |
| 131.125 | London Control |
| 131.15 | Shannon Control (Cork Sector) |
| 131.25 | Rome Control |
| 131.30 | Lydd Approach/Scottish Control (Stornoway) |
| 131.325 | Birmingham Radar |
| 131.35 | Paris Control North |
| 131.40 | Air India/CSA Ops |
| 131.425 | Saudia Ops (Heathrow)/Air NZ/Virgin Atlantic |
| 131.45 | Air Canada Ops/NLM/UK/Alitalia |
| 131.50 | Aer Lingus Ops/KLM London/Air France |
| 131.525 | American Manchester/Monarch Ops |
| 131.55 | Ryanair Ops Dublin |
| 131.575 | BMA Ops/El Al Ops |
| 131.60 | TWA Ops/Air India Ops/Field Aviation |
| 131.625 | Portishead Radio |

| | | | |
|---|---|---|---|
| 131.65 | KLM Ops | 133.55 | Plymouth Approach |
| 131.675 | Britannia Ops | 133.60 | London Control Strumble |
| 131.70 | Swissair Ops/SAS Ops | 133.70 | London Control Daventry West Sector |
| 131.75 | Aer Lingus Ops | 133.75 | Brize Radar |
| 131.775 | Aeroflot Heathrow/Air Foyle Luton | 133.80 | Oceanic Tracks Broadcast |
| 131.80 | British Airways Speedbird Ops (Shuttle) | 133.85 | Maastricht Control/Bristol Tower |
| | | 133.90 | London Military Radar/Brize Radar |
| 131.85 | British Airways Ops | 133.95 | Maastricht Control |
| 131.875 | Qantas Heathrow | 133.975 | London Control Departures via |
| 131.90 | British Airways Speedbird Ops (Overseas) | | Detling |
| | | 134.00 | Scottish FIS |
| 131.925 | Lufthansa Heathrow/Finnair Heathrow | 134.05 | Culdrose Approach |
| | | 134.10 | Highland Radar |
| 131.95 | Iberia Heathrow/Sabena Ops/El Al Ops | 134.125 | London Control |
| | | 134.15 | London Mil West/Londonderry Tower |
| 131.975 | British Airways Ops (Glasgow) | 134.20 | Rome Control |
| 132.00 | Paris Control | 134.225 | Gatwick Tower |
| 132.075 | Edinburgh ATIS | 134.25 | London Control North Sea Sector |
| 132.10 | Paris Control | 134.30 | Brize Radar/Scottish Military |
| 132.15 | Shannon Control | 134.35 | Valley Radar/Farnborough Radar |
| 132.175 | Glasgow ATIS | 134.40 | Reims Control |
| 132.20 | Reykjavik Oceanic (Polar Tracks) | 134.425 | London Control Pole Hill/Irish Sea |
| 132.30 | London Control Hurn Sector | 134.45 | London Control Hurn Sector |
| 132.325 | Full Sutton A/G | 134.55 | Chelmsford Heliport/Rivenhall |
| 132.35 | Dutch Military/Bristol (Filton) Tower | | Heliport |
| 132.40 | Shoreham ATIS | 134.75 | London Control Upper Sector West |
| 132.45 | London Control Lydd Sector | 134.775 | Scottish Control |
| 132.525 | Dutch Military | 134.80 | Biggin Tower/Belfast City Radar |
| 132.55 | Luton Tower | 134.90 | London Control Dover Sector |
| 132.60 | London Control SW Approaches | 134.925 | Cranfield Tower |
| 132.65 | Coastguard/Kent Air Ambulance | 134.975 | Heathrow Director |
| 132.70 | Thames Radar | 135.00 | CAA Flight Test |
| 132.75 | Maastricht UAC | 135.05 | London Control Hurn Sector |
| 132.80 | London Control Bristol Sector | 135.15 | London Military radar |
| 132.85 | Maastricht UAC | 135.175 | Dunsfold Approach |
| 132.95 | London Control | 135.20 | Wattisham Approach |
| 133.00 | Brest Control | 135.25 | London Control Cardiff Sector |
| 133.05 | Manchester Control A25/B3 | 135.275 | London Military East |
| 133.075 | London Control Cowly Sector | 135.30 | Paris Control North |
| 133.10 | Bordeaux Control | 135.325 | London Control |
| 133.15 | Cotswold Radar | 135.35 | Dusseldorf Information |
| 133.175 | London Control | 135.375 | London Volmet Main |
| 133.20 | Scottish FIS | 135.40 | Clacton A/G |
| 133.25 | Maastricht Control | 135.425 | London Control |
| 133.30 | London Military Radar | 135.45 | Maastricht Control |
| 133.35 | Maastricht UAC | 135.50 | Reims Control |
| 133.40 | Manchester Control/Stafa | 135.525 | Shanwick Oceanic (Clearances) |
| 133.45 | London Control Clacton Sector | 135.575 | Gatwick Director |
| 133.50 | Paris Control North | 135.60 | Shannon Control |
| 133.525 | London Control North Sea | 135.65 | Brest Control |

*VHF air band frequencies*

| | | | | |
|---|---|---|---|---|
| 135.675 | Scottish Control | | 136.55 | London Control Clacton Sector |
| 135.70 | Lee-on-Solent A/G | | 136.60 | London Control |
| 135.80 | Paris Control | | 136.80 | Airtours Ops Manchester |
| 135.85 | Scottish Control (UIR) | | 136.85 | Britannia Ops Luton |
| 136.20 | London Control | | 136.90 | Datalink/ACARS |
| 136.275 | London Control | | 136.925 | Datalink/ACARS |
| 136.325 | London Control | | 136.950 | Datalink/ACARS |
| 136.40 | London Control | | 136.975 | Datalink/ACARS |

# Appendix 4

# UHF air band frequencies

This listing has been compiled from official sources available to the general public. There are of course many other allocations, including air-to-air, TADs, Ops and satellite communications. An anomaly is the increased use of parts of the sub-band 137.0–149.9, officially allocated as 'Government Mobile', for air band purposes. A further wave of military cutbacks since the last edition of this book has seen the sad demise of many familiar bases including Alconbury, Chivenor, Finningley, Machrihanish and Scampton.

Note that some of the London Mil frequencies rebroadcast aircraft transmissions so that when a single controller is handling more than one channel, aircraft on one frequency are able to hear those on another and thus not inadvertently interrupt. An example is the Northwest ICF (Initial Contact Frequency) 231.625 on which civil aircraft transmitting on its sister VHF channel 127.45 can also be heard. London Mil has a number of unpublished UHF frequencies that are allocated by the ICF controller as required.

## Frequencies of military airfields and radar units

*Aberdeen:* Approach/Radar: 353.55

*Aberporth:* AFIS: 259.0 Range: 356.2/379.2

*ACMI Range North Sea:* 252.1/340.55/290.95/359.4

*Aldergrove:* Tower/Approach: 310.0 Ops: 241.825

*Barkston Heath:* Tower: 342.075 GMC: 340.525 Approach: 340.475 (Cranwell) PAR: 360.725
    Radar: 261.05/291.7 ATIS: 351.825

*Benson:* Tower: 279.35 GMC: 340.325 Approach/Radar: 268.825/358.8/315.75 PAR: 259.875/241.625

*Boscombe Down:* Tower: 370.1 GMC: 299.4 Approach/Radar: 291.65/380.025/276.85 PAR: 381.125
    ATIS: 263.5

*Boulmer:* A/G: 299.1/282.8

*Bristol Filton:* Tower: 342.025 Approach/Radar: 256.125/336.475

*Brize Norton:* Tower: 381.2 GMC: 370.3 Approach/Radar 342.45/356.875 PAR: 338.65 Ops: 357.475
    ATIS: 254.475

*Cambridge:* Tower/Radar: 372.425

*Cardiff:* Approach/Radar: 277.225

*Chetwynd:* Tower (Ternhill): 309.55 Approach (Ternhill): 365.075

*Chivenor:* A/G: 252.8

*Church Fenton:* Tower: 262.7 GMC: 340.2 Approach/Radar: 254.525/375.325 PAR: 386.725

*Colerne:* Tower: 344.6 GMC: 360.75 Approach: 277.275

*Coltishall:* Tower: 339.95/142.29 GMC: 296.725 Approach/Radar: 379.275/342.25/293.425
    PAR: 275.975/254.25 Ops: 364.8

*Coningsby:* Tower: 275.875 GMC: 358.55 Approach/Radar: 312.225/344.625/262.95
    PAR: 300.925/337.975

*Cosford:* Tower: 357.125 Approach: 276.125
*Cottesmore:* Tower: 370.05 GMC: 336.375 Approach/Radar: 312.075/340.575/358.725/376.575
    PAR: 262.9/337.875 ATIS: 242.325
*Cowden Range:* 241.775/260.0
*Cranwell:* Tower: 379.525 GMC: 297.9 Approach/Radar: 340.475/250.05/282.0 PAR: 383.475/285.15
    ATIS: 311.825
*Croughton:* A/G: 343.6
*Culdrose:* Tower: 380.225 GMC: 299.4 Approach/Radar: 241.95/339.95 PAR: 358.7/259.75 ATIS: 372.3
*Dishforth:* Tower: 259.825 GMC: 379.675 Approach (Topcliffe): 357.375 Ops: 252.9
*Donna Nook Range:* 232.075/342.175
*Dunsfold:* Tower: 375.4 Approach/Radar: 367.375/312.625
*Eastern Radar:* 229.975
*Edinburgh:* Tower: 257.8 Radar: 362.3
*Eskmeals Range:* 288.95
*Fairford:* Tower: 337.575/142.225 GMC: 259.975 Approach/Radar (Brize): 342.45/376.625
    Ops: 379.475/307.8/371.2/358.6
*Farnborough:* Tower: 357.4 Approach/Radar: 336.275/312.525 PAR: 259.0
*Garvie Range:* 337.95
*Glasgow:* Radar: 362.3
*Halton:* Aero Club: 356.275
*Hawarden:* Tower: 336.325
*Holbeach Range:* 343.375/360.45
*Honington:* Tower: 282.275 Approach: 309.95/254.875
*Inverness:* Approach: 362.3
*Kinloss:* Tower: 336.35 Approach/Radar: 259.975/311.325 PAR: 370.05/376.525 Ops: 358.475
*Lakenheath:* Tower: 358.675 GMC: 397.975 Approach/Radar: 242.075/264.675/398.35
    PAR: 309.075/290.825/338.675/264.1/279.25 Ops: 300.825/269.075/257.75 ATIS: 249.7
*Larkhill Range:* 345.2/358.55
*Leconfield:* A/G: 244.875/282.8
*Leeming:* Tower: 344.575 GMC: 338.85 Approach/Radar: 337.825/292.7/358.65 PAR: 336.35/309.875
    Ops: 356.725 ATIS: 249.525
*Leuchars:* Tower: 258.925 GMC: 259.85 Approach/Radar: 255.4/292.475 PAR: 370.075/268.775
    Ops: 285.025 ATIS: 249.575
*Linton-on-Ouse:* Tower: 300.425 GMC: 340.025 Approach/Radar: 362.675/292.8/344.475/381.075
    PAR: 358.525/259.875 ATIS: 241.65
*Llanbedr:* Tower: 380.175 Approach/Radar: 386.675 PAR: 370.3
*London Military:* Initial Contact Frequency: Northwest: 231.625 Central: 275.35 Clacton: 233.8
    Dover/Lydd: 230.05 Seaford/Hurn: 251.225 London Upper: 235.05 ICF (West): 275.475
    (East): 299.975
*Lossiemouth:* Tower: 337.75 GMC: 299.4 Approach/Radar: 376.65/258.85/259.975/311.325
    PAR: 250.05/312.4 ATIS: 344.45
*Luce Bay Range:* 358.825/376.525
*Lyme Bay Range:* 381.15/300.175
*Lyneham:* Tower: 386.825 GMC: 340.175 Approach/Radar: 359.5/345.025/300.475 PAR: 375.2
    Ops: 254.65 ATIS: 381.0
*Manorbier Range:* 360.775/366.225
*Manston:* Tower: 344.35 Approach/Radar: 379.025/338.625 PAR: 312.325
*Marham:* Tower: 337.9 GMC: 336.35 Approach/Radar: 291.95/293.775 PAR: 379.65 Ops: 312.55
    ATIS: 261.2
*Merryfield:* Tower: 312.7
*Middle Wallop:* Tower: 372.625 Approach/Radar: 312.0/312.675 PAR: 364.825

*Mildenhall:* Tower: 258.825 GMC: 380.15 Ops: 365.1/312.45/344.8 Metro: 257.75 ATIS: 277.075 142.275
*Mona:* Tower: 358.75 Approach: 379.7
*Netheravon:* Tower: 290.95 Approach: 362.225 A/G: 282.25 (Salisbury Plain)
*Newcastle:* Approach/Radar: 284.6
*Newton:* Tower: 375.425 GMC: 258.975 Approach: 251.725
*Northolt:* Tower: 312.35 Approach/Radar: 344.975/379.425 PAR: 375.5 Ops: 244.425 ATIS: 300.35
*Odiham:* Tower: 309.625 Approach/Radar: 386.775 PAR: 300.45 ATIS: 276.175 FIS: 315.975
*Otterburn Range:* 257.2/280.4
*Pembrey Range:* 336.35/379.875
*Plymouth Military Radar:* 379.85
*Portland:* Tower: 337.75 Approach/Radar: 300.175 PAR: 312.4 A/G: 282.8 ATIS: 343.475
*Predannack:* Tower: 338.975/370.0 Approach (Culdrose): 241.95
*Prestwick:* Ops: Navy Prestwick: 337.75
*Rosehearty Range:* 337.7
*St Athan:* Tower: 336.525 GMC: 386.5 Approach/Radar: 357.175 PAR: 340.1/380.125
*St Mawgan:* Tower: 241.825 GMC: 376.625 Approach/Radar: 357.2/360.55 PAR: 336.55 Ops: 260.0
    ATIS: 316.875
*Salisbury Plain:* A/G: 282.25/362.05
*Scottish Military:* 249.475
*Shawbury:* Tower: 269.1 GMC: 337.9 Approach/Radar: 276.075/254.2/386.875 PAR: 356.975 ATIS: 340.7
*Spadeadam Range:* 369.15/340.3/257.0
*Stanford:* A/G: 307.8
*Stornoway:* Tower: 362.3
*Tain Range:* 383.275
*Teesside:* Tower: 379.8 Approach/Radar: 296.725
*Ternhill:* Tower: 338.825 Approach: 276.825/365.075 Chetwynd Traffic: 309.55
*Topcliffe:* Tower: 309.725 GMC: 241.85 Approach/Radar: 357.375/255.6 PAR: 344.35
*Upavon:* Tower: 275.8
*Valley:* Tower: 340.175 GMC: 386.9 Approach/Radar: 372.325/268.775/337.725 PAR: 358.675
    SAR: 282.8
*Waddington:* Tower: 285.05 GMC: 342.125 Approach/Radar: 312.5/296.75/300.575/249.85
    PAR: 309.675 Ops: 244.275 ATIS: 291.675
*Wainfleet Range:* 340.05/356.8
*Warton:* Tower: 311.3 Approach/Radar: 336.475/311.3/343.7
*Wattisham:* Tower: 343.425 Approach/Radar: 291.125/283.575 PAR: 356.175/359.825
*West Freugh:* Tower: 337.925 Approach/Radar: 383.525/259.0
*Wittering:* Tower: 357.15 GMC: 311.95 Approach/Radar: 380.95/376.575 PAR: 383.225/337.95
*Woodford:* Tower: 358.575/269.125 Approach/Radar: 269.125/358.575
*Woodvale:* Tower: 259.95 Approach: 312.8
*Yeovil:* Tower: 372.425 Approach/Radar: 369.975/300.675
*Yeovilton:* Tower: 372.65 GMC: 311.325 Approach/Radar: 369.875/338.875 PAR: 339.975 ATIS: 379.75

# Miscellaneous

*NATO Common Frequencies:* Tower: 257.8 Approach: 362.3 Radar: 344.0 PAR: 385.4 Fixer: 317.5
    Royal Navy Air/Ship: 278.3 Low Flying (NATO/RAF): 300.8 Army: 253.9 Distress: 243.0
    Scene of Search: 282.8/156.0 (FM)/156.8 (FM)

# UHF air band frequencies in numerical order

*MHz*

| | |
|---|---|
| 142.225 | Fairford Tower |
| 142.275 | Mildenhall ATIS |
| 142.29 | Coltishall Tower |
| 230.05 | London Mil Dover/Lydd |
| 230.60 | London Mil |
| 231.625 | London Mil Northwest |
| 232.075 | Donna Nook Range |
| 233.80 | London Mil Clacton |
| 235.05 | London Mil Upper |
| 241.625 | Benson PAR |
| 241.65 | Linton ATIS |
| 241.775 | Cowden Range |
| 241.825 | Aldergrove Ops/St Mawgan Tower |
| 241.85 | Topcliffe GMC |
| 241.95 | Culdrose Radar/Predannack Approach |
| 242.075 | Lakenheath Depcon |
| 242.325 | Cottesmore ATIS |
| 243.00 | Distress |
| 244.275 | Waddington Ops |
| 244.375 | London Mil |
| 244.425 | Northolt Ops |
| 244.875 | Leconfield Rescue |
| 249.475 | Scottish Mil |
| 249.525 | Leeming ATIS |
| 249.575 | Leuchars ATIS |
| 249.675 | London Mil |
| 249.70 | Lakenheath ATIS |
| 249.85 | Waddington Radar |
| 250.05 | Cranwell Radar/Lossiemouth PAR |
| 251.225 | London Mil Seaford/Hurn |
| 251.625 | London Mil |
| 251.725 | Newton Approach |
| 252.10 | ACMI Range |
| 252.475 | Scottish Mil |
| 252.80 | Chivenor Rescue |
| 252.90 | Dishforth Ops |
| 253.80 | SAR Training |
| 254.20 | Shawbury Radar |
| 254.225 | London Mil |
| 254.25 | Coltishall PAR |
| 254.475 | Brize ATIS |
| 254.525 | Church Fenton Radar |
| 254.65 | Lyneham Ops |
| 254.825 | London Mil |
| 254.875 | Honington Approach |
| 255.40 | Leuchars Radar |
| 254.65 | Lyneham Ops |

| | |
|---|---|
| 255.60 | Topcliffe Radar |
| 256.125 | Filton Radar |
| 257.00 | Spadeadam Range |
| 257.20 | Otterburn Range |
| 257.225 | London Mil |
| 257.75 | Mildenhall Metro |
| 257.80 | Nato Common Tower |
| 258.825 | Mildenhall Tower |
| 258.85 | Lossiemouth Radar |
| 258.925 | Leuchars Tower |
| 258.975 | Newton GMC |
| 259.00 | Farnborough PAR/Aberporth AFIS/West Freugh Radar |
| 259.175 | Scottish Mil |
| 259.725 | Scottish Mil |
| 259.75 | Culdrose PAR |
| 259.775 | Scottish Mil |
| 259.825 | Dishforth Tower |
| 259.85 | Leuchars GMC |
| 259.875 | Linton PAR/Benson PAR |
| 259.95 | Woodvale Tower |
| 259.975 | Fairford GMC/Kinloss Radar/Lossiemouth Radar |
| 260.00 | Cowden Range/St Mawgan Ops |
| 260.025 | London Mil |
| 261.05 | Barkston Heath Radar |
| 261.20 | Marham ATIS |
| 262.70 | Church Fenton Tower |
| 262.90 | Cottesmore PAR |
| 262.95 | Coningsby Radar |
| 262.975 | London Mil |
| 263.075 | London Mil |
| 263.50 | Boscombe Down ATIS |
| 264.10 | Lakenheath Radar |
| 264.675 | Lakenheath Radar |
| 268.575 | Scottish Mil |
| 268.775 | Leuchars PAR/Valley Radar |
| 268.825 | Benson Radar |
| 268.925 | Scottish Mil |
| 269.075 | Lakenheath Ops |
| 269.10 | Shawbury Tower |
| 269.125 | Woodford Radar |
| 270.00 | London Mil |
| 275.35 | London Mil Central |
| 275.475 | London Mil West |
| 275.675 | London Mil |
| 275.80 | Upavon Tower |
| 275.875 | Coningsby Tower |
| 275.975 | Coltishall PAR |
| 276.075 | Shawbury Radar |
| 276.125 | Cosford Approach |

| | |
|---|---|
| 276.175 | Odiham ATIS |
| 276.775 | London Mil |
| 276.825 | Ternhill Approach |
| 276.85 | Boscombe Radar |
| 277.075 | Mildenhall ATIS |
| 277.125 | London Mil |
| 277.225 | Cardiff Approach |
| 277.275 | Colerne Approach |
| 277.775 | London Mil |
| 278.025 | London Mil |
| 279.175 | London Mil |
| 279.25 | Lakenheath Radar |
| 279.30 | London Mil |
| 279.35 | Benson Tower |
| 279.475 | London Mil |
| 280.40 | Otterburn Range |
| 282.00 | Cranwell Radar |
| 282.25 | Salisbury Plain A/G |
| 282.275 | Honington Tower |
| 282.80 | Boulmer A/G/Leconfield A/G/ Portland A/G/Valley SAR Ops |
| 283.475 | Anglia Radar |
| 283.525 | London Mil |
| 283.575 | Wattisham Radar |
| 284.30 | London Mil |
| 284.60 | Newcastle Radar |
| 285.025 | Leuchars Ops |
| 285.05 | Waddington Tower |
| 285.15 | Cranwell PAR |
| 285.175 | London Mil |
| 288.95 | Eskmeals Range |
| 290.575 | London Mil |
| 290.60 | London Mil |
| 290.70 | London Mil |
| 290.825 | Lakenheath PAR |
| 290.925 | London Mil |
| 290.95 | Netheravon Tower/ACMI Range |
| 291.125 | Wattisham Radar |
| 291.65 | Boscombe Radar |
| 291.675 | Waddington ATIS |
| 291.70 | Barkston Heath Radar |
| 291.775 | London Mil |
| 291.95 | Marham Radar |
| 292.475 | Leuchars Radar |
| 292.525 | London Mil |
| 292.60 | London Mil |
| 292.675 | Scottish Mil |
| 292.70 | Leeming Radar |
| 292.80 | Linton Radar |
| 293.425 | Coltishall Radar |
| 293.475 | London Mil |

| | |
|---|---|
| 293.775 | Marham Radar |
| 296.725 | Coltishall GMC/Teesside Radar |
| 296.75 | Waddington Radar |
| 297.90 | Cranwell GMC |
| 299.10 | Boulmer A/G |
| 299.40 | Culdrose GMC/Lossiemouth GMC/Boscombe Down GMC |
| 299.975 | London Mil |
| 300.175 | Portland Radar |
| 300.35 | Northolt ATIS |
| 300.425 | Linton Tower |
| 300.45 | Odiham PAR |
| 300.475 | Lyneham Radar |
| 300.575 | Waddington Radar |
| 300.675 | Judwin (Yeovil) Radar |
| 300.80 | NATO Low Flying |
| 300.825 | Lakenheath Ops |
| 300.925 | Coningsby PAR |
| 307.80 | Fairford Ops/Stanford A/G |
| 309.075 | Lakenheath PAR |
| 309.55 | Ternhill (Chetwynd Traffic) |
| 309.625 | Odiham Tower |
| 309.675 | Waddington PAR |
| 309.725 | Topcliffe Tower |
| 309.875 | Leeming PAR |
| 309.95 | Honington Approach |
| 310.00 | Aldergrove Tower/Approach |
| 311.30 | Warton Tower |
| 311.325 | Kinloss Radar/Lossiemouth Radar/Yeovilton GMC |
| 311.95 | Wittering GMC |
| 312.00 | Middle Wallop Radar |
| 312.075 | Cottesmore Radar |
| 312.225 | Coningsby Radar |
| 312.325 | Manston PAR |
| 312.35 | Northolt Tower |
| 312.40 | Lossiemouth PAR/Portland PAR |
| 312.45 | Mildenhall Ops |
| 312.50 | Waddington Radar |
| 312.525 | Farnborough Radar |
| 312.55 | Marham Ops |
| 312.625 | Dunsfold Radar |
| 312.675 | Middle Wallop Radar |
| 312.70 | Merryfield Tower |
| 312.80 | Woodvale Approach |
| 315.525 | Farnborough Radar |
| 315.75 | Benson Radar |
| 315.975 | Odiham Info |
| 316.875 | St Mawgan ATIS |
| 329.15– 335.00 | ILS Glidepath Transmitters |

| | |
|---|---|
| 336.275 | Farnborough Radar |
| 336.325 | Hawarden Tower |
| 336.35 | Kinloss Tower/Leeming PAR/Marham GMC |
| 336.375 | Cottesmore GMC |
| 336.475 | Filton Radar/Warton Radar |
| 336.525 | St Athan Tower |
| 336.55 | St Mawgan PAR |
| 337.575 | Fairford Tower |
| 337.70 | Rosehearty Range |
| 337.725 | Valley Radar |
| 337.75 | Lossiemouth Tower/Portland Tower/Navy Prestwick |
| 337.825 | Leeming Radar |
| 337.875 | Cottesmore PAR |
| 337.90 | Marham Tower/Shawbury GMC |
| 337.925 | West Freugh Tower |
| 337.95 | Garvie Range/Wittering PAR |
| 337.975 | Coningsby PAR |
| 338.625 | Manston Radar |
| 338.65 | Brize PAR |
| 338.675 | Lakenheath PAR |
| 338.825 | Ternhill Tower |
| 338.85 | Leeming GMC |
| 338.875 | Yeovilton Radar |
| 338.975 | Predannack Tower |
| 339.95 | Coltishall Tower/Culdrose Radar |
| 339.975 | Yeovilton PAR |
| 340.025 | Linton-on-Ouse GMC |
| 340.05 | Wainfleet Range |
| 340.10 | St Athan Radar |
| 340.175 | Lyneham GMC/Valley Tower |
| 340.20 | Church Fenton GMC |
| 340.25 | London Mil |
| 340.30 | Spadeadam Range |
| 340.325 | Benson GMC |
| 340.475 | Cranwell Radar |
| 340.525 | Barkston Heath Approach |
| 340.55 | ACMI Range |
| 340.575 | Cottesmore Radar |
| 340.70 | Shawbury ATIS |
| 342.025 | Filton Tower |
| 342.075 | Barkston Heath Tower |
| 342.125 | Waddington GMC |
| 342.175 | Donna Nook Range |
| 342.25 | Coltishall Radar |
| 342.45 | Brize Radar |
| 343.375 | Holbeach Range |
| 343.425 | Wattisham Tower |
| 343.475 | Portland ATIS |
| 343.60 | Croughton Radio |
| 343.70 | Warton Radar |
| 344.00 | Nato Common Radar |
| 344.35 | Manston Tower/Topcliffe PAR |
| 344.45 | Lossiemouth ATIS |
| 344.475 | Linton Radar |
| 344.575 | Leeming Tower |
| 344.60 | Colerne Tower |
| 344.625 | Coningsby Radar |
| 344.80 | Mildenhall Command Post |
| 344.975 | Northolt Radar |
| 345.025 | Lyneham Radar |
| 345.20 | Larkhill Range |
| 351.825 | Barkston Heath ATIS |
| 353.55 | Aberdeen Approach |
| 356.175 | Wattisham PAR |
| 356.20 | Aberporth Range |
| 356.275 | Halton Aero Club |
| 356.725 | Leeming Ops |
| 356.80 | Wainfleet Range |
| 356.875 | Brize Radar |
| 356.975 | Shawbury PAR |
| 357.125 | Cosford Tower |
| 357.15 | Wittering Tower |
| 357.175 | St Athan Radar |
| 357.20 | St Mawgan Radar |
| 357.375 | Topcliffe Radar |
| 357.40 | Farnborough Tower |
| 357.475 | Brize Ops |
| 358.475 | Kinloss Ops |
| 358.525 | Linton PAR |
| 358.55 | Coningsby GMC/Larkhill Range |
| 358.575 | Woodford Tower |
| 358.60 | Fairford Metro |
| 358.65 | Leeming Radar |
| 358.675 | Lakenheath Tower/Valley PAR |
| 358.70 | Culdrose PAR |
| 358.725 | Cottesmore Radar |
| 358.75 | Mona Tower |
| 358.80 | Benson Radar |
| 358.825 | Luce Bay Range |
| 359.40 | ACMI Range |
| 359.50 | Lyneham Radar |
| 359.825 | Wattisham PAR |
| 360.45 | Holbeach Range |
| 360.55 | St Mawgan Radar |
| 360.725 | Barkston Heath PAR |
| 360.75 | Colerne GMC |
| 360.775 | Manorbier Range |
| 362.05 | Salisbury Plain Ranges |
| 362.225 | Netheravon Approach |
| 362.30 | Nato Common Approach |

| | |
|---|---|
| 362.675 | Linton Radar |
| 364.80 | Coltishall Ops |
| 364.825 | Middle Wallop PAR |
| 365.075 | Ternhill Approach |
| 365.10 | Mildenhall Ops |
| 366.225 | Manorbier Range |
| 367.375 | Dunsfold Radar |
| 369.15 | Spadeadam Range |
| 369.875 | Yeovilton Radar |
| 369.975 | Judwin (Yeovil) Radar |
| 370.00 | Predannack Tower |
| 370.05 | Cottesmore Tower/Kinloss PAR |
| 370.075 | Leuchars PAR |
| 370.10 | Boscombe Tower |
| 370.30 | Brize GMC/Llanbedr PAR |
| 371.20 | Fairford Ops |
| 372.30 | Culdrose ATIS |
| 372.325 | Valley Radar |
| 372.425 | Cambridge Tower/Radar/Judwin (Yeovil) Tower |
| 372.625 | Middle Wallop Tower |
| 372.65 | Yeovilton Tower |
| 375.20 | Lyneham PAR |
| 375.325 | Church Fenton Radar |
| 375.40 | Dunsfold Tower |
| 375.425 | Newton Tower |
| 375.50 | Northolt PAR |
| 376.525 | Kinloss PAR/Luce Bay Range |
| 376.575 | Cottesmore Radar/Wittering Radar |
| 376.625 | Fairford Radar/St Mawgan GMC |
| 376.65 | Lossiemouth Radar |
| 379.025 | Manston Radar |
| 379.20 | Aberporth Range |
| 379.275 | Coltishall Radar |
| 379.425 | Northolt Radar |
| 379.475 | Fairford Ops |
| 379.525 | Cranwell Tower |
| 379.65 | Marham PAR |
| 379.675 | Dishforth GMC |
| 379.70 | Mona Approach |
| 379.75 | Yeovilton ATIS |
| 379.80 | Teesside Tower |
| 379.85 | Plymouth Military Radar |
| 379.875 | Pembrey Range |
| 380.025 | Boscombe Radar |
| 380.125 | St Athan PAR |
| 380.15 | Mildenhall GMC |
| 380.175 | Llanbedr Tower |
| 380.225 | Culdrose Tower |
| 380.95 | Wittering Radar |
| 381.00 | Lyneham ATIS |
| 381.075 | Linton/Church Fenton Radar |
| 381.125 | Boscombe PAR |
| 381.15 | Lyme Bay Range |
| 381.20 | Brize Tower |
| 383.225 | Wittering PAR |
| 383.275 | Tain Range |
| 383.475 | Cranwell PAR |
| 383.525 | West Freugh Radar |
| 385.40 | Nato Common PAR |
| 386.50 | St Athan GMC |
| 386.675 | Llanbedr Radar |
| 386.725 | Church Fenton PAR |
| 386.775 | Odiham Radar |
| 386.825 | Lyneham Tower |
| 386.875 | Shawbury Radar |
| 386.90 | Valley GMC |
| 397.975 | Lakenheath GMC |
| 398.35 | Lakenheath Radar |

# *ICAO aircraft type designators*

The designators below are used for flight planning purposes and also by ATC on flight progress strips. The aircraft name or designation in full is normally used on the R/T, but many of the abbreviated versions may also be heard. This list is a sample of the most common ones.

| | |
|---|---|
| AA5 | Gulfstream American AA5 |
| AC6T | Turbo Commander |
| AC12 | Rockwell 112 |
| AC14 | Rockwell 114 |
| B73F | Boeing 737-400 |
| B73S | Boeing 737-300 |
| B74F | Boeing 747-400 |
| B74S | Boeing 747SP |
| B707 | Boeing 707 |
| B727 | Boeing 727 |
| B737 | Boeing 737 |
| B747 | Boeing 747 |
| B757 | Boeing 757 |
| B767 | Boeing 767 |
| BA10 | BAe 125-1000 |
| BA11 | BAC 111 |
| BA31 | Jetstream 31 |
| BA41 | Jetstream 41 |
| BA46 | BAe 146 |
| BATP | BAe ATP |
| BE10 | Beech King Air 100 |
| BE20 | Super King Air 200 |
| BE40 | Beechjet 400 |
| BE55 | Beech Baron |
| BE60 | Beech Duke |
| BE76 | Beech Duchess |
| BE90 | Beech King Air 90 |
| BH06 | Bell Jet Ranger |
| BN2 | BN-2 Islander |
| BN3 | BN-3 Trislander |
| BT12 | Beagle Pup |
| C130 | C-130 Hercules |
| C150 | Cessna 150 |
| C172 | Cessna 172 |

| | |
|---|---|
| C310 | Cessna 310 |
| C401 | Cessna 401 |
| C421 | Cessna 421 |
| C500 | Cessna Citation |
| C550 | Citation II |
| CONC | Concorde |
| CV58 | Convair 580 |
| D228 | Dornier 228 |
| DA20 | Falcon 20 |
| DA50 | Falcon 50 |
| DH6 | DHC-6 Twin Otter |
| DH7 | DHC-7 Dash 7 |
| DH8 | DHC-8 Dash 8 |
| E110 | Bandeirante |
| E121 | Xingu |
| EA30 | Airbus A300 |
| EA32 | Airbus A320 |
| EA33 | Airbus A330 |
| EA34 | Airbus A340 |
| FK27 | Friendship |
| FK50 | Fokker 50 |
| FK10 | Fokker 100 |
| G2 | Gulfstream II |
| G3 | Gulfstream IV |
| G159 | Gulfstream I |
| GA7 | Cougar |
| HAR | Harrier |
| HP7 | Herald |
| HR10 | Robin HR100 |
| HS04 | Dove |
| HS25 | BAe 125 |
| HS74 | BAe 748 |
| IL62 | Ilyushin IL-62 |
| IL76 | Ilyushin IL-76 |

| | | | | |
|---|---|---|---|---|
| JAGR | Jaguar | | S601 | Corvette |
| L101 | Tristar | | S880 | Rallye |
| L188 | Lockheed Electra | | SC3 | Bulldog |
| LR24 | Learjet 24 | | SF34 | Saab SF340 |
| LR35 | Learjet 35 | | SHAR | Sea Harrier |
| MD80 | MD80 variants | | SH5 | Belfast |
| ND16 | C160 Transall | | SH33 | Shorts SD3-30 |
| ND26 | Nord 262 | | SH36 | Shorts SD3-60 |
| PA28 | Piper Cherokee | | SW2 | Merlin IIA |
| PA31 | Piper Navajo | | SW3 | Merlin III |
| PARO | Piper Arrow | | SW4 | Merlin IV/Metro |
| PASE | Piper Seneca | | TB09 | TB-09 Tampico |
| PAYE | Piper Cheyenne I/II | | TB10 | TB-10 Tobago |
| PAZT | Piper Aztec | | TU34 | Tupolev TU-134 |
| PN68 | Partenavia P68 | | TU54 | Tupolev TU-154 |
| S210 | Caravelle | | VC8 | Viscount 800 |

# Appendix 6

# Aircraft radio call-signs

The call-sign prefixes below include many officially allocated to various British operators, although in practice some are rarely used. A few military call-signs to be heard over Britain have been incorporated as they have remained unchanged for many years.

The three-letter codes are allocated by ICAO, the International Civil Aviation Organisation, on a worldwide basis and are listed separately as many operators use them rather than the allocated company designator. An example is 'RDK' instead of 'Irish Tours', either being permissible. There are now so many of them to be heard over Britain that the computer at London Area Terninal Control Centre has been programmed to print the spoken call-sign as well as the three-letter code on the controllers' flight progress strips, to make things easier for them. Unfortunately, new operators are appearing so fast that confusion still occurs at times, particularly when a call-sign is spoken in a foreign accent.

Military call-signs are further explained in Chapter 17, many being changed frequently for security reasons. This is not a problem for training aircraft, and many three-letter prefixes reflect their bases, examples being 'VYT' and 'WIT' for the Valley and Wittering Flying Training Units respectively; these have been assimilated into the ICAO three-letter system. I have endeavoured to include as many as possible of the civil prefixes heard over Britain and further afield on HF, but the list does not claim to be exhaustive.

| R/T call-sign | Operator |
| --- | --- |
| Abex | Airborne Express (USA) |
| ABG | Abelag (Belgium) |
| Aceforce | Allied Command Europe |
| Actair | Air Charter & Travel |
| Adria | Adria Airways |
| Aer Arann | Aer Arann |
| Aerial | Aerial Enterprises |
| Aerocancun | Aerocancun (Mexico) |
| Aerocarga | Carga Mexicana |
| Aerocaribbean | Aerocaribbean |
| Aerocharter | Aero Charter Midlands |
| Aerocom | Compagnie Aeronautique Européenne |
| Aeroflot | Aeroflot |
| Aero Lloyd | Aero Lloyd |
| Aeromar | Aeromaritime (France) |
| Aeromexico | Aeromexico |

| R/T call-sign | Operator |
| --- | --- |
| Aeromonterrey | Aeromonterrey (Mexico) |
| Aeronaut | Cranfield Institute |
| Aer Turas | Aer Turas |
| African Airlines | African Airlines (Kenya) |
| African Express | African Express |
| African West | African West (Senegal) |
| Afro | Affretair |
| Aigle Azur | Aigle Azur |
| Airafric | Air Afrique |
| Air Alba | Air Alba (UK) |
| Airals | Air Alsie (Denmark) |
| Air Atlantis | Air Atlantis |
| Air Belgium | Air Belgium |
| Air Berlin | Air Berlin |
| Air Cadet | RAF Air Cadet Schools |
| Aircam | Aircam Aviation |
| Air Canada | Air Canada |

| R/T call-sign | Operator | R/T call-sign | Operator |
|---|---|---|---|
| Air Charter | Air Charter (France) | All Weather | CAA Aerodrome Standards |
| Air Club | Air Club International (Canada) | Aly Aviation | Aly Aviation |
| | | Alyemda | Yemen Airlines |
| Air Discovery | Discovery Airways | American | American Airlines |
| Airevac | USAF Ambulance | Amex | Aero Market Express (Spain) |
| Air Experience | Air Experience Flight | Amtran | American Trans Air |
| Air Exports | EI Air Exports (Eire) | Appollair | Appollo Airlines (Greece) |
| Air Force One | US President | Aravco | Aravco |
| Air Force Two | US Vice-President | Argentina | Aerolineas Argentinas |
| Air France | Air France | Armyair | Army Air Corps |
| Airgoat | Airborne School of Flying | Ascot | RAF No 1 Group |
| Air Hanson | Air Hanson | Astel | Air Service Training |
| Air Hong Kong | Air Hong Kong | Aston | Chequair |
| Air India | Air India | Atlanta | Air Atlanta Iceland |
| Air Inter | Air Inter | Atlantic | Air Atlantique |
| Air Jet | Air Jet (France) | Atrans | Aviatrans (Russian Fed) |
| Air Kibris | Kibris Turkish | Audeli | Audeli Air Express (Spain) |
| Air Lanka | Air Lanka | Augsburg Air | Augsburg Airways (Germany) |
| Airlease | Aero Leasing France | | |
| Air Liberté | Air Liberté | Austrian | Austrian Airlines |
| Air Limousin | Air Limousin | Austrian Charter | Austrian Air Transport |
| Air Littoral | Air Littoral | Aviaco | Aviaco (Spain) |
| Air London | Air London | Avianca | Avianca (Colombia) |
| Air Malta | Air Malta | Avianova | Avianova (Italy) |
| Air Martinique | Air Martinique | Avon | Avon Flying School |
| Air Mauritius | Air Mauritius | Avro | Avro Woodford |
| Airmed | Air Medical Ltd | Ayflight | Ayflight Aviation Ltd |
| Air Mil | Spanish Air Force | Ayjay Services | AJ Services Ltd |
| Air Mike | Continental Micronesia (Guam) | Ayline | Aurigny Air Services |
| | | Aztec | Air Bristol |
| Airmorique | Air Armorique (France) | Backer | British Charter |
| Air Nav | Air Navigation & Trading | Balair | Balair (Switzerland) |
| Air Portugal | Air Portugal | Balkan | Balkan-Bulgarian |
| Air Rwanda | Air Rwanda | Baltic | Baltic International (Latvia) |
| Airshot | Birmingham Aerocentre | Bangladesh | Bangladesh Biman |
| Air South | Air South (UK) | Batman | Ratioflug Frankfurt |
| Air Sweden | Air Sweden | Beaupair | Aviation Beauport |
| Airtax | Warwickshire Aerocentre | Bee Med | British Mediterranean Airways |
| Air Tahiti | Air Tahiti | | |
| Air Truck | Air Truck (Spain) | Belgair | Trans European Airways |
| Air Vendé | Air Vendé | Belgian Carriers | Belgian International |
| Airwork | Airwork Services | Belgochallenge | Challengair (Belgium) |
| Air Zaire | Air Zaire | Belstar | Eurobelgian Airlines |
| Air Zimbabwe | Air Zimbabwe | Beryl | Emerald Air |
| Alderney | European Aviation Services | Big A | Arrow Air (USA) |
| Alitalia | Alitalia | Big Eff | Fine Airlines (USA) |
| Alkair | Alkair (Denmark) | Bird Dog | Crispe Aviation |
| All Charter | All Charter | Birmex | Maersk Air Ltd |
| All Nippon | All Nippon | Biscayne | Miami Air International |

| R/T call-sign | Operator | R/T call-sign | Operator |
|---|---|---|---|
| Bizair | Business A/C Users | Ceebee | CB Executive Helicopters |
| Bizjet | Hamlin Jet | Cega | Cega Aviation |
| Blackbox | Boscombe Down | Centennial | Centennial (Spain) |
| Blue | IBM Euroflight (Switzerland) | Chad | Chad Air Services |
| Blue Eagle | Eagle Flying Services | Challair | Challeng'air (France) |
| Blue Jet | Flyair (Spain) | Channex | Channel Express |
| Bluestar | Maerskair Ltd | Chaser | Enterprise Consultants |
| Bodensee | Delta Air (Germany) | Chauffair | Chauffair |
| Bond | Bond Helicopters | Cheshair | Cheshire Air Training |
| Bonus | Bonus Aviation Ltd | Cheyne | Cheyne Motors Ltd |
| Box | Tiphook PLC | China | CAAC |
| Boxer | HQ Air National Guard | China Eastern | China Eastern Airlines |
| Braathens | Braathens (Norway) | Chivenor | Chivenor SAR |
| Brenex | Welsh Dragon Aviation | Chukka | Polo Aviation Ltd |
| Brintel | British International Helicopters | Cimber | Cimber Air |
| Bristow | Bristow Helicopters | City | KLM Cityhopper |
| Britannia | Britannia Airways | Citybus | City Airbus Ltd |
| British Medical | British Medical Charter | Citylink | Citylink Air Taxi |
| British World | British World Airlines | City Jet | City Jet (Ireland) |
| Brittany | Brit Air | Clan | Transatlantic Fighter Deployment |
| Broadsword | Air Foyle Charter Airways | Clan King | Air Sinclair |
| Broadway | Fleet Requirements Unit | Clansman | Airwork |
| Brunei | Royal Brunei Airlines | Clifton | Bristol Flying Centre |
| Brymon | Brymon European | Clowes | Clowes Estates |
| Budget Jet | Ryanair (UK) | Clue | HQ EUSCOM (USAF) |
| Buffalo Air | Buffalo Airways (USA) | Coastguard | HM Coastguard |
| Bul Air Cargo | Bulgarian Air Cargo | Coastrider | Base Regional (Netherlands) |
| Busy Bee | Busy Bee of Norway | Compass | Compass Aviation |
| Buzzard | Butane Buzzard Aviation | Conair | Conair (Canada) |
| Cabair | Cabair Air Taxis | Condor | Condor Flugdienst |
| Caledonian | Caledonian | Contactair | Contactair Flugdienst |
| Calibrator | CAA Calibration Flight | Conti | Conti-Flug International |
| Calypso | Regal Bahamas International | Continental | Continental Airlines |
| Cam-Air | Cameroon Airlines | Corporate | Connect Aerienne Ltd |
| Cameo | Cam Air | Corsair | Corse Air |
| Canada | Worldways Canada | Corsemedi | Corse-Mediterranée |
| Canadian | Canadian Airlines | Costock | East Midlands Helicopters |
| Canforce | Canadian Armed Forces | Cotam | French AF Transport |
| Cargo | Safair Freighters (S Africa) | Coyne Air | Coyne Aviation |
| Cargolux | Cargolux Airlines | Cranwell | Cranwell FTU |
| Caribjet | Caribbean Airways (Barbados) | Croatia | Croatian Airlines |
| Carill | Carill Aviation Ltd | Cross Air | Cross Air |
| Catbird | US Navy Italy | Crusader | Firebird Aerobatics |
| Cathay | Cathay Pacific | CSA Lines | Czech Airlines |
| Cavalier | Chiltern Airways | CTA | CTA (Switzerland) |
| Cecil | Cecil Aviation | Cubana | Cubana |
| Cedarjet | Middle East Airlines | Cygnet | BAe Flying College |
| | | Cyprus | Cyprus Airways |

| R/T call-sign | Operator |
|---|---|
| Dagobert | Quick Air Jet (Germany) |
| Dahl | DHL Airways (USA) |
| Dairair | Dairo Air Services (Uganda) |
| Dantrans | Danish Air Transport |
| Debonair | Debonair Airways |
| Delta | Delta Airlines |
| Deltair | Delta Air Transport |
| Denim | Denim Air (Netherlands) |
| Direct Flight | Air Direct |
| Disco | David See Flying Services |
| Dominicana | Dominicana |
| Donair | Donair Flying Club |
| Drake | Air Care (SW) |
| Duke | Jubilee Airways |
| Dynamite | Dynamic Air (Holland) |
| Eagle Air | Eagle Air (Iceland) |
| Eastex | Eastern Air-Executive |
| Easyjet | Easyjet Airlines |
| Eclipse | World Airlines Ltd |
| Ecuatoriana | Ecuatoriana (Ecuador) |
| Edelweiss | Edelweiss Air (Switzerland) |
| Egyptair | Egyptair |
| El Al | El Al |
| Electricity | SWEB Helicopter Unit |
| Elite | Canada 3000 |
| Emerald | Westair Aviation (Ireland) |
| Emery | Emery Worldwide |
| Emirates | Emirates |
| Empress | CP-Air (Canada) |
| Engiadina | Air Engiadina (Switzerland) |
| Envoy | Air World |
| Estonian | Estonian Air |
| Ethiopian | Ethiopian Airlines |
| Euralair | Euralair (France) |
| Eurocat | Cat Aviation (Switzerland) |
| Eurocharter | European Aviation |
| Eurocypria | Eurocypria Airlines |
| Eurofly | Eurofly (Italy) |
| Eurojet | Eurojet (Spain) |
| Euromanx | Manx Airlines (Europe) |
| Europa | Europe Air (France) |
| European | European Airways |
| Eurotrans | European Air Transport |
| Eurowest | Euroflight (Sweden) |
| Eurowings | Eurowings (Germany) |
| Evergreen | Evergreen International |
| Exam | CAA Flight Examiner |
| Execujet | Execujet (UK) |
| Executive | Night Express (Germany) |

| R/T call-sign | Operator |
|---|---|
| Exel Commuter | Air Exel (Netherlands) |
| Exxon | 43rd Air Refuelling Wing |
| Falcon | Falcon Aviation (Sweden) |
| Falcon Jet | Falcon Jet Centre |
| Farner | Farner Air Transport (Switzerland) |
| Faster | Fast Air (Chile) |
| Fedex | Federal Express |
| Finnair | Finnair |
| First City | First City Air |
| Firestone | Dravidian Air Services |
| Flagship | Express Airlines |
| Flightline | Flightline |
| Flint Air | Flight Services Intl |
| Flo West | Florida West Airlines |
| Fly Cargo | African International (Swaziland) |
| Flyer | Cityflyer Express |
| Food | Food Brokers Ltd |
| Fordair | Ford Motor Co |
| Fortress | Fortess Flying Club |
| Foxclub | Leicester Aero Club |
| Foxtrot Mike | French Air Force |
| Foyle | Air Foyle (TNT) |
| France Cargo | EFIS Cargo |
| Frans Air Force | French Air Force |
| Fred Olsen | Fred Olsen (Norway) |
| French Lines | AOM Minerve |
| Frevag | Frevag (Belgium) |
| Funjet | LTE International (Spain) |
| Futura | Futura (Spain) |
| Gabon Cargo | Air Gabon Cargo |
| Gama | Gama Aviation |
| Gauntlet | Boscombe Down MoD/PE |
| Geeair | G Air Aviation Services |
| Geetee Avia | GT Airways |
| Geevax | Geevax Ltd |
| Gemstone | Emerald Airways |
| Genesis | Eastern Executive |
| Genex | Aviogenex |
| German Air Force | German Air Force |
| Germania | Germania |
| Ghana | Ghana Airways |
| Giant | Atlas Air (USA) |
| Gibair | GB Airways |
| Gillair | Gill Aviation |
| Gojet | Eurojet Aviation |
| Gold | 28th Air Refuelling Sqdn |
| Gram Air | Grampian Helicopters |

| R/T call-sign | Operator | R/T call-sign | Operator |
|---|---|---|---|
| Grand Prix | Williams Grand Prix Racing | JAT | Jugoslovenski Aerotransport |
| Granite | Business Air | Jay | J & J Air Charters |
| Grantex | Grantex Aviation | Jersey | Jersey European |
| Green Air | Green Air (Turkey) | Jes Air | Jes Air (Bulgaria) |
| Greenbird | Skyjet (Belgium) | Jet | European Jet Ltd |
| Greenlandair | Greenlandair | Jetplan | Memrykord Ltd |
| Grid | National Grid Co | Jet Set | Air 2000 |
| Griffon | The 955 Preservation Group | Jetwing | All Leisure |
| Gulf Air | Gulf Air | Jolly | USAF HH-53 Rescue |
| Gypo | Red Arrows Transit No 2 | | Helicopters |
| | Section | Jordanian | Royal Jordanian |
| Gypsy | Eagle Aviation (UK) Ltd | Kabo | Kabo Air Travels (Nigeria) |
| Hamburg Air | Hamburg Airlines | Karair | Kar-Air (Finland) |
| Hamilton | Air Nova | Keenair | Keenair Charter Ltd |
| Hansaline | Lufthansa Cityline | Kenya | Kenya Airways |
| Hapag Lloyd | Hapag-Lloyd | Key Air | Key Airlines (USA) |
| Harvard | Scientific Industries UK | Kilro | Air Kilroe |
| Hawker | BAe Dunsfold | King | 67th Rescue Sqn, USAF |
| Head-Dancer | EC-135 Comms Escort for | Kittyhawk | 32 (The Royal) Sqn (HM the |
| | Transatlantic Fighter | | Queen on board or certain |
| | Deployments | | other members of the Royal |
| Heavylift | Heavylift Cargo | | Family) |
| Helimed | First Air | Kitty | Royal positioning flights |
| Heli Southern | Southern Air Ltd | Kiwi | Royal New Zealand Air |
| Heritage | Jet Heritage | | Force |
| Herky | 37th Airlift Sqn | KLM | KLM |
| Hotel Yankee | Liberia World Airlines | Knightway | Knightair Ltd |
| Humber Air | Humber Aviation | Koreanair | Korean Airlines |
| Hunting | Hunting Cargo | Kris | Air Foyle Charters |
| Hyde | Hyde Helicopters | Kuwaiti | Kuwait Airways |
| Iberia | Iberia | Lair | Lionair (Luxembourg) |
| Iceair | Icelandair | Laker | Laker Airways |
| IDS | IDS Aircraft | LAN | LAN Chile |
| Images | Air Images | Lark | 55th Weather Recce Sqn, |
| Indonesia | Garuda Indonesian | | USAF |
| Info | Independent Nuclear Forces | Lauda | Lauda Air |
| | Observers | LCN | Lineas Aereas Canarias |
| Instone | Instone Airlines | Leck | Lec Refrigeration |
| Interflight | Interflight Ltd | Leeds | Northern Helicopters |
| Intersun | Intersun (Turkey) | Leisure | Air UK (Leisure) |
| Iona | Iona Airways | Lencon | Mala Services Ltd |
| Iranair | Iran Air | Leopard | 32 (The Royal) Sqn (Duke |
| Irish Air Corps | Irish Air Corps | | of York) |
| Irish Tours | Irish Air Tours | Libair | Libyan Arab |
| Isis | City Air Ltd | Lifeline | Aeromedicaire Ltd |
| Isle Avia | Island Aviation | Linton on Ouse | Linton-on-Ouse FTU |
| Istanbul | Istanbul Airlines | Lithuania | Lithuanian Airlines |
| Jambo | Alliance (Uganda) | Logan | Loganair |
| Japanair | Japan Airlines | Lomas | Lomas Helicopters |

| R/T call-sign | Operator | R/T call-sign | Operator |
|---|---|---|---|
| London Flights | London Flights (Biggin Hill) | Navcal | Hunting Aviation Services |
| Lonex | London Executive Aviation | Neat | European Air Taxi |
| Longtail | Imperial Air Services | Neatax | Northern Executive |
| Loveair | London Flight Centre | Netherlands | Royal Netherlands Air Force |
| LTS | LTU Sud | Air Force | |
| LTU | Lufttransport | Netherlands Navy | Netherlands Navy |
| Lufthansa | Lufthansa | Netherlines | Netherlines |
| Luxair | Luxair | Newdan | Newair (Denmark) |
| Lynton | Lynton Aviation | Newpin | Raytheon Hawarden |
| Macair | Macair Ltd | New Zealand | Air New Zealand |
| Macline | McAlpine | Nile Safaris | Nile Safaris (Sudan) |
| Maerskair | Maerskair (Denmark) | Nimbus | Nimbus Aviation |
| Magec | Magec Aviation | Nippon Cargo | Nippon Cargo Airlines |
| Magic | NATO AWACS | Nitro | TNT International |
| Majan | Royal Omani AF | NOAA | National Oceanographic and |
| Malawi | Air Malawi | | Atmospheric Administration |
| Malaysian | Malaysian Airline System | Nordic Air | Nordic (Sweden) |
| Malev | Malev (Hungary) | Norspeed | Norway Airlines |
| Mann | Alan Mann Helicopters | Northwest | Northwest Orient |
| Manta | Woodford Flight Test | Norton | Northants School Of Flying |
| Manx | Manx Airlines | Norving | A/S Norving (Norway) |
| March | March Helicopters | Norwegian | Royal Norwegian Air Force |
| Marocair | Royal Air Maroc | Nugget | RAe Farnborough |
| Marshall | Marshall of Cambridge | Oasis | Oasis International |
| Martin | Martin-Baker | Odiham | Odiham FTU |
| Mash | Foldpack Ltd | Okada Air | Okada Airlines (Nigeria) |
| Matair | Matair Ltd | Olympic | Olympic Airways |
| Maverick | Helicopter Training and Hire | Omega | Aeromega Ltd |
| Medic | Medical Air Services | Oman | Oman Royal Flight |
| Medivac | London Helicopter | Onur | Onur Air (Turkey) |
| | Emergency Medical Service | Orange | Air Holland |
| Merair | Meridiana (Italy) | Osprey | PLM-Dollar Group |
| Merlin | Rolls Royce (Military) | Osprey | Open Skies Consultative |
| Merrix | Merrix Air | | Commission |
| Metman | Met Research Flight | Oxoe | Oxaero |
| Midland | British Midland | Oxford | CSE Aviation |
| Mike Romeo | Air Mauritanie | Pacific | Air Pacific (Fiji) |
| Minair | CAA Flying Unit | Pakistan | Pakistan International |
| Minister | Business European Airways | Para | Army Parachute Centre |
| Monarch | Monarch Airlines | Parachute | UK Parachute Centre |
| Moonrun | Benelux Falcon (Belgium) | Paraguaya | Lineas Aereas Paraguayas |
| Morefly | Morefly (Norway) | Pat | US Army Priority Air |
| Moth | Tiger Fly | | Transport |
| Mozambique | LAM-Mozambique | Pathfinder | Leeds Central Helicopters |
| Multi | Air Transport Schipol | Peacock | H. E. Peacock & Sons |
| Myson | Myson Group | Pearl | Oriental Pearl Airways |
| Nacar | Air Sur (Spain) | Pegasus | Pegasus (Turkey) |
| Namibia | Namib Air | Pektron | Pektron Ltd |
| Navy | Royal or US Navy | Philippine | Philippine Airlines |

| R/T call-sign | Operator | R/T call-sign | Operator |
|---|---|---|---|
| Picture | Flying Pictures Ltd | Roman | R. M. Aviation Ltd |
| Pipeline | Helicopter inspection flight | Rook | 9th Recce Wing |
| Pirate | Air South West | Royal Nepal | Royal Nepal Airlines |
| Pleasure Flights | Manchester Helicopter Centre | Roycar | Rolls Royce Ltd |
| | | Rubens | VLM (Belgium) |
| Pointscall | Points of Call Airlines | Rushair | AVIAL (Russian Fed) |
| Polar Tiger | Polar Air Cargo (USA) | Rushton | FR Aviation |
| Police | Police Aviation Services | Ryanair | Ryanair |
| Pollot | LOT (Poland) | Sabena | Sabena |
| Port | Skyworld Airlines (USA) | Sabre | Sabre Airways |
| Portugalia | Portugalia | Safiran | Safiran Airlines (Iran) |
| Powerline | Helicopter inspection flight | Saint Athan | St Athan MU |
| Predator | Eagle Airways | Sam | Special Air Mission (USAF) |
| Premiere | First European Airways | Samson | Samson Aviation |
| Prestige | Capital Trading Aviation | Sandair | Fly Ltd |
| Proflight | Langtry Flying Group | Sapphire | Bristol BAe |
| Proteus | Proteus Airlines (France) | Sarnair | Channel Aviation |
| Provost | Bearing Supplies Ltd | Saudi | Saudi-Arabian Airlines |
| Python | Performance Executive | Scandinavian | Scandinavian Airlines System |
| Qantas | Qantas | | |
| Qatari | Qatar Airlines | Scanvip | Air Express (Norway) |
| Quick | Quick Airways (Holland) | Scanwing | Malmo Aviation |
| Quid | 43rd Air Refuelling Sqdn | Schreiner | Schreiner Airways |
| Rabbit | Rabbit-Air Zurich | Scillonia | Isles of Scilly Sky Bus |
| Rafair | Royal Air Force | Scotair | Euroscot Airways |
| Rainbow | 32 (The Royal) Sqdn (HRH Prince Philip) | Seacoat | SE College of Air Training |
| | | Sea Devon | Sea Devon Flight |
| Rangemile | Rangemile Ltd | Seagreen | Seagreen Air Transport |
| Ranger | Defence Products Ltd | Seeline | Barnes Olson Aeroleasing |
| Rapex | BAC Aircraft | Selair | Sierra National Airlines (Sierra Leone) |
| Raven | Raven Air | | |
| Reach | USAF Air Mobility Command | Seltex | J. Selwyn Smith (Shepley) |
| | | Semitrans | Semitool Europe Ltd |
| Readymix | RMC Group Services | Senair | Senair Charter Ltd |
| Redair | Redhill Aviation | Sentry | USAF AWACS |
| Red Devils | Red Devils Parachute Team | Seychelles | Air Seychelles |
| Redstars | Redstar Formation Team | Shamrock | Aer Lingus |
| Regal | Crown Air (Canada) | Shawbury | Shawbury FTU |
| Relief | Relief Transport Services | Shell | Shell Aircraft |
| Rescue | RAF Rescue | Shopair | Shoprite Group Ltd |
| Retro | Transatlantic Fighter Deployment | Short | Short Brothers |
| | | Shuttle | British Airways Shuttle |
| Rheinland | Rheinland Air Service | Silverline | Sterling Helicopters |
| Rhinoair | Heathrow Jet Charter | Simflight | Simulated Flight Training |
| Rhody | Rhode Island Air National Guard | Singapore | Singapore Airlines |
| | | Skydive | Activity Aviation |
| Richair | Rich International | Skyjet | Panair Spain |
| Riverside | Universal Air Transport | Skyking | Skyking Ltd |
| Rolls | Rolls Royce (Bristol) | Skyline Helicopters | Skyline Helicopters |

| R/T call-sign | Operator | R/T call-sign | Operator |
|---|---|---|---|
| Sky Service | Sky Service (Belgium) | Tat | Tat-European (France) |
| Skywork | Scottish Airways Flyers | Tayside | Tayside Aviation |
| Slip | Transatlantic Fighter Deployment | Tee Air | Tower Air (USA) |
| | | Teebird | West Freugh FTU |
| Sloane | Sloane Aviation Ltd | Teessair | North British Airlines |
| Snoopy | Air Traffic GMBH | Tennant | Jetstream Aircraft Ltd |
| Sobelair | Sobelair (Belgium) | Tester | Empire Test Pilots School |
| Somalair | Somali Airlines | Thai | Thai International |
| Southern Air | Southern Air Transport | Thanet | TG Aviation Ltd |
| Southern Comfort | Laka Motors Ltd | Til | Tajikistan International |
| Spar | 58th Airlift Sqdn, USAF | Tomcat | Cologne Commercial Flight |
| Special | Metropolitan Police Air Support Unit | Topcat | Helicopter Services |
| | | Topcliffe | Topcliffe FTU |
| Spectrum | Spectrum Aviation | Tourjet | Airtours |
| Speedbird | British Airways | Transamerica | Transamerica Airlines |
| Speedfox | Jet Air (Denmark) | Trans Arabian | Trans Arabian (Sudan) |
| Speedway | Deutsche BA | Trapper | Tempest Aviation |
| Spider | Ibis (Belgium) | Transat | Air Transat |
| Spotter | RUC Air Support | Transavia | Transavia (Holland) |
| Springbok | South African Airways | Transcon | Trans Continental (USA) |
| Stampede | Holidair (Canada) | Trans Europe | Air Transport (Slovakia) |
| Standards | CAA Training Standards | Translift | Translift Airways (Eire) |
| Stapleford | Stapleford Flight Centre | Transwede | Transwede |
| Star | Star Aviation (UK) | Triangle | Atlantic Island Air (Iceland) |
| Starburst | Glenair Helicopters | Tropic | Tropair (UK) |
| Stellair | Stellair (France) | Truman | Truman Air Charter |
| Sterling | Sterling European Airlines | Tulip | Tulip Air (Netherlands) |
| Streamline | Streamline Aviation | Tunair | Tunis Air |
| Suckling | Suckling Airways | Tune | 435th Airlift Wing |
| Sudanair | Sudan Airways | Turbine | Turbine Helicopters Ltd |
| Sunshine | Sunshine Aviation (Switzerland) | Turkair | Turkish Airlines |
| | | Turnhouse | Turnhouse Flying Club |
| Sunways | Sunways Airlines (Sweden) | TWA | Trans World Airlines |
| Sunwing | Spanair | Tyne | Aero Tours (Newcastle) |
| Surinam | Surinam Airways | Tyrolean | Tyrolean Airways |
| Surrey | Surrey and Kent Flying Club | Uganda | Uganda Airlines |
| Surveyor | Cooper Aerial Surveys | Ukay | Air UK |
| Swan | Inflite Ltd | Ukraine Cargo | Air Ukraine Cargo |
| Swazi Cargo | Air Swazi | Ukraine International | Air Ukraine International |
| Swedic | Swedish Air Force | | |
| Swissair | Swissair | Uni Air | Uni Air (France) |
| Swiss Ambulance | Swiss Air Ambulance | Unique | Helicopter Management Ltd |
| Sword | Thomas R Green | United | United Airlines |
| Syrianair | Syrian Arab Airlines | Universair | Universair (Spain) |
| Tajikair | Tajikair | UPS | United Parcel Service (USA) |
| Tango Lima | Trans Mediterranean | US Air | US Air |
| Tarmac | Tarmac Aviation | UTA | UTA (France) |
| Tarnish | BAe Warton | Uzbek | Uzbekistan Airways |
| Tarom | Tarom (Rumania) | Vale | Woodvale Aviation |

| R/T call-sign | Operator | R/T call-sign | Operator |
|---|---|---|---|
| Varig | Varig Brazil | Wizard | Merlin Executive |
| Vectis | Pilatus Britten Norman | Woodair | Woodgate Executive |
| Veritair | Veritair Ltd | | Aviation |
| Viasa | VIASA (Venezuela) | Woodpecker | Howarth Timber (Air |
| Vickers | Vickers Shipbuilding | | Charter) |
| Victor Victor | US Navy | Woodstock | Oxford Air Services |
| Viking | Premiair (Denmark) | World | World Airways |
| Virgin | Virgin Atlantic | Wycombe | Wycombe Air Centre |
| Viva | Viva Air (Spain) | Yellow | European Expedite |
| Volare | Volare (Russian Fed) | | (Belgium) |
| Volga-Dnepr | Volga-Dnepr Airline | Yemeni | Yemen Airways |
| | (Russian Fed) | Yeoman | Foster Yeoman |
| Warrior | RS Pilot Training | Yorkair | Yorkshire Flying Services |
| Watchdog | Ministry of Fisheries | Yugair | Air Yugoslavia |
| WDL | WDL Flugdienst | Zambia | Zambia Airways |
| Wessex | Wessex Air Services | Zap | Titan Airways |
| West Indian | British West Indian Airways | ZAS Airlines | ZAS Airlines (Egypt) |
| Westland | Westland Helicopters | Zebra | African Safari (Kenya) |
| Whitestar | Star Air (Denmark) | Zeus | Heliview |
| Willowair | Willowair | Zimex | Zimex (Switzerland) |
| Witchcraft | Flugdienst Fehlhaber | | |

Suffixes to the flight number have various meanings:

| A | Extra flight on the same route. If more than one, B, C etc, may be used |
| F | Freight |
| P | Positioning flight |
| T | Training flight |
| **Heavy** | Reminder to ATC that aircraft is wide-bodied with a strong vortex wake |

*Note that British Airways Shuttle call-signs, for example 'Shuttle 6Z', are unique to this operation.*

Some operators have their own system of suffixes, an example being Gillair of Newcastle, one of whose flights, GIL04L, indicates a Liverpool mail flight; an A suffix indicates one that originates from *Aldergrove*. Britannia Airways uses the suffixes A and B to signify outbound and inbound flights respectively, for example BAL513A is Manchester to Rhodes, and BAL513B Rhodes to Manchester.

British Airways' domestic services employ a two- or three-digit number denoting the route, and a suffix letter identifying the particular service. This is a development of the Shuttle call-signs that have been in use for many years as follows: Shuttle 2 – London to Manchester; Shuttle 3 – Manchester to London; Shuttle 4 – London to Belfast; Shuttle 5 – Belfast to London; Shuttle 6 – London to Glasgow; Shuttle 7 – Glasgow to London; Shuttle 8 – London to Edinburgh; Shuttle 9 – Edinburgh to London. The letter suffixes change alphabetically for each service throughout the day.

The US Army in Germany is required by its regulations to use a different suffix for each leg of a series of communications flights, eg Duke 12A for the first, Duke 12B for the second, and so on, and this practice is continued for flights within the UK.

# ICAO company designators

| 3-letter code | Operator |
|---|---|
| AAB | Abelag Aviation |
| AAC | Army Air Corps |
| AAF | Aigle Azur |
| AAG | Atlantic Aviation |
| AAL | American Airlines |
| AAN | Oasis International |
| AAT | Austrian Air Transport |
| ABB | Air Belgium |
| ABX | Airborne Express |
| ACF | Air Charter International |
| ACW | RAF Air Cadet Schools |
| ADB | Antonov Design Bureau (Ukraine) |
| ADI | Audeli Air (Spain) |
| ADR | Adria Airways |
| AEA | Air Europa |
| AED | Air Experience Flight |
| AEF | Aero Lloyd |
| AEK | African Express Airways |
| AFB | Belgian Air Force |
| AFC | African West |
| AFM | Affretair |
| AFN | African International |
| AFP | Portuguese Air Force |
| AGL | Air Angouleme |
| AGS | Air Gambia |
| AGX | Aviogenex |
| AHK | Air Hong Kong |
| AHR | Air Holland |
| AIH | Airtours |
| AIJ | Air Jet |
| AIK | African Airlines (Kenya) |
| ALK | Air Lanka |
| ALS | Air Alsie (Denmark) |
| AMC | Air Malta |
| AME | Spanish Air Force |
| AML | Air Malawi |
| AMM | Air 2000 |
| AMR | Air America |
| AMT | American Trans Air |
| AMX | Aeronaves De Mexico |
| ANA | All Nippon Airways |
| ANZ | Air New Zealand |
| AOA | Apollo Airlines (Greece) |
| AOM | AOM Minerve |
| APR | Air Provence |
| APW | Arrow Air |

| 3-letter code | Operator |
|---|---|
| ARG | Aerolineas Argentinas |
| ATJ | Air Traffic GMBH |
| ATQ | Air Transport Schiphol |
| ATT | Aer Turas Teoranta |
| AUA | Austrian Airlines |
| AUI | Air Ukraine |
| AVA | Avianca |
| AVB | Aviation Beauport |
| AVD | Air Vendé |
| AVT | ATS Charter |
| AXP | Air Express (Norway) |
| AYC | Aviaco |
| AYR | British Aerospace Flying College |
| AZR | Air Zaire |
| AZW | Air Zimbabwe |
| BAC | BAC Leasing |
| BAL | Britannia Airlines |
| BBB | Balair |
| BBC | Bangladesh Biman |
| BBL | IBM Euroflight (Switzerland) |
| BCR | British Charter |
| BCS | European Air Transport |
| BDN | Boscombe Down MoD/PE |
| BEE | Busy Bee of Norway |
| BER | Air Berlin |
| BEX | Benin Air Express |
| BHL | Bristow Helicopters Group |
| BHY | Birgenair (Turkey) |
| BIC | Belgian International Air Carriers |
| BIH | British International Helicopters |
| BLM | The Black Magic Project |
| BMA | British Midland |
| BRA | Braathens (Norway) |
| BRY | Brymon European |
| BSK | Miami Air International |
| BVA | Buffalo Airways |
| BWA | BWIA International |
| BWY | Fleet Requirements Air Direction Unit |
| BZH | Brit Air |
| BZN | Brize Norton FTU |
| CAT | Cat Aviation (Switzerland) |
| CBY | Coningsby FTU |
| CCA | Air China |
| CCF | Cologne Commercial Flight |
| CDN | Canadian Airlines International |
| CEG | Cega Aviation |
| CFD | Cranfield Institute of Technology |
| CFG | Condor Flugdienst |

| 3-letter code | Operator |
|---|---|
| CFU | CAA Flying Unit |
| CHX | Air Charter Express |
| CIM | Cimber Air |
| CKS | American International |
| CKT | Caledonian Airways |
| CLC | Classic Air (Switzerland) |
| CLG | Challeng'Air (France) |
| CLX | Cargolux Airlines |
| CMI | Continental Micronesia |
| CMM | Air 3000 (Canada) |
| CNA | Centennial (Spain) |
| COA | Continental Airlines |
| CPA | Cathay Pacific |
| CRL | Corse Air International |
| CRN | Aero Caribbean |
| CRX | Cross Air |
| CSA | Czech Airlines |
| CTN | Croatia Airlines |
| CUB | Cubana |
| CUL | Culdrose SAR Training Unit |
| CUS | Cronus Airlines (Greece) |
| CWL | Cranwell FTU |
| CWS | Air Swazi Cargo |
| CYP | Cyprus Airways |
| DAH | Air Algerie |
| DAL | Delta Airlines |
| DAT | Delta Air Transport |
| DCN | German Federal Armed Forces |
| DMA | Maersk Air |
| DSR | Dairo Air Services (Uganda) |
| DUN | BAe Dunsfold |
| DYA | Alyemda Democratic Yemen Airlines |
| EAX | Eastern-Air Executive |
| EBA | Eurobelgian |
| ECA | Eurocypria |
| EEB | Euroberlin |
| EFF | Westair Aviation (Ireland) |
| EIA | Evergreen International |
| EIN | Aer Lingus |
| EIX | EI Air Exports (Eire) |
| ESA | Seagreen Air Transport |
| ETH | Ethiopian Airline Corp |
| ETP | Empire Test Pilots School |
| EUA | Europe Air |
| EUL | Euralair International |
| EUX | European Expedite (Belgium) |
| EWG | Eurowings |
| EWW | Emery Worldwide |

| 3-letter code | Operator |
|---|---|
| EXS | Channel Express |
| EXT | Night Express (Germany) |
| EYT | Europe Aero Service |
| FAF | French Air Force |
| FAT | Farner Air Transport |
| FBF | Fine Airlines (USA) |
| FCN | Falcon Aviation (Sweden) |
| FDX | Federal Express |
| FEU | Compagnie Aeronautique Européenne |
| FFG | Flugdienst Fehlhaber |
| FGN | Gendarmerie Nationale |
| FIN | Finnair |
| FJC | Falcon Jet |
| FJI | Air Pacific (Fiji) |
| FNY | French Navy |
| FOF | Fred Olsen |
| FOX | Jetair (Denmark) |
| FRA | Flight Refuelling |
| FSB | Flight Services International |
| FST | Fast Air Carrier (Chile) |
| FUA | Futura (Spain) |
| FVG | Frevag (Belgium) |
| FWC | Freeway Air (Netherlands) |
| GAF | German Air Force |
| GAL | Gemini Airlines (Ghana) |
| GBL | GB Airways |
| GEC | Lufthansa Cargo |
| GFA | Gulf Air |
| GHA | Ghana Airways Corp |
| GIA | Garuda Indonesian Airlines |
| GMI | Germania |
| GRL | Gronlandsfly |
| GRN | Green Air (Turkey) |
| HAF | Greek Air Force |
| HAS | Hamburg Airlines |
| HJC | Heathrow Jet Charter |
| HLA | Heavylift Cargo |
| HLF | Hapag-Lloyd |
| HRN | Airwork |
| IAW | Iraqi Airways |
| ICE | Icelandair |
| ICG | Icelandic Coastguard |
| IDS | IDS Aircraft |
| IFT | Interflight |
| IMX | Zimex Aviation (Switzerland) |
| IND | Iona National Airways |
| IQQ | Caribbean Airways |
| IRA | Iran Air |

| 3-letter code | Operator |
|---|---|
| ISL | Eagle Air |
| ITF | Air Inter |
| IYE | Yemen Airways |
| JAL | Japan Air Lines |
| JAT | Jugoslovenski Aerotransport |
| JCL | Jet Cargo Liberia |
| JES | Jes Air (Bulgaria) |
| KAC | Kuwait Airways |
| KAL | Korean Airlines |
| KAR | Kar-Air (Finland) |
| KEY | Key Airlines (USA) |
| KIS | Contactair Flugdienst |
| KQA | Kenya Airways |
| LAA | Libyan Arab Airlines |
| LAM | Linhas Aereas Mocambique |
| LAN | LAN Chile |
| LAP | Lineas Aereas Paraguayas |
| LAZ | Balkan-Bulgarian Airlines |
| LCN | Lineas Aereas Canarias |
| LDA | Lauda Air |
| LEA | Lead Air (France) |
| LGL | Luxair |
| LIB | Air Liberté |
| LIL | Lithuanian Airlines |
| LIR | Lionair (Luxembourg) |
| LIT | Air Littoral |
| LKA | Alkair (Denmark) |
| LME | Lyneham FTU |
| LOP | Linton-on-Ouse FTU |
| LOS | Lossiemouth FTU |
| LOT | Lot Polskie |
| LTE | LTE International Airways |
| LTN | Latinas (Venezuela) |
| LTS | LTU Sud |
| LTU | Lufttransport |
| LWA | Liberian World |
| MAH | Malev |
| MAS | Malaysian Airline System |
| MAU | Air Mauritius |
| MEA | Middle East Airlines |
| MET | Meteorological Research Flight |
| MIN | Business European |
| MKA | MK Air Cargo (Nigeria) |
| MON | Monarch Airlines |
| MOR | A/S Morefly |
| MPH | Martinair Holland |
| MRT | Air Mauritanie |
| MSC | Moscow Airways |
| MSR | Egyptair |

| 3-letter code | Operator |
|---|---|
| MTQ | Air Martinique |
| MUK | Muk Air Taxi (Denmark) |
| NAD | Noble Air (Turkey) |
| NAF | Royal Netherlands Air Force |
| NAN | National Airlines |
| NCA | Nippon Cargo |
| NCR | Air Sur (Spain) |
| NDC | Air Nordic |
| NGA | Nigeria Airways |
| NMB | Namib Air |
| NOR | A/S Norving (Norway) |
| NOS | Norway Airlines |
| NOW | Royal Norwegian Air Force |
| NRN | Royal Netherlands Navy |
| NSA | Nile Safaris (Sudan) |
| NTR | TNT Aviation |
| NVY | Royal Navy |
| NWA | Northwest Orient |
| OAL | Olympic Airways |
| ODM | RAF Odiham |
| OJA | Oriental Pearl Airways |
| OKJ | Okada Airlines (Nigeria) |
| PAC | Polar Air Cargo |
| PAL | Philippine Airlines |
| PBU | Air Burundi |
| PGA | Portugalia |
| PGT | Pegasus (Turkey) |
| PIA | Pakistan International |
| PJS | Jet Aviation (Switzerland) |
| PLC | Police Aviation Services |
| PNR | Panair (Spain) |
| PRB | Proteus (France) |
| PTS | Points of Call Airlines |
| QAH | Quick Airways (Holland) |
| QFA | Qantas |
| QKL | Aeromaritime (France) |
| QNK | Kabo Air Travels (Nigeria) |
| QSC | African Safari Airways |
| RAM | Royal Air Maroc |
| RAT | Ratioflug |
| RAX | Royal Air Freight (USA) |
| RAZ | Rijnmond (Netherlands) |
| RBA | Royal Brunei Airlines |
| RBH | Regal Bahamas |
| RDK | Irish Air Tours |
| RFR | Royal Air Force |
| RGI | Regional Airlines (France) |
| RIA | Rich International |
| RJA | Royal Jordanian |

| 3-letter code | Operator |
|---|---|
| RKA | Air Afrique |
| RLC | AVIAL (Russian Fed) |
| RLD | Rheinland Air Service |
| ROT | Tarom (Romania) |
| RQX | Air Engiadina |
| RRL | Rolls Royce (Military Aviation) |
| RRR | Royal Air Force |
| RRS | Boscombe Down RAE |
| RTS | Relief Transport Services |
| RWD | Air Rwanda |
| RYR | Ryanair |
| SAY | Suckling Airways |
| SAZ | Swiss Air Ambulance |
| SCH | Schreiner Airways |
| SCW | Malmo Aviation (Sweden) |
| SDC | Swedish Air Force |
| SEY | Air Seychelles |
| SFR | Safair Freighters |
| SHF | Support Helicopter Flight NI |
| SHS | Sunshine Aviation |
| SIA | Singapore Airlines |
| SJM | Southern Air Transport |
| SKS | Sky Service |
| SLK | Silkair (Singapore) |
| SLM | Surinam Airways |
| SLR | Sobelair |
| SOM | Somali Airlines |
| SPC | Skyworld Airlines (USA) |
| SPP | Spanair |
| SRR | Star Air (Denmark) |
| STM | Streamline Aviation |
| STN | St Athan MU |
| STP | Holidair (Canada) |
| STR | Stellair (France) |
| SUD | Sudan Airways |
| SVA | Saudi Arabian Airlines |
| SWN | West Air Sweden |
| SWR | Swissair |
| SYR | Syrian Arab Airlines |
| SYS | Shawbury FTU |
| TAP | TAP (Portugal) |
| TAR | Tunis Air |
| TAT | TAT-European |
| TCN | Trans Continental |
| TCP | Transcorp Airways |
| TCS | Transcaesa (Mexico) |
| TEA | Trans European Airways |
| THA | Thai Airways |
| THY | Turk Hava Yollari |

| 3-letter code | Operator |
|---|---|
| TIL | Tajikistan International |
| TLA | Translift Airways |
| TLP | Tulip Air |
| TMA | Trans Mediterranean Airlines |
| TOF | Topcliffe FTU |
| TOW | Tower Air |
| TRA | Transavia (Holland) |
| TRT | Trans Arabian Air Transport |
| TSC | Air Transat (Canada) |
| TSO | Transaero Airlines (Russia) |
| TSV | Tropair Air Services |
| TWA | Transworld Airlines |
| TWE | Transwede |
| TYR | Tyrolean Airways |
| UAA | Leuchars UAS/AEF |
| UAD | Colerne UAS/AEF |
| UAE | Emirates |
| UAG | Cambridge UAS/AEF |
| UAH | Newton UAS/AEF |
| UAI | Uni Air International |
| UAJ | Glasgow UAS/AEF |
| UAM | Woodvale UAS/AEF |
| UAO | Benson UAS/AEF |
| UAQ | Leeming UAS/AEF |
| UAS | Belfast UAS/AEF |
| UAU | Boscombe Down UAS/AEF |
| UAW | St Athan UAS/AEF |
| UAX | Church Fenton UAS/AEF |
| UAY | Cosford UAS/AEF |
| UGA | Uganda Airlines |
| UKA | Air UK |
| UKC | Air Ukraine Cargo |
| UKL | Air UK (Leisure) |
| UNA | Universair (Spain) |
| UPA | Air Foyle |
| UTA | Union Des Transports Aeriennes |
| UYC | Cameroon Airlines |
| UZB | Uzbekistan Airways |
| VAS | Aviatrans (Russian Fed) |
| VDA | Volga-Dnepr Airline |
| VER | Venus (Greece) |
| VIA | Viasa (Venezuela) |
| VIR | Virgin Atlantic |
| VLL | Valley SAR Training |
| VLM | VLM (Belgium) |
| VLR | Volare (Russian Fed) |
| VRG | Varig |
| VTA | Air Tahiti |
| VYT | Valley FTU |

| 3-letter code | Operator | 3-letter code | Operator |
|---|---|---|---|
| WDL | WDL Flugdienst | WSX | Wessex Air Services |
| WFD | Avro International | WTN | BAe Warton |
| WHE | Westland Helicopters | YRG | Air Yugoslavia |
| WIT | Wittering FTU | ZAC | Zambia Airways |
| WOA | World Airways | ZAS | ZAS Airlines of Egypt |

# Appendix 7

# UK SSR Code Allotment Plan

| Codes/Series | Controlling Authority/Function |
|---|---|
| 0000 | SSR data unreliable |
| 0001–0017 | Allotted to France and Denmark |
| 0020 | Air Ambulance Helicopter Emergency Medivac |
| 0021 | Fixed-wing aircraft (receiving service from a ship) |
| 0022 | Helicopter(s) (receiving service from a ship) |
| 0023 | Aircraft engaged in actual SAR Operations |
| 0024 | Radar Flight Evaluation/Calibration |
| 0025 | MET research flight – DRA Boscombe Down |
| 0026 | London Fire Brigade Helicopter |
| 0027 | Lancashire Police Helicopter |
| 0030 | FIR Lost |
| 0031 | Lost aircraft subsequently identified |
| 0032 | Aircraft on police air support ops |
| 0033 | Aircraft Paradropping |
| 0040 | Civil Helicopters North Sea |
| 0041–0057 | Allotted to Belgium |
| 0060–0077 | Allotted to Ireland, Netherlands and Norway |
| 0101–0137 | ORCAM Brussels |
| 0140–0177 | ORCAM Amsterdam |
| 0201–0220 | RAF Leuchars |
| 0201–0257 | RNAS Portland |
| 0260–0267 | RAF Mildenhall |
| 0270–0277 | Plymouth Radar |
| 0301–0305 | ORCAM Heathrow |
| 0306–0377 | ORCAM London |
| 0401–0430 | Leeds Bradford Approach |
| 0401–0437 | Ireland Domestic |
| 0401–0476 | DRA Farnborough |
| 0401–0477 | RAF Lakenheath |

| Codes/Series | Controlling Authority/Function |
|---|---|
| 0404 | Leeds Bradford conspicuity purposes |
| 0440–0457 | Edinburgh Approach |
| 0440–0467 | ACMI (NSAR) |
| 0470–0477 | RN South West Approaches |
| 0477 | RAF Odiham |
| 0501–0577 | ORCAM London |
| 0601–0677 | ORCAM Frankfurt |
| 0701–0777 | ORCAM Maastricht |
| 1000 | Autonomous FTR Ops |
| 1001–1077 | ORCAM Paris |
| 1100 | Autonomous FTR Ops |
| 1101–1137 | ORCAM Frankfurt |
| 1140–1177 | ORCAM Scottish |
| 1200 | Autonomous FTR Ops |
| 1201–1277 | Channel Islands Domestic |
| 1300–1317 | Aircraft receiving service from AEW aircraft |
| 1320–1327 | Autonomous FTR Ops |
| 1330–1377 | ORCAM Bremen/Dusseldorf |
| 1400 | Autonomous FTR |
| 1401–1407 | UK Domestic |
| 1410–1417 | RAF Coltishall/Norwich Approach |
| 1420–1457 | Shannon inbound UK Domestic |
| 1460–1477 | Pennine Radar, Guernsey Approach, RAF Coltishall, Bristol Approach |
| 1500–1567 | RAF Buchan |
| 1570–1576 | RAF Benbecula |
| 1600–1627 | RAF Boulmer |
| 1630–1647 | No 1 ACC |
| 1650–1657 | Special Events |
| 1660–1677 | Plymouth Radar |
| 1700–1727 | Special Events |
| 1730–1777 | RAF Valley |
| 1730–1757 | RAF Waddington/Lossiemouth/ Kinloss/Benson |

| Codes/Series | Controlling Authority/Function |
| --- | --- |
| 1760–1777 | RAF Wattisham, RAF Chivenor |
| 2000 | Aircraft from non-SSR environment |
| 2001–2077 | ORCAM Shannon |
| 2100 | Autonomous FTR Ops |
| 2101–2177 | ORCAM Amsterdam |
| 2200 | Autonomous FTR Ops |
| 2201–2210 | ORCAM Manchester |
| 2211–2215 | ORCAM Gatwick |
| 2216–2277 | ORCAM London |
| 2300 | Autonomous FTR Ops |
| 2301–2327 | ORCAM Brest |
| 2330–2377 | ORCAM Reims |
| 2400–2477 | RAF Neatishead |
| 2500 | Autonomous FTR Ops |
| 2501–2577 | ORCAM Rhein (Karlsruhe) |
| 2600 | Autonomous FTR Ops |
| 2601–2617 | RAF Marham |
| 2601–2620 | Aberdeen Approach |
| 2601–2631 | Cardiff Approach |
| 2601–2657 | RAF Linton-on-Ouse |
| 2601–2657 | Irish Domestic Westbound departures and Eastbound arrivals |
| 2620–2637 | Luton Approach |
| 2621–2630 | Sumburgh Approach |
| 2632 | S and E Wales Police Air Support Unit |
| 2633–2654 | Cardiff Approach |
| 2640–2657 | RAF Marham |
| 2640–2657 | Northern North Sea Offshore |
| 2660–2677 | BAe Warton, RAF Marham |
| 2700 | Autonomous FTR Ops |
| 2701–2737 | ORCAM Shannon |
| 2740–2777 | ORCAM Zurich |
| 3000 | Autonomous FTR Ops |
| 3001–3077 | ORCAM Zurich |
| 3100 | Autonomous FTR Ops |
| 3101–3177 | ORCAM Rhein (Karlsruhe) |
| 3200 | Autonomous FTR Ops |
| 3201–3277 | LJAO |
| 3300 | Autonomous FTR Ops |
| 3301–3307 | London Radar Special Tasks (Sector 38) |
| 3310–3337 | London Radar |
| 3340–3377 | London Radar |
| 3400 | Autonomous FTR Ops |
| 3401–3477 | RNAS Yeovilton |
| 3410–3427 | RAF Leeming, Stansted Approach |
| 3430–3473 | Anglia Radar |

| Codes/Series | Controlling Authority/Function |
| --- | --- |
| 3475 | Essex Police Helo |
| 3476–3477 | Stansted Approach |
| 3500 | Autonomous FTR Ops |
| 3501–3507 | ORCAM Berlin |
| 3510–3537 | ORCAM Maastricht |
| 3540–3577 | ORCAM Berlin |
| 3601–3617 | Southampton Approach |
| 3601–3677 | Northern North Sea Offshore |
| 3620–3637 | Manchester Approach |
| 3640–3657 | Exeter Approach |
| 3661–3663 | Heathrow (Met Police Air Support Unit) |
| 3665–3677 | DTEO Aberporth |
| 3670–3676 | London Special Tasks |
| 3701–3717 | DTEO Boscombe Down |
| 3701–3727 | Teesside Approach |
| 3720–3727 | RAF Northolt |
| 3730–3731 | Not allocated |
| 3732 | Vale of York AIAA conspicuity |
| 3733 | RAF Leeming/Linton-on-Ouse |
| 3734 | Vale of York AIAA conspicuity |
| 3735–3736 | Northumbria Police ASU |
| 3740–3753 | RAF St Mawgan |
| 3740–3777 | RAF Cranwell |
| 3755–3777 | RAF Shawbury |
| 4001–4047 | ORCAM Brest |
| 4050–4077 | ORCAM Bordeaux |
| 4101–4177 | ORCAM Frankfurt/Dusseldorf |
| 4201–4214 | Heathrow Domestic |
| 4215–4245 | Dublin inbound UK |
| 4246–4253 | CCF Special Tasks |
| 4254–4625 | Gatwick Domestic |
| 4266–4277 | UK Domestic |
| 4301 | RSRE Malvern/ARE Portsdown |
| 4302 | Blackpool Approach |
| 4303 | RSRE Malvern/ARE Portsdown |
| 4304 | Marconi, Rinvenhall |
| 4305 | Royal Flights – Helicopters |
| 4306 | Selected Flights – Helicopters |
| 4307 | Cambridge Approach |
| 4310 | East Midlands Police Helicopter |
| 4311 | Antenna trailing/target towing |
| 4312 | MATO Special Tasks |
| 4313/4314 | Coventry Approach |
| 4315 | Cambridge Approach |
| 4316 | MATO Special Tasks |
| 4323–4341 | Manchester Domestic |
| 4342 | Merseyside Police Air Support Unit |

| Codes/Series | Controlling Authority/Function |
|---|---|
| 4343 | Morecambe and Liverpool Bay Helicopters |
| 4344 | Cheshire Police Air Support Unit |
| 4345 | RAF Woodvale local area conspicuity |
| 4346–4377 | Manchester Domestic |
| 4401–4477 | UK Domestic |
| 4501–4507 | Scottish Special Tasks |
| 4510–4527 | Westland Helicopters Yeovil |
| 4530–4537 | BAe Filton |
| 4540–4546 | London D&D Cell |
| 4550–4553 | Heathrow CCF |
| 4560–4567 | BAe Woodford |
| 4560–4577 | London City Airport Approach |
| 4570–4576 | Filton Special Tasks |
| 4577 | Avon and Somerset Police Helicopter |
| 4601–4677 | Brize Radar |
| 4640–4677 | Northern North Sea Offshore |
| 4701–4720 | Heathrow Approach |
| 4701–4777 | RNAS Culdrose |
| 4721–4740 | Birmingham Approach |
| 4740–4776 | Newcastle Approach |
| 4740–4777 | RAF Coningsby |
| 4777 | Newcastle Approach VFR conspicuity |
| 5001–5077 | UK Domestic |
| 5101–5177 | UK Domestic |
| 5201–5270 | ORCAM London |
| 5271–5277 | ORCAM Jersey |
| 5301–5377 | ORCAM Barcelona |
| 5401–5477 | UK Domestic |
| 5501–5577 | ORCAM Barcelona |
| 5601–5637 | ORCAM Bordeaux |
| 5640–5677 | ORCAM Paris |
| 5701–5777 | ORCAM Geneva |
| 6001–6007 | DTEO Llanbedr |
| 6001–6077 | Guernsey Approach |
| 6010–6077 | London Radar (Sectors 1–7) |
| 6030–6077 | Jersey Approach |
| 6101–6177 | London Radar (Sectors 10–17) |
| 6201–6210 | Shannon Eastbound Landing UK |
| 6211–6224 | Gatwick Approach (CCF) |
| 6201–6207 | London Radar (Sector 20) |
| 6225–6237 | Scottish ATSOCA purposes |
| 6240–6277 | UK Domestic |
| 6301–6317 | Glasgow Approach/Humberside Approach |
| 6301–6337 | RAF Lyneham |

| Codes/Series | Controlling Authority/Function |
|---|---|
| 6320 | Strathclyde Police Helicopter |
| 6340–6377 | Superdomestic – London to Paris |
| 6401–6477 | UK Domestic |
| 6501–6577 | Scottish Military/DTEO Boscombe Down |
| 6501–6507 | RAF Wittering/RAF Cottesmore |
| 6550–6577 | RAF Cottesmore |
| 6601–6627 | ORCAM Frankfurt |
| 6630–6677 | ORCAM Dusseldorf |
| 6701–6777 | ORCAM Marseille |
| 7000 | Conspicuity code |
| 7001 | Military Low Level Climbout/Conspicuity |
| 7002 | Danger Areas General |
| 7003 | Red Arrows Transit/Display |
| 7004 | DTEO Boscombe Down |
| 7007 | Open Skies Observation Aircraft |
| 7010–7046 | RAF Spadeadam |
| 7047 | Cumbria Police Air Support Unit |
| 7010–7057 | RNAS Yeovilton |
| 7010–7067 | RAF Wattisham |
| 7060–7067 | BAe Dunsfold, BAe Brough, BAe Warton |
| 7070–7077 | SAR Exercises/Special Events |
| 7100–7177 | ORCAM Brussels |
| 7250–7257 | UK Superdomestic for destinations in France and Barcelona FIR |
| 7260–7267 | Dublin Superdomestic for destinations in France and Barcelona FIR |
| 7270–7277 | Plymouth Radar Superdomestic for destinations in UK and France |
| 7301–7317 | Superdomestic – London to Amsterdam |
| 7320–7347 | Superdomestic – Amsterdam to London |
| 7330–7337 | Not allocated |
| 7350/7351 | BAe College Prestwick |
| 7340–7353 | Gatwick Approach (CCF) |
| 7354–7357 | Gatwick Approach/Tower |
| 7360–7377 | Bournemouth Approach, East Midlands Approach, Prestwick Approach |
| 7400–7437 | UK Domestic |
| 7440–7477 | UK Domestic |
| 7500 | Hi-jacking |
| 7501–7537 | ORCAM Geneva |
| 7540–7547 | ORCAM Rhein |
| 7550–7577 | ORCAM Paris |

| Codes/Series | Controlling Authority/Function |
|---|---|
| 7600 | Radio Failure |
| 7601–7617 | ORCAM Reims |
| 7620–7647 | ORCAM Paris |
| 7650–7677 | ORCAM Marseille |
| 7700 | Emergency |
| 7701–7710 | Not allocated |
| 7711–7717 | SAR Operations |

| Codes/Series | Controlling Authority/Function |
|---|---|
| 7720 | Not allocated |
| 7721–7727 | SAR Operations |
| 7730–7757 | Superdomestic – Shannon Eastbound Landing UK |
| 7777 | SSR Monitors |

**Squawk Code allocations (see page 63)**

# Magazines for the enthusiast and air band listener

Although anti-terrorist measures have reduced spectator opportunities at some major airports, the reverse is true at many military bases. There are now official viewing enclosures at Coningsby, Lakenheath, Mildenhall, Waddington and Yeovilton, some with enthusiasts' shops and other facilities. Almost every part of the United Kingdom has an active aviation society, most of which produce a magazine detailing local airfield movements and overflights.

## Addresses for enthusiasts' magazines

*Air-Britain News* and *Air-Britain Digest*, David Crook (Membership Secretary), 36 Nursery Road, Taplow, Maidenhead, Berkshire SL6 0JZ.

*Air Strip* Midland Counties Aviation Society Honorary Registrar, 113 Ferndown Road, Solihull, West Midlands B91 2AX.

*Aviation Ireland* Aviation Society of Ireland, 31 Shanrath Road, Whitehall, Dublin 9, Eire.

*Aviation Letter* John R. Roach, 8 Stowe Crescent, Ruislip, Middlesex HA4 7SS.

*Aviation News and Review* LAAS International, M. W. Tatner, Mikalian, Blackmore Road, Kelvedon Hatch, Brentwood, Essex CM15 0AP.

*British Aviation Review* and *Roundel* British Aviation Research Group, Paul Hewins, 8 Nightingale Road, Woodley, Berkshire RG5 3LP.

*Channel Islands Aviation News* Dave Bougourd, 5 Rue du Douit, Marais Lane, Vale, Guernsey, CI.

*Contact* Air-Britain Gwent Branch, K. Thomas, 47 Queens Hill Crescent, Newport, Gwent NP9 5HG.

*Hawkeye* Gatwick Aviation Society Registrar, 144 The Crescent, Horley, Surrey RH6 7PA.

*Humberside Air Review* Humberside Aviation Society, Pete Wild, 4 Bleach Yard, Beverley, East Yorkshire.

*Irish Air Letter* P. Cunliffe, 20 Road Five, Kempton Navan Road, Dublin 7, Eire.

*North West Air News* Air-Britain Liverpool Branch, Peter Sloan, 50 Rathmore Road, Oxton, Birkenhead L43 2HF.

*Osprey* Air-Britain Southampton Branch, Doreen Eaves, 84 Carnation Road, Bassett, Southampton SO50 5QJ.

*Prestwick Airport Letter* Prestwick Airport Aviation Group, D. Reid (Editor), 45 Bellesleyhill Avenue, Ayr KA8 9BJ.

*Scottish Air News* Central Scotland Aviation Group, 12 Pearson Drive, Renfrew, PA4 0BD.

*Skyward* West Country Aviation Society, 54 Radcliffe Close, Southway, Plymouth PL6 6JZ.

*South East Air Review* West London Aviation Group, 18 Green Lawns, Ruislip, Middlesex HA4 9SP.

*Southwest Aviation News* Southwest
  Aviation Society, Richard Hodgkinson
  (Registrar), Marsh Farm, Salford Priors,
  Near Evesham, Worcestershire.

*26 Threshold* Air-Britain Luton Branch,
  Chris Alton, 27 Margery Wood, Welwyn
  Garden City, Herts AL7 1UN.

*Ulster Air Mail* Ulster Aviation Society, c/o
  Broomhill Park, Belfast, Co Down.

*Winged Words* The Aviation Society, 6
  Martin Drive, Darwen, Lancs BB3 2HW.

There are currently three commercial
magazines that publish air band
information in a regular column: my own
'Radio Watch' in the 'Aviation News'
section of *Air Pictorial*, Godfrey Manning's
'Airband' and Graham Tanner's 'SSB
Utility Listening', both in *Short Wave
Magazine*, and Graham Duke's 'Airband' in
*Aircraft Illustrated*. *Pilot* magazine also
publishes useful NOTAM summaries,
although of course not aimed specifically at
air band listeners. Finally, one must not
forget the several limited circulation
newsletters that cover military air band
topics – no mainstream publication would
dare to print such detailed information!

# Index